BLOOD COLD

FAME, SEX, AND MURDER IN HOLLYWOOD

DENNIS McDOUGAL AND MARY MURPHY

AN ONYX BOOK

ONYX
Published by New American Library, a division of Penguin Putnam Inc.,
375 Hudson Street, New York, New York 10014, U.S.A.
Penguin Books Ltd, 80 Strand, London WC2R 0RL, England
Penguin Books Australia Ltd, Ringwood, Victoria, Australia
Penguin Books Canada Ltd, 10 Alcorn Avenue, Toronto, Ontario,
Canada M4V 3B2
Penguin Books (N.Z.) Ltd, 182–190 Wairau Road, Auckland 10, New
Zealand

Penguin Books Ltd, Registered Offices: Harmondsworth, Middlesex,
England

First published by Onyx, an imprint of New American Library, a
division of Penguin Putnam Inc.

First Printing, September 2002
10   9   8   7   6   5   4   3   2   1

Copyright © Dennis McDougal and Mary Murphy, 2002
Cover Photos: Bonny Lee Bakley photo by ZUMA Archive/ZUMA
Press. Copyright © 2002 by ZUMA Archive. Robert Blake photo by
Pool Photo/ZUMA Press. Copyright © 2002 by Pool Photo.
All rights reserved

 REGISTERED TRADEMARK—MARCA REGISTRADA

Printed in the United States of America

Without limiting the rights under copyright reserved above, no part of
this publication may be reproduced, stored in or introduced into a
retrieval system, or transmitted, in any form, or by any means
(electronic, mechanical, photocopying, recording, or otherwise), without
the prior written permission of both the copyright owner and the above
publisher of this book.

BOOKS ARE AVAILABLE AT QUANTITY DISCOUNTS WHEN USED TO PROMOTE
PRODUCTS OR SERVICES. FOR INFORMATION PLEASE WRITE TO PREMIUM
MARKETING DIVISION, PENGUIN PUTNAM INC., 375 HUDSON STREET,
NEW YORK, NEW YORK 10014.

If you purchased this book without a cover you should be aware that this
book is stolen property. It was reported as "unsold and destroyed" to
the publisher and neither the author nor the publisher has received any
payment for this "stripped book."

For our own children,
Jen, Amy, Kate, Fitz, and Andrea,
and also for Megan and Nicholas . . .
and for every child who deserves our love, attention
and protection, no matter what

Acknowledgments

Together, we must first express our gratitude to Steve Reddicliffe and Vince Cosgrove at *TV Guide,* who recognized early on the import of a murder mystery that most in the mainstream media wrote off as just another tabloid flavor-of-the-month tragedy. It is thanks to the two of them that the authors were paired on the Blake-Bakley story over a year ago and were given carte blanche to follow the story wherever it took them: Nutley and Dover, New Jersey; Manhattan and Long Island, New York; Memphis, Tennessee; St. Louis, Missouri; New Orleans, Louisiana; northern Mississippi and, of course, the breadth and length of Southern California.

In an age of pecuniary multimedia conglomerates when ignorant "suits" squeeze every last penny out of their newspaper and magazine subsidiaries and leave investigative reporting to starve in favor of fluff, bilge and gossip, there isn't enough praise to heap on editors like Vince and Steve who damn the torpedoes and order their reporters to keep on the story—full speed ahead.

Thanks to our crack researcher, Jesse Oppenheimer, whose dogged diligence turned up dozens of nuggets about the Bobby and Bonny story. His old man had better watch out; the lad's got *cojones* the size of basketballs and can spin a story better than Scheherazade.

When the chips are down, the Bob Zellers, Pat Broeskes and Diane Goldners of this world always come through—not for money or glory or praise, but because of friendship and a common commitment to telling the whole story, as accurately and as well as possible. If this book reads well and names are spelled correctly, it is because of them. Finer, more conscientious editors do not walk the earth. Pat also ran a close second to Jesse in the research department.

And speaking of research, applause to Dorothy Korber for providing assistance in Sacramento; the archivists at *Entertainment Tonight;* the able, amiable men and women of the Shelby County courts who directed us to records both readily apparent and confoundingly obscure; likewise, the folk who labor in the basement of the Los Angeles County Hall of Records and even deeper in the earth (three stories) at the County Archives; the staffs of the Museum of Television and Radio Broadcasting, the Margaret Herrick Library of the Academy of Motion Picture Arts and Sciences, the Long Beach Public Library, the UCLA libraries, the Los Angeles Public Library and the Angelo Iacobani branch of the Los Angeles County Library.

Thanks also to our agents extraordinaire, Alice Martell and Irv Schwartz, attorney John David, and Dan Slater, a patient, attentive and supportive editor.

A special thanks to Dawn Dupré for sharing her memories of her late uncle DeMart Besly as well as his sage observations about Bonny Bakley.

Individually, Mary thanks News Corp. executive vice president Anthea Disney, for her candor and support, and Lois Draegin for her encouragement during preparation of the first *TV Guide* article on the Blake-Bakley story. Thanks too to the magazine's fact hawks, Robin Honig and Matthew Larson, for the countless hours that added detail and authenticity to the project; to Tim Williams, who helped immeasurably with research; to Celina Martin who guided the flow of information between the authors and made it all seem effortless; to Nancy Schwartz, the tireless and determined finder of photographs, giving our efforts pictures to complement the words; and to Ben Grossman, publicist without peer.

Journalists who were generous with their observations include Jim Bellows, Ted Johnson, Frank and Carole Lalli, Mark Schwed, Richard Reeves, Steve Sonsky, Janet Weeks and Michele Willens.

But the core of Mary's appreciation goes to family: her mother, Jean Begley, and her fourteen brothers and sisters, who taught Mary the meaning of perseverance and dignity; Mary's own children, Megan and Nicholas (who helped transcribe interview tapes); her cousins Jack and Joan Bray; and Mary's very own Ya-Ya sisterhood: Keven Bellows, Cathy O'Neill, Evelyn Prever, Marion Wallien, Mary Ann King, Kathy Mooney Munsch, Ciji Ware, Diana Gould, Annie Gilbar and Marjorie Bernard.

But if Mary had to thank the one person who has encouraged her, believed in her, nudged her, and put the fire inside to always do her best, it would have to be Clancy Imislund, the managing director of the Midnight Mission in Los Angeles. A girl could not have a better friend.

Sharon McDougal does that same kind of believing in Dennis, and has done so through eight books now. Writing is such a tenuous and fragile craft, particularly when it is of the length and complexity of a book, that it cannot happen without a strong, patient and nurturing support group. Sharon gets first prize in that regard, but Dennis also owes his walkin' bud John Beshears; his fab family, Colleen, Patrick, Carl, Lola, Don and Neal McDougal; Ray and Jen Dominguez; Mike and Amy Riley; Kate (another transcriber!) and Id; the little people in descending order, Austin, Megan, Cody, Alex, Devin and Ryan; the Whooshes, especially Leslie Lazar (Big Time transcriber!); Pierce O'Donnell; Corey Mitchell, Dana Holliday, Bill Knoedelseder, Susan Daniels, Margaret Leslie Davis, Jim Broeske, Richard Kyle, David Cay Johnston, and Irv Letofsky, who edits like the wind.

Overture

The calendar said spring, but winter still loomed.

On the overcast morning of the day when the police finally came for actor Robert Blake, Southern California's familiar desert winds, the trademark palm trees and the steady sunshine that lit up the L.A. basin like klieg lights were all absent.

News helicopters were already hovering overhead. They had an unobstructed view of the street where Blake lived. His lavish home, which he owned jointly with his grown daughter, Delinah, was tucked away inside the gated community of Hidden Hills, and it was there that he was raising his twenty-two-month-old toddler, Rose Lenore Sophia. The copters stayed in place because all morning long, rumors of the sixty-eight-year-old actor's impending arrest for the murder of Rose's mother, Bonny Lee Bakley, had been leaking out of Parker Center police headquarters.

One news copter captured an aerial shot of the actor climbing into his beige Chevy Suburban for what appeared to be a routine trip to the store. Blake drove to a security gate checkpoint that kept the public—and the media—at arm's length. Only when the former star of TV's *Baretta* spotted the small convoy of news vans lying in wait just on the other side of the fence did he abandon his trip. He immediately made a U-turn and headed back home.

As the afternoon wore on, the number of copters, vans and reporters multiplied. From the sky, Blake could be seen out on his front lawn at one point, almost in defiance of the stalking camera crews. Since moving into the home the previous summer, he'd put up two swing sets and a play-house in the yard for Rosie and a patio and porch swing, where he could relax while he watched her play. But as the whirlybird buzz matched the televised buzz spreading across the country, and as channel after channel sprouted talking heads who speculated on Blake's fate, the dark, diminutive actor retreated inside the sprawling ranch-style house and shut the door. As close pal Mark Canavi once noted, Blake behaved much like a bear when under attack, withdrawing to his cave until the worst blew over.

But for Robert Blake, there was nowhere to hide on April 18, 2002. Police were already on their way.

"I am really surprised," Harland Braun, Blake's attorney, told CNN. "I got a call from the police just before they got to his house to have me call Robert and alert him that they were coming. He was shocked, but I just said, 'Remain calm. Come on out and cooperate.'"

As the cold spring sun dropped toward the nearby Pacific Ocean, a convoy of police cars led by an unmarked white sedan rolled to a stop in front of the Blake home. Four LAPD officers climbed out, advancing en masse toward his front door. All four car doors remained wide open while the plain-clothesmen entered the Blake residence, as though each officer knew that he would be returning momentarily, quarry in hand. Instead, the quartet remained inside for the better part of an hour. Blake stalled them long enough to call Delinah home from work early to watch the baby.

The car doors gaped. The copters hummed. To fill the dead air, TV commentators recounted what they could of the events leading to this moment. L.A. radio reporter Brad Pomerance—who grew up with both of Blake's adult children, Delinah and Noah Blake—described the scene as surreal. "A lot of the homes have horses out there, and the whole place is pretty serene with lots of trees. It's almost like a beautiful part of Texas," he said. "Dr. Laura [Schlesinger] lives there, and so does one of the Jackson Five. It's not a thoroughfare to anywhere, and a lot of people live there for that very reason. And then to all of a sudden have both gates shut so you're closed off from the world and then to have helicopters circling, it's pretty unnerving."

By now the sky overhead was thick with news copters capturing every move down on the ground and broadcasting the scene across the nation. It was already prime time on the East Coast, where sitcoms were interrupted with news bulletins, but California was still coming up on its evening newscasts. News directors at every station in Southern California understood that the arrest of Robert Blake for allegedly killing his wife after nearly a yearlong LAPD investigation was a guaranteed showstopper.

TV experts began weighing in—video attorneys of every stripe, whose analysis of all things criminal became a running counterpoint to the play-by-play from Rather, Jennings and Brokaw. Comparisons to a similar LAPD celebrity arrest from eight years earlier were rife. The reprise of the O.J. Simpson case ricocheted from CNN to MSNBC to FOX and back again even before police hauled Blake out in handcuffs.

Simpson himself had offered up ironic advice to Blake months earlier via the syndicated TV show *Extra!*: Don't take a polygraph test and don't smear your dead wife, but above all, don't turn on the television set. "I know that watching TV is only going to frustrate him," Simpson explained, adding, "As far as I'm concerned, this man is innocent until a jury comes back and calls him guilty."

Against the eerie aerial shot of the open-doored white sedan yawning in front of the Blakes' manicured $1.4 million home, the linking of Blake to O.J. became irresistible to commentators, tele-attorneys, and news anchors alike.

"Now some of you, perhaps even most of you, are whispering to yourselves, 'O.J.,'" said CNN's Aaron Brown. "Yes, I hear that too. How this plays out over time, how media crazy we all go on this, what lessons we learned or didn't are for another day. This is a well-known person and a case with lots of little twists and turns."

Though acquitted in a sensational televised eight-month trial in 1995, Simpson had been subsequently found responsible for the death of his wife, Nicole, and her young friend Ron Goldman during a nontelevised civil trial, and while Simpson remained officially not guilty, the prevailing belief from coast to coast was that the ex-NFL running back, comic co-star of the *Naked Gun* film trilogy and airport broad jumper from countless Hertz Rent-a-Car TV commercials had literally gotten away with murder.

And now pundits wondered out loud: Was history about to repeat itself?

ABC News interrupted its broadcast just before six o'clock, Pacific Daylight Time, with a sky video of a hand-cuffed Blake in a green ball cap, dark trousers and clean white sweatshirt that declared I SURVIVED MALIBU CANYON across its back. He was passive—even friendly. As Harland Braun later explained, his client had spoken frequently over the months with detectives investigating Bonny's death, and was fully prepared if this day ever came.

After Blake climbed into the rear of the waiting white sedan, all four doors finally slammed shut and the car drove off slowly through the pleasant suburban streets of Hidden Hills—hidden, appropriately enough, at the westernmost end of the sprawling San Fernando Valley. The car picked up speed as it ducked out a side gate, far away from the security checkpoint, where the news crew encampment was quickly dismantling. Few were fast enough to catch up to the un-marked police vehicle as it neared the Ventura Freeway and headed into rush-hour traffic, but copters never lost sight of the white sedan, prompting TV's talking heads to comment again on the similarity to another media chase back in June 1994. O.J. Simpson had made a freeway run for the Mexican border, riding in a white Bronco that was also trailed by news copters, as well as more than a dozen police cars. Simpson finally made a U-turn and headed home to Brent-wood, where he was taken into custody without further incident.

Unlike Blake, Simpson alone was charged with murdering his wife. According to police, Robert Blake had an ac-complice. At the same time detectives were arresting a dark, diminutive and defiant Blake in Hidden Hills, another cadre of cops arrived at an apartment in Burbank, where Blake's burly forty-six-year-old chauffeur and bodyguard lived. Earle Caldwell, the subservient handyman who had been at Blake's side since he married Bonny eighteen months earlier, was charged with conspiring with Blake to kill her. A half head taller and more than half a hundred pounds heavier than

Blake, Caldwell held his head high, but put up no resistance to police. His wraparound sunglasses and a black T-shirt with SEZ WHO? emblazoned over the heart pretty much said it all. In addition to arresting Caldwell, detectives hauled boxes, a shotgun and two gun cases out of his second-floor apartment.

As night fell over Los Angeles, the cars containing Blake and Caldwell both pulled up at the booking entrance at the rear of Parker Center. Blake faced a small army of men and women armed with boom mikes, Minicams, notepads and floodlights. As a star of film and television for most of his life, the one-time TV icon of the hit cop series *Baretta* was accustomed to media tumult, but this time there was no red carpet waiting, and the rude questions tossed at him could in no way be construed as celebrity softballs.

"What are you being charged with?"

"Mr. Blake, did the arrest come as a surprise?"

"Did you do it, Bob? Did you kill your wife?"

Robert Blake said nothing, keeping his blank eyes focused straight ahead and maintaining the self-imposed silence he'd kept since the day he buried Bonny Bakley ten months earlier.

Her May 25, 2001, funeral at Forest Lawn Cemetery had been Blake's last public appearance. It was an odder quirk of fate that the unscrupulous celebrity-stalking Bonny Bakley finally wound up there. A shrewd groupie who had spent a lifetime trying to wedge herself into the Hollywood milieu now had a permanent berth on the artificially green hillside opposite the Hollywood sign and within sight of Warner Brothers, Disney and Universal studios. In his terse eulogy, however, Blake never once mentioned the irony to the cameras.

"It was [Bonny's] will, her conviction, not mine, her dedication that brought Rosie into this world," Blake pronounced solemnly over his dead wife's grave, dramatically removing a white rose from the spray atop her casket. Cradling Rose in the crook of her arm, Delinah also plucked a flower off the casket and handed it to the toddler.

After that, Robert Blake never spoke publicly about

Bonny or anything else again, and that didn't change now that he had been arrested for her murder.

He kept his head bowed and continued walking, flanked by Ron Ito[1] and Brian Tyndall, two LAPD detectives who had been investigating the case. For months they too had maintained their silence. Enduring speculation from both Harland Braun and a jaded L.A. news corps that the May 4, 2001, murder of Bonny Lee Bakley might never be solved, neither cop uttered a single substantive word about the case. During the early days of the investigation, the media flooded their offices in the elite Robbery Homicide division up on Parker Center's third floor with calls wanting to know the status of the case. After a couple months had passed, the flood became a trickle. Summer gave way to fall, and fall to winter, but the detectives' answer to the media was always the same: "The case remains under investigation."

Indeed, the killing of Bonny Lee Bakley, forty-four-year-old groupie-cum-wife of actor Robert Blake, had evolved into the most expensive and, arguably, the most extensive investigation in LAPD history. Of the 584 murders committed in the nation's second largest city during 2001, over half had gone unsolved, and police officials all the way to Chief Bernard Parks' office were painfully aware that the murder of Bonny Bakley had been among those that officially remained a mystery. Though Bonny's famous husband had been the obvious suspect from the start, the police had turned up no witnesses, no forensic evidence and no immediate clues that would fix the blame on Robert Blake beyond a reasonable doubt.

Indeed, the actor had behaved like a stricken and bereaved husband. While Bonny lay dying in an ambulance headed toward nearby St. Joseph's Hospital, Blake alternately wept and vomited into the gutter half a block from the murder scene while delivering the following story to investigators:

> Before they left Blake's home for Vitello's, a
> nearby neighborhood bistro, Bonny insisted that her

---

[1]The detective is no relation to Los Angeles Superior Court judge Lance Ito.

husband pack one of his pistols because she believed someone had been stalking her. The couple parked beside a vacant house that was under construction on a side street and walked a block to the restaurant, which had been a Blake haunt for close to twenty years. They arrived around 8:30 P.M., and sat in a corner booth. Bonny ordered seafood and wine while Blake had chicken soup.

The couple ate, Blake paid the bill, adding a 25 percent tip, and they left at about 9:30 P.M., but when they got to his car, Blake discovered he'd left his .38 caliber handgun behind. He returned to the restaurant, retrieved the gun, asked for two glasses of water, drank them and left.

When he returned to his car, Blake found that in his brief absence, Bonny had been shot twice. After discovering his mortally wounded wife, Blake went to a house around the corner from Vitello's parking lot and knocked. Actor/director Sean Stanek opened the door to a frantic Blake around 9:50 P.M. and, upon hearing his story, called 911. Then both men ran to the car, where Bonny lay slumped in the passenger seat. Blood was everywhere. Paramedics could not revive her. Bonny was declared DOA at St. Joseph's Hospital at 10:15 P.M.

While Blake's story seemed riddled with inconsistencies, after nearly five hours of questioning, police did not arrest him. They declined to even name him a suspect. Bonny's autopsy was sealed, Blake's Dodge Stealth was impounded and the murder weapon—a relatively rare 9 millimeter German military pistol called a Walther P38—was recovered from a nearby trash bin a couple of days later along with a pair of gloves.

But in the days, weeks and months that followed, neither Detectives Ito or Tyndall nor any of the other half dozen investigators who worked the case with them would even confirm that they had located the murder weapon. Stung by its rush to prosecute O.J. Simpson, the department wasn't about to make the same mistake twice. Police Chief Parks, who had risen to the top of the department as an indirect result of the housecleaning the LAPD had undergone following the 1992 L.A. riots and the O.J. trials, urged the public and media to have patience.

"It's a homicide that at least at this time has very few clues," Parks told a local radio station two weeks after the murder. "It's going to require an extensive amount of investigation."

Asked if Blake was a suspect, Parks said, "No one's been eliminated. It would not be an investigation if we just chose who should be a suspect and who shouldn't."

He vowed to provide whatever resources Robbery Homicide captain Jim Tatreau said his detectives needed to arrest, prosecute and convict Bonny's killer. In the meantime, Parks muzzled everyone but his media relations officers, and after little more than two months of tabloid speculation, the mystery surrounding the murder of Robert Blake's wife vanished from the headlines.

Over the following nine months, investigators traveled to twenty states, where they conducted more than 150 interviews and amassed 35,000 pages of evidence. They explored the seedy after-hours jazz joints on Beale Street in Memphis once haunted by starstruck Bonny Bakley and her gal pals; the High Sierra resort where Blake took Bonny—and Earle Caldwell—on a belated honeymoon just a week before she died; and the mean streets of northern New Jersey towns where Bonny and Robert Blake were both born into very different but equally dysfunctional families.

The detectives traveled to Montana, Vegas, Arkansas, New York, Mississippi, Phoenix and Florida, speaking with many of the men whom Bonny had bilked of money, property and insurance during a pornographic career that stretched over two decades. They interviewed transvestites, stuntmen, musicians, thieves, prostitutes, lawyers, bouncers and at least one professional Elvis impersonator. They waded hip deep into Bonny's disturbing netherworld of phone sex, dirty pictures and gutter erotica and entered into Blake's dark, obsessive and equally disturbing twilight zone—a bitter world of "what ifs" and missed opportunities that Blake himself called "the third act" of his fast-fading television and movie star's life.

It was here, inside the tarnished imagination of the former child actor who refused to grow up and leave the stage, that Ito and Tyndall believed they finally found their killer. On April 18, 2002, the detectives concluded that the brooding screen persona that Little Rascal Bobby Blake nurtured into a lead role in the big screen adaptation of Truman Capote's *In Cold Blood* and continued to cultivate for half a Hollywood century finally crossed over from tough guy fantasy to killer reality.

"Robert Blake shot Bonny Bakley," Captain Tatreau told a hastily gathered news conference that Thursday night after Blake had been fingerprinted, photographed, booked and transferred to a holding cell. "We believe his motive is that Robert Blake had contempt for Bonny Bakley. He felt that he was trapped in a marriage that he wanted no part of."

Outside Parker Center, after an hour-long meeting with his client, attorney Harland Braun held his own impromptu press conference. A veteran defense lawyer who first gained national recognition twenty years earlier successfully defending director John Landis in the *Twilight Zone* manslaughter case, Braun was as media savvy as any attorney in Los Angeles. He knew how to spin and he knew when he was being spun, just as he was at this very moment.

Braun vented his frustration over being kept in the dark about Blake's arrest, which appeared to have been made just in time for the evening news. In answer to questions shouted at him about Blake's reaction, the sandy-haired criminal defense veteran peered out over his trademark tortoiseshell half lenses and told reporters: "His main concern right now is his children."

Ironically that's how the whole saga had begun to unwind. Bonny Bakley had trapped Robert Blake by becoming pregnant with his child—the oldest trick in the starchaser's book. But little did she know the difficulty he had in separating fantasy from reality.

Braun didn't speculate though. He called it a night and bid the ladies and gentlemen of the Fourth Estate a good evening. It had been a long, cold, difficult day and the days to follow promised to be equally long, equally challenging and equally chilling.

ACT I

The Seduction

All the lonely people, where do they all belong?

—John Lennon

1

One hot summer night at the end of August, Robert Blake attended a birthday party for comedian Chuck McCann at Chadney's Restaurant. A onetime steak and chop shop, the Burbank nightspot was located on a sliver of prime real estate directly across the street from the NBC studios, where Blake had once enjoyed many of his finest hours as a regular guest on the *Tonight Show* with Johnny Carson.

But it was now the summer of 1998. Carson was retired, and Chadney's had long since gone to seed, just like many of its patrons. In its waning days, the downstairs level of the venerable old eatery still served as one of Southern California's few well-known jazz venues[2] and Blake had come to hear pianist Ross Tompkins accompanying renowned trumpet master Jack Sheldon. Observed Sheldon with affection, "Bobby's always been a great fan."

But Bonny Bakley wasn't. She preferred doo-wop and rockabilly to jazz, Chubby Checker to Charles Mingus. She remembered Chuck McCann when he was younger, thinner and had more hair, hosting an afternoon kiddies' show on TV in New York. That was back in the 1960s when Bonny herself was a kid growing up impoverished in rural north-

---

2. But not for much longer. Four months later, just before Christmas 1998, torrential rains soaked the roof so badly at Chadney's that it collapsed. A year later, Burger King applied for a conditional use permit to demolish the landmark nightclub and replace it with a drive-through restaurant.

east New Jersey. She watched McCann and she watched *American Bandstand*—two of her favorite after-school TV escape valves in a childhood that included incest, rape and regular beatings from an alcoholic father—a general Dickensian lifestyle that would have given Oliver Twist night sweats.

Now that Bonny was all grown-up, McCann seemed a lot older to her. So did the trumpet player and the dozens of other fogies who had gathered at Chadney's to listen, schmooze and reminisce. They were flabby and wrinkled and showed their age—something that Bonny simply could *not* abide. She fought growing old, gracefully or otherwise. The old guys up on the dais with McCann and Sheldon weren't bothered by age, though. They had come that night to remember how sweet it all was, and Robert Blake was very much a part of their crowd.

Bonny—or Leebonny, as she was known on the Hollywood party circuit—had come for entirely different reasons. She was powdered and perfumed and ready to romp and roll with a star. The forty-two-year-old bleached blonde lived in Memphis, but she'd been flying in and out of L.A. regularly since Dean Martin died on Christmas Day 1995. Martin had everything Bonny had been looking for in a man: money, celebrity and an insatiable sex drive. She stalked Martin at his favorite watering holes in Beverly Hills and West Hollywood. She'd finally managed to sidle up to the aging crooner at La Familia or the Hamburger Hamlet, where he ate once a week, and even got him to pose with her once for a snapshot. Bonny giggled about the moment with all her girlfriends, staying on the phone for hours the way bobbysoxers do when one has just been felt up for the first time by the captain of the football team. "He told me he loved my legs," said best friend Judy Howell. "'Wouldn't you just love to hug those legs?' he told me." Bonny was jealous.

Bonny calculated that she was within weeks of seducing Dean Martin into dropping his trousers and making her his mistress. Thus, the day that the seventy-eight-year-old ex–Rat Packer finally expired from decades of inhaling martini-flavored cigarettes, Bonny wept as long and as loud back at home in Tennessee as did Martin's ex-wife Jeanne in Beverly Hills, who maintained the death vigil at Martin's bedside.

"Bonny took his dying real hard," recalled Bonny's ex-husband Paul Gawron. "She didn't stop crying for a week."

But despite her broken heart and bitter disappointment, Bonny had also fallen in love with Southern California. Her frequent visits to L.A. had given her a taste for the moderate weather and the perpetual sunshine. Los Angeles had none of the snow she'd grown up with in northern New Jersey, nor the smelly sauna heat of summertime in Memphis.

Throw in the celebrity-strewn night life, the thousands of horny, well-heeled septuagenarian males, and the loosey morality of an aging motion picture colony powered by the twin engines of Viagra and easy money, and Bonny thought she'd simply died and gone to grifter's paradise.

She never did anything by halves, so she announced her decision to become an Angeleno as ostentatiously as possible. She paid $3,500 to rent a billboard on the Sunset Strip, where she displayed her smiling portrait and her phone number, should any bright young talent scout be shrewd enough to want to snap her up and sign her to a contract. None did, but Bonny Bakley had never been easily discouraged.

A year after Dean Martin's death, she even purchased a house in Thousand Oaks just beyond the northernmost end of the San Fernando Valley, about an hour's drive from downtown Los Angeles. She rented it out temporarily, though her eventual plan was to move her three children, ex-husband Paul, and her "mail order" business out to California.

Everyone Bonny knew agreed that her business was a natural for El Lay and the San Fernando Val-Lay in particular. As commemorated in the docudrama *Boogie Nights* (1997), the Valley had evolved over the last decades of the twentieth century into the capital of American pornography. At one time or another behind warehouse walls from Reseda to Canoga Park, any and all sexual behaviors—no matter how stupid, demeaning, or disgusting—had been recorded on tape. Twosomes, threesomes, gruesomes . . . . you name it, the Valley had filmed it.

Bonny Lee Bakley had never held down a real job—not

because she was incapable, but because it became a point of honor not to. Jobs were for pinheads who couldn't earn a living any other way. Bonny supported herself, her three children, her ex-husband and a variety of friends, relatives and hangers-on by selling lurid photos of herself and other women through the classifieds in the back of swinger publications. She further fleeced the lonely men who wrote to her by promising sex but ultimately swindling them out of whatever money, credit, insurance or property they had.

"In one word, I'd describe her as a thief," said Gawron, her first cousin, second husband and father of three of her four children. "If she had put her mind on something else, she could have been a whiz. It's just a shame that everything she did was crooked."

Bonny started out in her teens with classifieds of the "lonely young thing seeking older man" variety, and soon she began creating her own database of prospective marks and branching out into a nationwide mail-order scam. She'd string her pen pals out as long as she could, milking them for everything from Greyhound bus fare or airline tickets to credit cards and money that she claimed she needed desperately for medical bills. There was a favorite aunt in the hospital or a sister who'd lost her welfare benefits and couldn't scrape up enough to feed her newborn.

If her victims continued to respond, Bonny would run property, asset and credit checks to determine their net worth. On the bigger scores, she worked Social Security scams, juggling numbers and forging signatures so that checks meant for her victims were rerouted instead directly to her. In rare cases, she'd even marry a mark if she thought his personal fortune or life insurance policy was big enough.

"Don't ask me how she did it," said Gawron, who remained her partner in the mail-order business long after they were divorced. "I can't even make a long-distance phone call."

While Bonny worked the mailing lists and lonely-hearts ads to pay the rent, her ultimate goal was to land a celebrity. Her grandmother advised her early to get herself a tough little rich guy, like James Cagney or Frank Sinatra, and do whatever it took to hold on to him. Grandma suggested Elvis, but he up and died too soon.

Bonny tried becoming a celebrity herself for a while, but concluded it was just too much work. "If I'd kept romance out of my life, it would have been possible," she said. "But I would have had to be like Katharine Hepburn and it was too hard. I kept falling for somebody. So I thought: 'Why not fall for a movie star instead of being one?' It's more fun. I like being around celebrities. It makes you feel better than other people."

As a teenager, Bonny felt a strong psychic bond with Frankie Valli, the lead singer for the 1960s pop group the Four Seasons. In her twenties she graduated from Valli to 1950s rock pioneer Jerry Lee Lewis. By her thirties she grew beyond childish rock and roll fancies and migrated to Hollywood, where fantasy was a way of life. Now she was in her early forties, and the same celebrity obsession had brought her to Chadney's on this fateful Sunday evening.

A parade of ancients took the stage and made birthday cracks about McCann. "They did bits," recalled Mark Canavi, a young stand-up impressionist who once worked as Robert Blake's personal assistant and who accompanied him to the restaurant that night. It wasn't a roast of the Dean Martin variety exactly. Bonny would have recognized that right away, having studied the Martin oeuvre well before she put her first moves on the old man. But there were still plenty of clever insults flying in Rickles fashion as the evening wore on.

Bonny had come with Will Jordan, a veteran New York comic who'd made a career of impersonating Ed Sullivan. Nearly twice her age, Jordan had been Bonny's entrée to parties before. He asked her to come along this night because he didn't drive and Bonny did. They'd known each other since she was seventeen, and while any romance between them had cooled long ago, Bonny still used him to get close to celebrities.

"They used each other," said her sister Margerry. "Whenever Will needed a young woman on his arm for a party or something, he'd call Bonny."

Jordan introduced her to Blake, who was in rare form that

night. While everyone else wore evening clothes, Robert had on a sleeveless black T-shirt and jeans. He might have been facing his sixty-fifth birthday in less than three weeks, but his daily exercise regimen had paid off in a well-muscled torso and thick, tanned biceps. Add to that the face-lift he'd gotten five years earlier and the weekly dyeing ritual that kept his thinning gray hair thick and black, and—presto! Robert Blake was a virile young leading man once again.

Bonny had her own wrinkling to contend with. She'd just celebrated her forty-second birthday, and the flesh she'd depended upon to earn a living since she was a teenager had begun to lose its youthful vitality, drooping, swelling and gathering in folds. Prescription pills and fad diets helped, but only temporarily. She too had been through cosmetic surgery, and years of peroxide, dye and color rinse had left her hair as blowsy as a fright wig. When she let it go too long, she could see the occasional silver weed growing among her natural brunette roots.

When Canavi excused himself to the men's room, Bonny followed him. She was waiting outside the door when he emerged.

"You're with Robert Blake?" she asked.

Canavi nodded and smiled.

"Could I have his telephone number?"

Canavi was taken aback by her brass for a moment, but recovered enough to answer: "If you want his phone number, you'd better ask him yourself."

Apparently she took his advice because when he returned from the bar, she was all over Blake. On this magic evening, deception seemed to work just fine for both Bonny and Robert. Bonny sidled up, giggling every time Blake opened his mouth. Blake sat up a little straighter, clowned a little more convincingly and fell into his surefire *Baretta* banter, peppering his punch lines with Jersey-esque "dese" and "dat's."

New Jersey was something they had in common. He was born north of Newark, in an older Italian neighborhood with tree-lined streets and a pub on every other corner. She was born farther west, out in Morristown, where the Irish and German riffraff mixed with the horsy crowd.

Blake and Bonny left early, and they left together, laughing and leering. Once they were alone in the parking lot, according to Bonny's sister, Blake behaved like a teenager in heat. He was all over her before they even climbed into the front seat of his SUV. Bonny left her car behind at Chadney's. Will Jordan would get back to the hotel somehow. He was a resourceful old coot. What was important right now was fending off Robert Blake's advances, but not too hard.

"At every stoplight he'd stop and grab her and, like, make out with her," said Margerry.

Blake mentioned nothing about prostate problems that occasionally made it hard for him to get an erection, and Bonny did not reveal that she wore a support corset to ease the pain of a slipped disc and keep her weighty breasts from sliding around like pudgy jellyfish. As they drove east, back toward Bonny's hotel, it was summer and there was passion in the night.

Bonny was half naked before they even pulled into the parking lot of the Beverly Garland Holiday Inn. Named for the blond B-movie "scream queen"[3] who appeared in *My Three Sons*, *Gunsmoke*, *Remington Steele* and a host of other *TV Land* chestnuts, the down market hotel was located at the crotch of the Hollywood and Ventura Freeways—the perfect spot for Bonny and Blake to consummate their passion. In fact, Robert took her right there, in the rear of his SUV. If the windows weren't tinted it didn't matter because they more than made up for it with aerobic breathing. By the time they finished rutting like happy, healthy terriers pent up far

---

3. Beverly Garland, born Beverly Lucy Fessenden, was probably best known as Fred MacMurray's wife on *My Three Sons* (1960–72) and as Kate Jackson's mother on *Scarecrow and Mrs. King* (1983–87). Her nickname came from a string of horror movies she made in the 1950s, including *It Conquered the World* (1956), *Not of This Earth* (1957), and *The Alligator People* (1959). Unlike many of her contemporaries, Garland learned early that even an actor steadily in demand rarely retires rich. In 1959, she married developer Fillmore Crank and built the Beverly Garland Hotel and Convention Center within blocks of Universal Studios. While she continues to act well into the twenty-first century, Garland's fortune is grounded in real estate, not filmed fantasy.

too long in separate kennels, the windows were damp with condensation.

Sated and happy, Bobby then said a fond good night. He did not offer, nor did she request, a service fee of any kind. Instead, they exchanged telephone numbers and promised to keep in touch. As her newest paramour drove off into the night, she saw his personalized license plate: SAYZWHO.

Bonny quickly made her way back to her room. She couldn't wait to call her friends back home in Memphis.

2

By the end of the 1990s, Robert Blake no longer needed to work. Shrewd investing and a frugal lifestyle had ensured him a secure retirement.[4] In late 1998, he made preparations to deed over a pair of homes he'd owned for years to Noah and Delinah, his two grown children from his first marriage. Meanwhile, he continued to live comfortably and alone at his self-styled "Mata Hari Ranch," working out in his home exercise room each morning and dancing occasionally in the mirrored tap dancing salon next to his gym.

"He would get up in the morning at six A.M. and work out," said Mark Canavi. "And he wouldn't just work out. He would be in his gym for four hours, working on all kinds of stuff. He had a sauna in there, and he would listen to ragtime or jazz during the whole time. He loved Alice Faye, Doris Day, the Mills Brothers. He'd listen to this stuff for hours while he was working out."

Blake avoided junk food and steered clear of drugs or excessive alcohol. He'd admitted years earlier that he was an addict and could never do anything in moderation. "If a Hershey bar makes me feel better, I'll have a bathtub of them tomorrow," he once told a reporter. "I stopped smoking twenty-five years ago, and just started smoking again a week ago, and I went to an A.A. meeting this morning. Anything

---

4. A financial statement dated May 31, 2000, put his net worth at $8,365,500.

that takes me out of how I feel, I abuse. I don't give a fuck what it is—food, alcohol, nicotine, sleeping pills, uppers, downers, sideways, whatever. If it changes how I feel, I use a lot of it."

So he stuck only to those addictions that he believed were good for him. No fast food. No lethargy. He might be getting older, but Blake refused to "lay around the house and become like a piece of Italian sausage," as he told one acquaintance.

For the most part, Robert Blake kept to himself. His was the only place at the west end of Dilling Street that was surrounded by a six-foot wrought iron fence.[5] Visitors were stopped at the locked front gate until they identified themselves. If the wiry actor lapsed into one of his infrequent glooms, he'd stay indoors and seldom open the door. Once, in a poem he liked to quote, he'd even described himself to friends as an old, blind bear, wandering the winter woods alone:

> *Too mean to die; too lost to care;*
> *But show some caution, he's still the bear.*

Blake was no brooding hermit, however. Reclusive though he might be, he was just as often quite sociable. He smiled and waved at his Studio City neighbors when he came out to pick up the newspaper or the mail, and he could be heard in the front room on occasion playing his old Gibson guitar. He could be funny, cracking a joke or delivering a punch line, and he could also be dreamy, almost as though in a trance when he puttered around the yard or sat on the front porch. He'd glide on his porch swing and stare off into the distance, absently crooning sea chanteys or a cowboy lullaby.

Robert loved the desert. He often drove his Winnebago out to the Mojave on weekends. He'd stop in the middle of

---

5. Just a few doors down from Blake's house was the two-story house used as the exterior of the Bradys' home on *The Brady Bunch*.

nowhere to inhale the clean air and soak in the heat. Though fast approaching seventy, Blake still loved to go biking aboard his Harley, opening up full throttle on the open road. He camped sometimes in the High Sierras and often took along one of his guns for target practice.

He went out regularly for walks around the neighborhood, usually with a pal like sixty-year-old actor John Solari, an ex-con who did time for burglary in both Attica and Sing Sing when he was younger. Blake wore a long black leather coat and he always packed a gun and kept it in his car on the floor beside his seat—a practice that didn't bother Solari in the least. He'd grown up poor and Italian. He understood.

"Robert liked to dance and sing," said Solari. "He always said if he could do it over, he'd be a singer."

In town, Blake did a little clubbing for recreation. There was dancing at the Derby in the Los Feliz Hills or sometimes he'd shoot pool up at the Playboy Mansion, where he'd been welcomed as one of Hefner's favored guests since his *Baretta* days. When musician pal Jack Sheldon played at L.A. area jazz clubs like Lunaria or Jax, Blake was there, shutting his eyes and nodding in rhythm to the beat.

Blake ate out a lot—sometimes at Frankie's on Melrose or nearby Vitello's, a favored Italian restaurant where he was so well-known to the Restivo brothers who owned it that they named one of their menu items for him: a $12.95 spinach and tomato pasta called "Fusilli e Minestra alla Robert Blake." Dozens of actors had contributed autographed 8x10 glossies to the Restivos over the years, and they decorated every square inch of the entry to the restaurant, but Blake's was not among them. His name might be printed on Vitello's menu, but he maintained that he preferred keeping a low profile.

Blake's guilty pleasure, whether eating out or in his own kitchen, was "gravy"—red sauce like the rich marinara Italian chefs drizzle over linguine. But on the whole, though, Blake watched the calories and developed a passion for fat-free health food. He did treat himself occasionally to a frozen dessert at Al Gelato's on Robertson over in Beverly Hills or a bagel at a favorite coffee shop spot near Paramount Studios. Sometimes he met there or at Bob's Donut Shop in

Farmer's Market to catch up on the weekly gossip with a loosely knit circle of other industry regulars. He flirted often with the idea of finding the perfect script that would crown his long and enviable career.

"People have always wanted him to do stuff," said his son, Noah. "For reasons that I don't know, he has chosen not to, or at least to work very infrequently in the last ten or fifteen years."

From time to time, Blake attended stage plays or showed up at charity events, as did any number of other aging celebrities. He joined a regular Wednesday-night poker game for a while and passed much of the rest of his days and evenings defying his dyslexia by reading copiously. He collected old pocket knives, BB guns and pistols as well as books, and visited a nearby firing range to keep up his shooting skills. Mostly, he worked hard at enjoying retirement. Indeed, the angry young screen persona that Robert Blake had cultivated over two generations seemed from the outside to have finally mellowed into a comfortable decline. Along with several of Robert's closer friends, Noah reckoned his father had lapsed into a kind of semipermanent nostalgia.

But nostalgia cuts both ways. There are triumphs and there are regrets. That may have accounted for the increase in his fits of gloom. Blake had taken to evaluating his life and career of late, and despite his many remarkable accomplishments, both always seem to come up wanting.

In one of his last TV appearances, on Roseanne Barr's short-lived daytime talk show, Robert boasted that he could teach anybody to act. When Roseanne's booker tried to get him to return and demonstrate on some nonactor from the studio audience, he declined. Boasts followed by retreats were not new to Blake. That was how he'd lived his life for more than half a century. As Robert himself might have observed in his best *Baretta* street cant, "Ya can lead a horse to water, but ya can't teach ol' dogs new tricks." Combining two opposing ideas into one oddly wise adage was a Blake specialty.

Perhaps it was the nostalgia that made Noah believe his father when he talked about starting up an actors' studio, much like the one that the blacklisted character actor Jeff

Corey opened in L.A. during the 1950s. Blake never tired of waxing on about those days in the McCarthy era, when he joined other young rebels like James Dean, Rita Moreno and Jack Nicholson to study, stretch and tune his acting "instrument" at Corey's Professional Actors Studio. It was a lofty-sounding institution, but it actually began quite modestly at the back of Corey's garage up in the Hollywood Hills.

Noah, who'd struggled to follow in the old man's footsteps since college, envisioned a father-son actors' master class that would similarly tap into L.A.'s vast talent pool. But as was all too frequently the case, Robert Blake's talk about opening an acting school was just that: talk. Noah wound up founding his own school without his father's help.

"I never acted with him. I never acted *near* him," said Noah, more weary than sour about his feckless famous father. "I was never on any of his shows. Basically, I never had anything to do with him, and that's unfortunate, I think. It's too bad."

Noah wasn't looking for a handout, just a hand up, like the one that Donald Sutherland gave to Kiefer, Lloyd Bridges gave to Jeff and Beau, or Martin Sheen gave to his boys Charlie and Emilio Estevez. "My dad always thought that helping his children would somehow cripple them, [keep] them from having to learn from 'the struggle,' which is very interesting," said Noah. "As if my life wasn't struggle enough, he had to impose some more."

When Noah and his sister were growing up, Robert loved to defend both of his children against injustice, whether real or imagined, just so long as that injustice came from the outside world and not from inside the troubled Blake household. Robert and their mother, actress Sondra Kerr, were constantly at war, either with each other or their neighbors. They were both quick to condemn outsiders, sometimes on the flimsiest evidence. Like the cockatoo that had once kept Tony Baretta company, Blake always carried an invisible chip on his shoulder.

"Both him and my mother were very emotional," said Noah. "I guess you could say 'dramatic.' That would be a good word. There was a lot of drama in our house. *Lots* of drama."

As Noah told one old family friend, growing up was often "like a ride in an ambulance." Because the adults seemed always to be at war, either with each other or the rest of the world, the children frequently found themselves drafted. Sometimes the target was Mom, sometimes Dad or sometimes any poor fool unlucky enough to knock at the wrong time at the front door.

According to Noah, neither of his parents hit him or his sister, but both were always wrought up, especially his father. Delinah developed her own wry self-confidence while Noah became sweetly diffident. There was no question that some of their parents' angst spilled over on them.

"There was not a lot of distinction between the adults and the children in our house," recalled Noah. "The roles were not very clear. My father would intermittently be very parental, and then *not* be a parent, and then basically just seem completely disinterested."

Throughout his long career, Robert Blake never seemed to learn that shooting from the lip was not always the best means of public expression. "He's definitely, you know, a type A kind of person," said Noah. "He's very opinionated. He's never been shy about saying how he feels or what he thinks." For instance, whenever the subject of child abuse came up during an interview or in one of his many appearances on the *Tonight Show*, Robert passionately invoked his own tortured childhood as an example of what happens when parents lash out rather than listen to their children. On the other hand, he didn't mind titillating Carson's audience with the revelation that he and Sondra had made love in front of their own children. How else were they going to learn, he wanted to know? As Noah put it, "Our family was like a twenty-four-hour crisis hotline."

The Blakes fought constantly. When Sondra enrolled both youngsters in North Hollywood's private Oakwood School along with other movie stars' children, Robert soon threw a fit, pulled them out and sent them to public school. He felt they needed to learn how to cope with the great unwashed middle class, just as he had been forced to do as a troubled though privileged child star.

But no sooner had Noah and Delinah adjusted to public school than their volcanic father fomented another crisis. Noah meekly suggested that his class march to the theme from *Rocky* during sixth-grade graduation exercises. When the principal politely vetoed the idea, Robert blasted the hapless educator in a national magazine.

And so the pendulum swung, through junior high, high school and on into college. After Sondra and Robert finally divorced in 1982, the Blakes fought over which of them would get custody of Delinah. And through it all, Robert was either overattentive or utterly uninterested in what his children did with their lives. Noah blamed his father's erratic parenting on his lousy upbringing. "He didn't come to the table too well equipped when my sister and I came around," he said.

Robert did get along far better with his daughter than with his son. Delinah was the apple of his eye. Blake even named one of his businesses Delinah Enterprises. Despite his early worry about spoiling her too much by sending her to private school, he continued to lavish star treatment on her well into her teens. For her eleventh birthday, Blake treated his little princess to dinner at venerable Chasen's Restaurant in Beverly Hills—all because Deli had expressed a wish to eat at a "fancy" restaurant. But Blake didn't stop there. He took the celebration up another notch by arranging to have actress Kate Jackson, then riding high as one of the stars of TV's *Charlie's Angels* (Deli's favorite show), emerge on cue from Chasen's kitchen singing "Happy Birthday" with a cake in her hands.

Deli responded in kind. She worshiped her old man and sided with him during the divorce. During one of Blake's several separations from Sondra, his daughter came to visit him in his dressing room on the Universal lot. In a corner she found a statuette of a clownish character with outstretched arms and a silly expression on its face. A small plaque at the base read: I LOVE YOU THIS MUCH! Deli set the figure on her father's desk and announced: "Daddy, you *must* keep this out at all times."

The father-daughter love fest didn't spare Delinah her own psychological challenges. In a 1983 interview that Blake gave *TV Guide,* he proudly announced that his daughter was a straight-A student and wanted to become a pediatric surgeon, but added that she had also been through psychotherapy. "Two years ago, shrinks told me she was neurotic," he said. "Since then she's pulled it back in place, got the show-biz kid out of her blood—doin' great."

With typical Blake bluster, he followed this report of his daughter's mental health with a blast at the precarious behavior of others' children. "Some of my movie friends, their kids're wandering the street, sellin' dope," he said. "They got green hair. *Green hair!*"

As he grew older, in a 1995 interview with *Detour Magazine,* he acknowledged his own failures as a parent. "I'll never make up for what I did to my kids," he said. "They have to go in therapy and they have to work that out. If I could, I would. If it would help me to go to my son and have him beat the shit out of me every day for a year, I'd do it gladly. But it wouldn't make any fucking difference. He's got to go back and take care of his business, the way we all do. All I can be now is the best friend I know how to be, and there's a huge difference between being a friend and a parent. I can't be a parent anymore—they're twenty-eight and twenty-nine years old—but I can be the best friend they have."

Both Blake children remained single well into their thirties—perhaps out of an unspoken fear that marriage might wind up as hideous for each of them as it had been for their parents. Being single didn't pose much of a problem for either Noah or Delinah. They each had their careers.

While Noah lived the semi-Bohemian existence of the West Hollywood wanna-be, running from audition to audition with small theater productions in between, Deli followed a more traditional academic path. She studied psychology at UCLA and Pepperdine, specializing in the very field that Robert had been exploring since he first sat in a psychologist's office back in the late 1950s.

Blake made no secret of his obsession with psychology. He was an early convert to Freud scholar Karen Horney and later Alice Miller, the Swiss psychologist who first linked adult dysfunction to early abuse of the "inner child." John Bradshaw, a Miller disciple, pioneered techniques to rid patients of their demons by helping them get in touch with that "inner child," and Blake was one of Bradshaw's earliest converts. "It's one thing to save an infant," he said. "It's another thing to save an adult with a tortured infant inside."

Delinah earned her psychology M.A. and went on to intern as a marriage, family and child counselor while she finished up her doctoral dissertation at UCLA. But once she graduated, even Delinah drifted out of her father's life. She made her home in Calabasas on the opposite end of the San Fernando Valley. She still saw her father far more frequently than her brother, but all three now lived separate lives. Robert Blake was very much on his own.

Blake was more likely to run into his ex than his kids. Sondra still lived in the neighborhood just a few blocks away. She had never remarried or changed her married name and, some acquaintances believed, alternately feared and still carried a torch for Robert.

Once, twenty years earlier, Blake delivered one of the many mini-lectures for which he developed minor fame among Hollywood journalists who were intent on digging beneath the surface of the well-rehearsed sound bytes of movie stars. Unlike most politically correct careerists who learn early how to spin the media and make no waves, Blake made a practice of letting it all hang out. When he spoke about family values long before it became fashionable to do so, even the most cynical newsman sat up and took notice.

"You can get a job, get an education, have good times, join the Pepsi generation and never have to have a family," Blake said. "But what happens is you end up with a life that has no third act. The hardest job in the world is being a parent or a husband or a wife. But if you walk away from it, there's nothin' left."

What Blake never counted on was his wife and children turning the tables and walking away from him. He had no grandchildren, nor were there any on the horizon. He was sixty-five, and it appeared as though he'd be playing out his vaunted "third act" all by himself.

Lately, he'd even taken up the odd practice of finding all the gifts and tokens that fans had sent him over the years, and sending them back to them. He'd never much cared for gifts, even at Christmas.

"I've never enjoyed Christmas for myself," he once told a TV interviewer for *Entertainment Tonight.* "I do not like the presents I get. When I was a kid we were very poor. The presents were like, 'Oh look! A new pair of pants, something you can use.' Nobody ever bought you a bicycle or anything. That's why I like buying presents for my kids. What I would really like for Christmas. I would like somebody to share the rest of my life with."

And that was it, really. That was what everything had boiled down to.

"He would say, within my hearing, 'Gosh, I'm lonely. I'm so damned lonely,'" recalled Canavi.

Still, life was not unpleasant. Friends dropped by; he answered letters and made the occasional run to the grocery store. A maid came in to clean twice a month, and a handyman/companion performed odd jobs. The house was plastered with film posters, constantly reminding him of his past as that Little Rascal Mickey, Red Ryder's Injun companion Li'l Beaver or *Mokey* (1942), the wide-eyed wonderful waif who won the heart of Donna Reed so many, many years ago.

A corner of his bedroom was an homage to the childhood he wished he'd had, filled with tapes of *The Lone Ranger*, a bunk bed with cowboy sheets, an old-time radio. Even the wallpaper had a Lone Ranger motif. Blake's inner child seemed to have turned interior decorator.

There were far fewer reminders inside the Dilling Street house of the many homicidal characters who grew out of Robert's "inner child," like the mass murderer Perry Smith in Truman Capote's *In Cold Blood* (1967) or Blake's Emmy-winning portrayal of notorious New Jersey killer John List, who slaughtered his entire family in *Judgment Day* (1993).

As 1998 wound to a close, he could count himself lucky. Despite a roller-coaster career whose downs could usually be traced to Blake's own explosive obstinance, the aging actor had everything he needed. The rest of his life looked equally comfortable clear up until the night he met Bonny Lee Bakley. Somehow he'd managed to forget the cautionary advice about sex being like any other addictive drug: the first fix was always free.

He picked up the phone and dialed Bonny's number.

3

Bonny had been waiting for Robert to call. She didn't call him first because that was not what a nice girl did. "It usually takes a man a week or two weeks to call you—sometimes a month—so you never panic," observed Bonny's sister Margerry, in whom Bonny confided.

At first Bonny did panic when she understood for the first time exactly who Robert Blake was. She had a vague notion that night at Chadney's that he was "somebody," but she had no idea how big a somebody! When she spilled the tale to her younger sister Margerry and her pal Judy Howell, they stayed up all night jabbering about the implications. This guy had once been on *Baretta*!

Judy was ten years older than Bonny, and she remembered Tony Baretta. Bonny slept with *Robert Blake*? This was so much bigger than that time in the late eighties when Bonny gave Jerry Lee Lewis oral sex backstage at an oldies concert.

"He's really kind of cute," said Bonny.

"He's ugly and short, but he is a star," said Judy.

Judy and Margerry agreed that it was imperative that Bonny follow through correctly. Bonny had read and reread the bestselling how-to book *The Rules*,[6] about the do's and don'ts of snaring a man. The very first rule was not to spook him. Let him make that all-important first move.

---

6. Her other dog-eared bible was *I'm with the Band: Confessions of a Groupie* by Pamela Des Barres.

A nail-biting few weeks passed, but eventually Blake did call. What was more, he was just as witty and clever and sexy as he had been that night in the parking lot. She loved his husky, distinctive voice with its faint hint of danger, his Jersey patter sprinkled with "ain't's" and "dat's". Funny how he'd never lost that accent, even after living in L.A. for sixty years.

She wanted to impress him, so "she played up her illegal activities to the hilt," said Margerry. "She made claims that just were untrue. She made her business out to be bigger and worse than it was because she thought it intrigued him. She told him her brother, Joey, was a hit man [and] she told him that I was a Colombian drug dealer."

Marge had, in fact, been convicted once in 1996 for stealing government property and using a false ID in connection with one of Bonny's Social Security scams—a mistake Marge had never made again. Joey's worst crime was getting drunk in Florida in 1992, snorting coke and stealing a car for a joyride. But if Bonny needed to exaggerate to land a celebrity, so be it. Blake apparently liked the idea of associating with a criminal enough to keep the romance going.

After she'd bedded Robert a few more times, Bonny returned home to Memphis in triumph. She regaled her friends with tales of a penny-pinching Hollywood oddball who took her up to a friend's mountain cabin and walked around the place in a pair of duct-taped slippers. She began to think that she might have made a mistake, that maybe he wasn't so well off after all. When they returned to his house in Studio City, she checked out his closet when he wasn't looking. She found nothing but jeans and black T-shirts similar to the outfit he'd had on at Chadney's the night they met. He spared no expense on neck and footwear, though. He wore Enrico Coveri ties and DiFabrizio boots with raised heels that made him appear several inches taller than five-foot-four.

"She figured he was just like her: when you find something you like, buy five of 'em and you'll always have something in the closet you're happy to wear," said Margerry.

Bobby and Bonny were alike in other ways too. When he told her about growing up abused, Bonny nodded sympathetically. She too had been abused by her own father. Here was a man capable of seeing beyond her fading bleached-blond charms to the real Bonny underneath—a sad, successful survivor of her own mean childhood.

One of the first things Bonny did was to run an asset check on him. There was no sense in chasing down a celebrity if the only thing he owned was his celebrity. Bonny smiled when she got the report back on Blake's portfolio. He checked out like a Dun & Bradstreet blue chip. The guy was loaded, with an eight-million-dollar portfolio spread out over real estate, stocks, business investments. A TV has-been he might be, but he was a well-heeled has-been.

She watched him dye his hair jet-black and torture his abs to delay the inevitability of old age. He lived in a ramshackle homestead on the flatlands of the San Fernando Valley, but he still stayed in shape in case that next big movie role turned out to be just around the corner. He had a room behind the house walled with mirrors like a ballet studio, where he stripped to the waist and danced in tights. She thought that was weird enough, but the even stranger thing was the gun cabinet. He had a padlocked display case next to the plié barre, stocked with bright, shiny rifles. He'd take them out and caress them. An odd duck, this Robert Blake. But then, Bonny liked a man with a hint of danger about him.

He was moody, just like her. Maybe not exactly in the same way, because Bonny's moods swung between happy wacky and can't-get-outta-bed depressed. Blake's moods could only be described as mercurial. One minute he was a pussycat; the next he was a panther. When he got angry, his eyes changed to pewter and that elastic face of his turned into a scowl. And yet, to Bonny, more than just another eccentric in a long line of characters who had waltzed in and out of her own strange life, Robert Blake was her alter ego. In short, she told her sister and Judy, they were soul mates. They were made for each other.

Of course, she and Christian Brando were made for each other too. She'd been chasing Marlon Brando's troubled eldest son even before he was paroled from prison in January 1996. She'd mailed him some of her photos and struck up a correspondence. Once he was out, she didn't let up. "She

hired this female private detective to find out where he lived
and then she wrote him again," recalled Judy Howell.

"The moment Christian got out of jail, she started pursuing him," added Margerry. "He was so cute."

He was also damaged from years of abuse at the hands of
a volcanic narcissist for a father and an angry alcoholic
mother. He'd grown up pampered one day and pummeled
the next. Before he was out of his teens, Christian had in-
gested all manner of drugs and after-dinner drinks. Marlon
himself called his grown son a "gun-toting alcoholic" long
before Christian shot his half sister's boyfriend to death in
the spring of 1990.

The darkly handsome Christian was then thirty-two.
Bonny read all about his terrible tragedy in the tabloids.
Convicted of shooting pregnant Cheyenne Brando's lover,
Dag Drollet, point-blank in the face during a squabble over
Drollet's alleged mistreatment of her, Christian wound up
spending half of a ten-year sentence at the California State
Men's Colony in San Luis Obispo.

It seemed like a short sentence for blowing someone's
face off, but it *was* L.A., after all, where celebrity counted
in the courtroom. When Marlon waddled to the witness
stand, it began to look bad for the prosecution. The master
Method actor wept for his lost son, and reporters out in the
corridor started to wonder whether Christian would get off
with a suspended sentence or simply walk. That he eventually pleaded guilty to voluntary manslaughter and did any
time at all seemed nothing less than a small miracle. As
Bonny and her circle of friends knew full well, celebrities
never got equal treatment under the law.

When Christian did get out of prison, his publicity-averse
father whisked him away from the tabloid vultures and put
his son into "treatment." Bonny translated that to mean he
kept Christian away from newspaper and television reporters. There would be no more painful public spectacles like
the trial or its media aftermath, which the elder Brando believed responsible for his daughter's suicide.[7]

---

7. In April 1995, Cheyenne hanged herself at the Brando family
compound in Tahiti, where she and Drollet met and where she returned

Bonny found Christian living temporarily in one of the many properties that his father owned in and around L.A., but before they could meet, he slipped from her grasp. He moved out of state with no forwarding address. Bonny believed that Marlon had found out about her. Not to be thwarted, she hired a private investigator. Bonny's intrepid detective tracked Christian down to the logging town of Kalama, Washington, thirty miles north of Portland. Bonny wrote to him and finally arranged to meet Christian face-to-face.

The beefy firstborn of Marlon Brando and fiery Irish/Indian actress Anna Kashfi was only a few years older than Bonny. Once his famous father finally died, she figured Christian would be worth a fortune.[8] She cooed over his burnt-out demeanor, much the same way she sympathized over Blake's confessions of childhood abuse. Christian made her feel maternal, in a horny sort of way. Just like Bonny, he had dropped out of school by the eleventh grade, and they had other things in common too, including a passion for rock and roll. Nor did Christian care about her having kids or being with other guys or having an ex-husband as a business partner either.

Unfortunately, Bonny told her pals, Christian Brando tended to have paranoid delusions about half the time. For this reason alone, Margerry, Judy and even her ex, Paul Gawron, were all relieved when she met Blake—if only slightly. "She was asking, 'Who do you think I should go with, Christian or Blake?'" said Margerry. "And obviously they're both lethal."

---

with their child after Christian was convicted. Like her half brother, she had spent much of her adult life addicted to drugs and alcohol, in and out of mental health facilities.

8. As it turned out, Bonny might have arrived too late for the Brando gravy train had she lived. In April 2002, Maria Cristina Ruiz, forty-three, filed a $100 million breach-of-contract lawsuit against Marlon Brando claiming the seventy-eight-year-old actor fathered three of her children during her fourteen years as his maid. If she wins, it might break Brando financially.

"Between the two of them, I would say Blake is probably the safer bet," said Gawron. "Christian has already killed somebody."

For the first time in her years of celebrity stalking, Bonny had two celebrities to choose from. She asked everyone from Margerry and Judy to Paul to her own two grown children, Holly and Glenn Gawron, to help her pick: the handsome hallucinating convicted killer or the smoldering former TV actor?

"I thought, well, when I met Blake, I kinda wanted him, but I kinda didn't, because he wasn't like up to par with the looks," said Bonny. "And I thought I was already in love with Christian."

Despite his wild mood swings, by the beginning of 1999, she found herself leaning toward Blake. "Think this guy's going to kill me?" she asked her ex.

"I never met the guy," Gawron told her. "I don't know nothing about him."

Bonny decided to move the selection process to a new level. Neither of her beaux liked to use condoms, so she started taking the fertility drug Clomid, telling them both that they were birth-control pills. Sooner or later, one of them would get lucky—and whoever the winner was got to marry her.

Bonny liked living dangerously.

4

In the meantime, Delinah wanted a baby.

Unlike her brother, the temperamental artist, Delinah was a cool-headed social scientist. When she knew what she wanted, she went after it with steely determination. The petite, pretty brunette was a successful psychotherapist, at the forefront of the highly competitive field of clinical psychology before she was even out of her twenties.

Still, the most successful career didn't make someone a mother.

Deli had just turned thirty-two, and her biological clock was ticking. A husband might have been nice, but what Deli was really looking for was a male to father her child. To further complicate matters, she had a "severe physical condition" she would not discuss.

In Michael Edward Johnson, a fellow she'd met in rehab years earlier, Deli believed she had found her man. On the marriage license he gave "music industry biller" as his profession, but friends said it was more accurate to call him a handyman. He was tall and had hair as long as Deli's, and had met with Robert's approval. Blake had even offered to put Johnson through college.

Lissa Hakim, a minister of the Universal Life Church,[9]

---

9. Founded in Modesto in 1959 by the Rev. Kirby Hensley, the Universal Life Church offers mail-order ordination to anyone who applies. A 1974 court decision granted tax exempt status to Hensley and his lucrative side business of accepting donations for a line of ministerial orders, doctorates of divinity and canonical certificates, all suitable for

married the couple at the Calabasas Inn on February 20, 1999. Robert paid for the reception and many of the wedding guests were the couple's friends from rehab. Delinah's mother, Sondra, was noteworthy by her absence. Still, there were testimonials and dancing, much gaiety and good wishes.

Then, one month after it began, the marriage ended.

"Before the marriage, I agreed and promised to have children right after marriage," Johnson later admitted to the judge when he agreed to an annulment. "Within one week after the date of the marriage, we stopped living together in the same house." In fact, said Johnson, he and Delinah had never even slept in the same room together, let alone the same bed.

"He told me he came home one night and she was lying on the sofa, frozen, comatose," said Gary Randall, an old friend who later became Johnson's boss in the film business. "She said she had misgivings about the wedding, about the marriage, and that it was over. Done."

And that wasn't all: the promise of putting him through school, the car that Blake had given him—everything dissolved with the marriage. Johnson was broke and homeless.

"He was sad but he got over it," said Randall, a set decorator who later got Johnson a union job moving furniture at one of the studios.

In court, both Delinah and Michael admitted that their marriage had been a sham.

"I changed my mind and decided not to have children," explained Johnson. Of course, he neglected to tell Deli any of this until after they were married. She told him to get out, hired her father's law firm and took Johnson to court, claiming she had not been thinking soundly when she married him. She charged Johnson with fraud and, by April, she was once again an unmarried woman.

---

framing. Citing First Amendment guarantees of religious freedoms, the courts also found that ULC ministers had the right to administer sacraments, including marriage.

But Deli was an unmarried woman who still had no child, or any prospect of getting one soon.

Bonny Bakley had no such problem. During the cold wet winter of 1999, just as she was first getting to know Robert Blake—his penchant for curling up into a fetal position while sleeping with a gun beneath his pillow, for example—Bonny's menstrual cycle suddenly pedaled to a halt. She was four months shy of forty-three, so she had to rule out menopause as the cause of her dry spell.

Those fertility drugs she began taking after her initial tryst with Blake appeared to have kicked in. Bonny was pretty sure by the timing that Baretta was the winner in the Blake-or-Brando sweepstakes.

At first she thought Blake might get mad. In their short time together, she'd seen him angry and it was not pretty. He wasn't as dumb as Brando either. He'd demand to check her prescription vials. She decided to break the news to him gently, suggesting at first that she was late and that she didn't think it was anything to get alarmed about.

He wasn't alarmed, though. In fact, she told her friends back in Memphis he actually seemed a little proud that he still had the juice to be a papa. "She said to him with the first pregnancy, 'Well, if I don't get an abortion, will you leave me? Will you break up with me?'" recalled Margerry. "And he said, 'No, I would never do that.' She said, 'Well, then why would I get an abortion?' I mean, she actually believed that he *wanted* her to get pregnant because he left the door open."

"He was overjoyed," said Judy. "He will do the right thing. We'll take care of the baby."

In the end, however, the whole thing turned out to be a false alarm. Her menstrual cycle kickstarted again, and she assured Blake that she wasn't pregnant.

By the spring of 1999, their odd relationship was well established. Bonny constantly stayed in touch, by phone or by mail, and looked forward to each California visit. That suited Blake fine. He had made one point clear from day one: he was not interested in any kind of bond beyond occasional sex.

While this obviously wasn't all that Bonny had in mind,

she had plenty to keep her busy. After all, her business motto printed on her office stationery read: "Life is a game. Play it."

As head of her thriving home-based pornography enterprise, Bonny was constantly on the road, either tending to her many mail drops or visiting prospective clients. She spent a lot of time back in Memphis, checking up on the welfare of her mother, her sister, her brothers and her three children, and assisting Paul in getting out porn letters each month so that the money kept rolling in.

There were galleys to review before each monthly copy deadline for the various regional swinger magazines she used to advertise her goods. The randy snapshots had to be reproduced so that they looked slick yet homespun. And she had hundreds of letters that had to be handwritten. In a pinch, they could be typed and signed, but Bonny knew that her customers preferred that personal touch. Lines like "I'd love to suck your hard, thick cock all night long while you eat my pussy" or "you make me wet when I think about licking your big hairy balls" just didn't read the same in typescript. Writing smutty lines in longhand added a certain level of sincerity to the whole process of assembly-line passion.

She also had to match the right photo to each client. It didn't do to simply toss any old vaginal display into an envelope and drop it in the mail. If she left it to Paul, that is exactly what would happen, and they would soon enough begin to lose their market share. No, after years of catering to the anonymous onanistic needs of all sorts of men, Bonny understood that properly second-guessing exactly what kind of female a man fantasized about could spell the difference between a onetime sale and a satisfied return customer.

There were the basics, of course, like the age-old question of blondes, brunettes or redheads. But it didn't stop there. There was black versus brown versus white skin. Ethnicity could be a big factor in snagging a subscriber. You want Italian or shall we send out for Chinese?

There was also body size. Were they into normal, hefty, obese, or hockey stick? Some guys fancied grandmothers old enough for dentures. Others liked them mature, beginning to wrinkle and certain to sag, but still barely holding on to a discernible waistline. Some looked for something in the twenty-something range, others way down the age scale to a barely legal Lolita.

Breasts were equally important. Lawyers and other white collar professionals seemed to savor little more than a pair of swollen bee stings while truckers and ex-cons wanted enough udder to choke Babe the Blue Ox. Go figure. After all these years, men never ceased to amaze her.

Once Bonny got the selection process down to the right type of woman, her own uncanny intuition took over. This was what separated her operation from that of mere amateurs. She studied each individual response to her ads for clues. Did this guy want lots of fur or did he prefer a clean shaven gal? Did he want a relatively tasteful peek-a-boo, reminiscent of Sharon Stone's "Mind if I smoke?" scene from *Basic Instinct*, or a close-up that resembled a *National Geographic* aerial shot of the mouth of the Amazon?

Inviting or sangfroid. Sometimes she'd have to spread out a dozen or more poses on the kitchen table to find just the right one. At first this practice bothered Paul. What with the kids and all their school friends wandering in and out at all hours of the day and night, wouldn't they be affected by seeing mom's privates go public? Apparently not. It was all part of the business, she explained, like the patient mother that she was. "She liked these guys having her picture," said Paul. "She enjoyed that."

Indeed, Bonny the exhibitionist preferred parading naked through the suburban Memphis home she shared with Gawron and the three children to wearing any clothing at all. Bonny would strip, skinny-dip in the pool out back, get herself a nice tall glass of Dr Pepper and stand in front of a floor fan.

She saw absolutely nothing wrong with using sex as a tool and said as much to her family. Bonny likened what she did to late night TV ads for X-rated phone conversations at $5 a minute. She taught them that sex is a natural part of life's many experiences.

Actually, Bonny had a great relationship with her children. At least, that's what she told herself. She bought whatever faddish electronic gadget or fashionable bauble that their instant gratification demanded, provided she wasn't on the road or a little short of cash that week.

She spent lots of quality time with them going to the movies, buying the extra-large pizza from Domino's or taking them along on one of her midnight mail runs. In fact, both Glenn and Holly were with her on that February night in 1996 when she got arrested by the feds.

With the kids were in the back of her 1990 Ford van, she was driving through Marion, Arkansas, just across the Mississippi River from Memphis, at two a.m. Bonny got pulled over for running a stop sign. It wouldn't have been much more than another traffic ticket to toss in the glove compartment with the rest, except this time she panicked. She was usually cool and coy in a traffic stop, flashing a little thigh—or more—if she thought it might help her situation, but this night nothing seemed to work out the way it should. Bonny was worried that Holly and Glenn had pot stashed in their backpacks. She'd told them countless times how opposed she was to using drugs of any kind, but kids would be kids. If they did have a Baggie or two, she would be busted as well.

Noticing how flustered she was, the policeman asked if he could search the van and started demanding ID. Unfortunately, Bonny had plenty. Seven driver's licenses and five Social Security cards, to be exact, for everyone from Bonny Lee Bakley to Elizabeth Baker to Lorraine Drake, Sylvia Stefanow, Alexandria King Daniela and Christina Scheier, a woman Bonny had known since grammar school back in New Jersey. Bonny had introduced Christina to the porn trade, but they'd had a recent falling-out, so Bonny got even by stealing Christina's identity and adding it to all of her others. All of it spilled out of her purse while Arkansas highway patrolman Nick Phillips examined it with his flashlight. He also found sixteen stolen credit cards and ten more that had been issued in variations of Bonny's name. He headed back to his squad car to call in her arrest.

Her case didn't go to court for another seventeen months. Then the judge fined Bonny $1,050 and took her driver's license collection away—all except her own. She put Bonny on probation for three years, beginning in February 1998. Bonny saw nothing to be gained by telling Blake or Brando about any of this. She shrewdly figured that what they didn't know couldn't hurt her.

After her sentencing, she rented an apartment in Little Rock so she could keep up with her probation requirements. She wasn't supposed to leave the state without permission, except to go home to see Paul and the kids in Memphis. Her probation officer suggested she get a job, and she did. The man who delivered the *Memphis Commercial Appeal* in the neighborhood told Bonny she could take over his route. She went to him with a proposal. What if she took over the route, but continued to pay him his old salary plus a premium to deliver the papers? That way she'd have pay stubs to show that she was holding down a job.

The deal was accepted and Bonny made plans to jet off to the West Coast once more. Through persistence, determination, good humor and sleight of hand, there was always a solution to even the most impossible situation. Like Frankie Valli used to sing: big girls don't cry.

5

In August, almost a year after they'd first met, Bonny was pregnant. For real this time. On top of that, she was pretty sure that the kid was Blake's. She'd timed it so that it would be. She sat down at the dining room table back in Memphis, trying to figure the best way to break the news. "I hate to tell you this, but the pill did not work for me," she wrote. "I was supposed to take them for a week or two at first. I didn't start them until a couple days before. Now you don't have to worry about it happening." She even told him to "forget the vasectomy or any means of birth control. All that stuff just turns me off. In fact, I may want to try for another."

"You can't have a baby!" Blake shrieked at her over the phone after he got her letter.

Seeing as the birth control pill didn't work, he told her to try a different kind of pill: RU-486, the abortion capsule that induces miscarriage even several weeks after conception.

No way, said Bonny. Such drugs were illegal in the U.S. and she was still on probation.

Blake switched tactics: he was dying. He hadn't told her because he didn't want to upset her, but he had both prostate cancer and colon cancer. He was going under the knife real soon because the chemo just wasn't doing the job. He couldn't be a father. He couldn't be a husband. He was a walking corpse.

"The therapy just wears me out," he told her. "I guess I'm lucky my hair hasn't fallen out. If this surgery doesn't work out, the end of the trail is a couple years off for me."

Bonny was not unsympathetic, but she couldn't help suspecting that he might be lying. She had learned that he did tend to exaggerate when agitated. She flew back out to L.A. to see him, to reassure him that she wanted him as much as she wanted the baby and to generally smooth the waters. When she called from her hotel, he told her he was coming over in the morning to get her pregnancy terminated. "We're gonna go to the clinic and get that out of the way," Blake said.

But he never showed up. He called later and explained that his cancer had kicked up again and he'd spent the night at the hospital.

Bonny was dubious. He didn't seem sick to her.

The next time he called, he had recovered enough to yell at her over the phone line. He couldn't believe what she had conned him into. He didn't even want to see her until the fetus was scraped out.

"Couldn't I just maybe give temporary custody to my mother or something?" she pleaded.

"Have the baby and give it to your mother? Why? What would that do, Bonny?"

"Because you don't want it around you."

"I'd rather you didn't have it."

Bonny broke into sobs. "Why can't you let me be with you and I'll make my mother watch it?" she begged.

Blake ignored her. "You know, if you are going to do it, you have to do it really soon."

"I don't want to do it!"

"You know all those crazy letters you wrote me?" he said, with a dangerous edge in his voice. "You already knew you were pregnant and all that stuff. You are who you are and you do what you do. If you can live with yourself doing stuff like that, it's gonna come down on you."

"All I wanted is to be with you," Bonny said. "I didn't know there was anything wrong."

"Deliberately getting pregnant is wrong," Blake replied. "You wrote letters to me about how you are going to get an abortion. You promised me. You said, 'I'll take pills. You don't have to worry. If I ever get pregnant, I swear on my life I'll get an abortion.' How can you lie to me like that?"

"Don't do this!" Bonny sobbed.

"I'm not the bad guy here. I didn't lie. I didn't cheat. I didn't hustle. I didn't do anything wrong."

Oh yeah? Bonny began clicking off the times she'd caught him in various lies.

Blake cut her short. "You got it all figured out in your head already. Getting pregnant deliberately and lying to me about abortions. That's who you are and that's what you do, and that is the name of that tune."

"You don't understand," Bonny protested. "I figured that maybe there would be a better connection between us."

"Oh, yeah," he answered sarcastically. "Getting pregnant when it is the one thing I'm terrified of. That's gonna be a better connection. You lied to me, you double-dealt me and that's who you are! You promised me! You said, 'Don't worry, Robert. No matter what, I'll have an abortion.' And it was all a lie!"

"If you don't want me out here, I won't . . . ."

He cut her off again, shouting into the receiver. "You swore to me on your life that no matter what, I didn't have to worry and that was a rotten, stinking, filthy lie, and you deliberately got pregnant. Your period ended on August 20 and you were out here fucking me on the exact day you were supposed to. For the rest of your life, you'll have to live with that, and for the rest of my life I'll never forget it."

By now Bonny knew when to be passive and let him vent. She wept into the receiver, pleading for mercy. He liked to blow his top. When he was finished, he settled right down. He was passive-aggressive. No question. He'd eventually give in.

They'd been through lovers' quarrels before. He'd yell and scream and carry on with the most horrible language, and Bonny would burst into tears and there would be phones slamming down and calls back and forth and more tears. Sometimes Blake wouldn't return her calls for weeks. But Bonny persevered. She waited and eventually he'd call or at least accept *her* call, and they'd make up and the whole cycle would start again.

"He'd come on really mushy and sweet, like he's really falling for me," she explained to one of her friends. "I was backing off then, and then all of a sudden I didn't know what happened. But I fell for him and then he started backing off and then I got those awful feelings."

Robert Blake, she had learned, could be manipulative, morose and explosively angry. According to friends and acquaintances alike, that pretty much described his behavior throughout most of his adult life. She was also learning that he could be kinky.

"He liked rough sex," said Judy Howell. "One night he strangled her while they were making love so hard that she nearly passed out."

"He almost went too far with the kinkiness," said Howell. "She told me it scared her but yet, there was that attraction."

"During sex he grabbed her by the hair and ripped it out by the roots," said Margerry.

Bonny told him that the only reason she wanted to have his baby was so that she could get close to him and become a part of his life. He accused her of using her pregnancy as a threat. At one point, he even suggested that she sell it. He knew where she could get $100,000 for it.

"If you wanted to be with me, all you had to do is be with me," said Blake. "Yeah, I'm neurotic and crazy and disappear from time to time, but I always come back and you know that."

"What about now?" she asked.

"Baby, the ball is in your court. I've told you, I know who you are and I know *what* you are," he said, referring to her pornography.

He made it sound like being a pornographer was a bad thing. What about Blake's old pal Hugh Hefner? What about Bob Guccione or Larry Flynt? They were pornographers. What made it so different for them? "You rob people."

"I don't do anything they don't want to do," she insisted. "I don't do anything illegal."

The more Blake learned about her business, the more he complained—and yet, he seemed fascinated too. Bonny had never tried to hide what she did because, in the beginning at any rate, Blake actually seemed intrigued. She shared some of the funnier stories about her customers. Bonny told her sister and other confidantes that her postal exhibitionism appeared to titillate Blake. Soon enough, however, titillation turned to revulsion.

After realizing Blake wouldn't give in, she decided to visit Christian Brando in Kamala, Washington. Although she knew the baby wasn't his, she took the necessary precautions while visiting Christian in case she needed to pass the kid off as his. "Of course, when she had it like six months later, she'd have to explain that it was a ten-pound preemie," Margerry said wryly.

After Bonny returned to Arkansas, she began to taunt Blake in her phone calls and letters, playing on his ego. "After all, it may not just be your money I'd miss out on by marrying you," she wrote. "It might be Marlon's . . . via Christian someday."

Around this time Bonny thought about buying a blouse that had GOLD DIGGER stitched across the front. "The next time we go to dinner, I'll wear it, because that's what he thinks [of me] anyway," she bitterly told her sister.

Bonny had already proven she could support herself very nicely without a man. The operation had grown so big in fact that she and Paul now had mail drops in a half dozen states. She talked about going international, starting with Australia, where she'd heard rich, love-starved old men dotted the Outback. She'd even looked into opening an account at a Mailboxes Etc. on Ventura Boulevard, a mile from where Blake lived.

Everything was computerized nowadays so that she could keep track of clients and not make the same stupid mistakes she'd made in earlier years, like sending out teasing form letters to established customers or getting her crotch shots mixed up. Very bad for business. Thanks to mail merge and her deep database, such grievous errors were now kept to a minimum.

"She was very entrepreneurial about it," observed attorney Jonathan Kirsch, a publishing expert who reviewed dozens of Bonny's letters a few years later. "She's a gifted pornographer, and she's very much in control. She's very calculating and does not come across as a victim. She's probably quite the opposite. She comes across as a victimizer. And it's like Robert Blake was her last victim."

Blake may have seen her as trailer trash, attaching herself to him like a famished lamprey, but Bonny never saw it that way at all. All she wanted was to become Mrs. Robert Blake.

For the time being, however, Blake ignored her phone calls, threw away her letters and retreated farther and farther into his cave. He felt trapped.

"People hurt each other all the time," Blake told Bonny. "But when you hurt somebody deliberately, somebody you care about, rip their fucking heart out, make them crawl and squirm, that's tough stuff. I mean, you have to live with yourself, and I don't know how you do it. . . .

"The one thing in the world you knew I was terrified of was anybody getting pregnant, and you did it deliberately. Why? Not because you wanted to be with me. It has something to do with some crazy shit that's going on in your head that you want Robert Blake's baby. And that's all on you, baby, and *you* have to live with that. You schemed this whole thing."

6

On June 2, 2000, Bonny gave birth to a beautiful blond girl at the University of Arkansas Medical Service in Little Rock. She named her Christian Shannon Brando, but anyone could tell just by looking at the infant that it was not Brando's. She had Robert Blake's dark, piercing stare and the same small rosebud mouth. The child uncannily resembled turn-of-the-century baby pictures of Blake's own mother.

Contrary to what some of her peers might have believed, peripatetic Bonny loved all of her children. She might leave them with Paul Gawron while she gallivanted all over the country chasing down celebrities or picking up her porn post, but she was not an absentee mom. She saw to it that her kids were well cared for. There was no way she'd ever do what her own mother had done and give her children up for adoption. Each one was very special to her for very different reasons. Sweet, sulky Holly. Big ol' lumbering Glenn. Little freckle-faced Jeri Lee.

Yet Bonny's attachment to Christian Shannon superceded the bond with her other three children. She insisted on breast-feeding the baby. She was Bonny's ticket to Hollywood. She was still trying to convince Blake that she was his daughter during the summer of 2000, but Blake remained in denial.

Her thoughts turned back to Christian Brando.

"I thought, well, when I met Blake I kinda wanted him, but I kinda didn't because he wasn't up to par with the looks," Bonny confessed over the phone to Ray Hale, a roadie who once worked with Frankie Valli and who had become one of Bonny's confidants over the years. "I thought, well, I don't know if I really would want him the rest of my life because he's going to get even older and worse-looking and I'm already in love with Christian."

Christian told Bonny he was prepared to accept this child as his daughter. He wanted to see the baby as soon as possible.

"Who would you go for?" Bonny asked Ray. "Blake or Christian? I'd probably feel more safe with Blake."

"Blake ain't gonna let you hustle him," said Ray. "Blake's too slick."

"You think Blake is like a genius?"

"I think he's hip. You ain't gonna get a dime out of him. . . . He's not a dummy. I think he's going to use you more than you use him."

"What would he use me for?"

"Just sex."

As if on cue, little Christian Shannon cried. She could be heard squealing in the background over the phone.

"I don't know if the baby is going to work for or against me," said Bonny. "Some guys don't like having a kid squalling around. They get on your nerves."

"Is it really his baby?"

"Yeah," said Bonny.

Over the summer, Bonny vowed she was going to wear Blake down. She sent him photos of the baby. He would have to accept that the child was his.

Hollywood's leading men had a tradition of impregnating women, publicly denying any wrongdoing and quietly paying off the mother. They had to uphold their public images at all costs. With the perfection of DNA blood-typing, denying paternity was becoming harder. Robert Blake would be convicted in the court of public opinion should he deny the kid and it turn out to be his. He also had another consideration. If this child was truly his, then he knew exactly what he wanted to do. After all, he had another daughter, and she wanted a baby.

In late August Blake agreed to the DNA test. Bonny violated her probation in Arkansas once again, and flew with the baby to L.A. the first week of September. Even before the results of the blood tests came back, though, Blake knew. This was his daughter. All ambiguity ended abruptly the moment he laid eyes on her.

Blake picked up Bonny and the baby at the airport and drove them back to the house. This was not the same Robert Blake who'd ranted over the phone and flat out ordered her to abort the child. This Robert Blake was downright solicitous. He melted, smiling and cooing all over the little girl. He'd already spent nearly $1,000 on a nursery and hired a live-in nanny. Funny how his cancer had cleared up too.

He drove Bonny to a nearby cafe, but just as they sat down for lunch, two policemen showed up. Bonny's eyes widened when they told her she was under arrest for leaving Arkansas while still on probation.

Bonny panicked, but Blake patted her hand. Not to worry. She'd have to go with them, but he'd take care of the baby until he could call his lawyer and bail her out.

Once Bonny and the cops were in the car and headed toward the North Hollywood station, one of the cops informed her that he was just a week away from retiring. All he needed was another arrest report to type up. He made her an offer. If he just put Bonny on a plane back to Little Rock, could she be trusted to report to her probation officer when she got there? They'd forget the whole thing ever happened.

Bonny heaved a sigh of relief. She was worried about little Christian Shannon, but guessed the baby would be all right with Blake, since he'd hired a nanny. It wasn't until hours later, when she was back in Arkansas, that she found she'd been had. When Bonny breathlessly called her probation officer with her abject apologies for violating the terms of her probation, he told her she was going to be under house arrest—a private investigator, hired by Robert Blake, had called to tell him that Bonny had violated her parole.

"He stole the baby the same day of the DNA test, and nobody's ever gotten to see her since," said Margerry.

That wasn't exactly true. Bonny got to see her a couple more times for an hour or two, but Blake did have the baby and he was not giving her up.

The nanny turned out to be Cody Blackwell, a woman who'd worked for Blake in the past as a maid. The two cops were not cops at all, though one of them, Will Jordan—not to be confused with Bonny's friend, actor Will Jordan—was a retired LAPD officer, a former sixteen-year veteran of the force, who worked for Blake as a private investigator.

While Bonny was spitting nails in Little Rock over Blake's duplicity, back in L.A. Robert had worked quickly. Once Bonny and the "cops" were out of sight, he drove up to Blackwell's apartment in the Hollywood Hills. On the off chance that the ruse didn't work at the restaurant and they had to revert to Plan B, Blake had instructed Blackwell to take the baby home with her.

As Blackwell later described it to *Star* magazine, Plan B involved a six-foot, 250-pound bruiser nicknamed Moose—his real name was Earle Caldwell, a forty-six-year-old car stereo installer whom Blake had hired the previous year as a gofer and bobyguard. Clad in camouflage fatigues and combat boots, Moose was waiting inside a utility closet at Blake's house to subdue Bonny if she came back to the house and started pitching a fit because her baby was missing.

Fortunately, Plan B wasn't necessary. Blake ordered Blackwell to strap the baby into the infant car seat in the cab of his truck. The next stop was Calabasas. Just off the Ventura Freeway, Blake dropped Blackwell at a McDonald's, gave her $10 and told her to buy herself a Happy Meal. She waited for him for close to an hour. He returned without the baby.

"I knew he must have left her with Delinah," said Blackwell.

For most of the next year Delinah's home would be the baby's home. Courtesy of her father, Delinah had her own infant to raise with neither the pain of childbirth nor the impediment of a husband.

All the way back to Studio City, Blake banged on the steering wheel, cursing, snarling. He swore he'd hold on to the baby no matter what. "Just let them come for me," he said. "Just let them try. I've got guns. I'll pick them off one by one as they come over my fence. I'll leave their bones in the yard for the birds."

When Blackwell tried to calm him and question him about the kidnapping, Blake shushed her, and paid her $300.

"The trouble with you, Cody, is that you live your life like Mary Poppins," he said. "Nice guys always finish last."

Back in Little Rock, fitted with a monitoring bracelet to ensure that she stayed under house arrest for the duration of her probation, Bonny fumed. She called Marvin Mitchelson, the famous divorce lawyer who tripped up Lee Marvin back in 1979 when he tried to deny his live-in girlfriend, Michelle Triola, a settlement.[10] Mitchelson told Bonny he was retired, but he suggested Beverly Hills attorney Cary Goldstein, who told Bonny he would be happy to threaten Blake with a paternity suit.

Bonny flew back to L.A. on October 1 with her parole officer's permission, and along with filing a police report accusing Blake of stealing her child, she delivered an ultimatum: marry her or pay $7,500 a month in child support. Furthermore, Bonny threatened to go public with the whole sordid story if her demands weren't met.

Blake gave in. By October 3, they had hammered out an eighteen-page prenuptial agreement that guaranteed that Blake would never have to pay her a dime and that Bonny could remain a mail-order pornographer as long as she did none of her business on Blake's property. They both agreed that community property would never be an issue because there wouldn't be any. Blake would keep what he owned and Bonny would keep hers. The same went for retirement plans, insurance benefits, real estate, investments. According to their agreement, everything was separate. To underscore this point, Blake's lawyers added a section called "Absolute Waiver of Spousal Support Forever." Neither Bonny nor

---

10. Actually, Mitchelson won only $104,000 for his client, but he did coin the term "palimony" in a decision seen by many unwed live-in mates as a precedent for reciprocal property rights. Upon winning her reduced cash award in April 1979, Triola spoke for thousands of other spurned lovers when she said, "If a man wants to leave a toothbrush at my house, he can damn well marry me."

Blake had any obligation to support the other "at any time, no matter what happens."[11]

Bonny also signed a temporary custody agreement, granting Blake physical custody of the baby. The paper also barred her from having friends or family visit without Blake's written permission. Delinah kept the baby. Strictly temporary, however, until Bonny finished up her probation and she and Blake could get acquainted better as husband and wife.

Bonny didn't get to see her daughter that trip, but that seemed a small price to pay. She had finally landed a movie star. On October 4, everyone signed off, including attorneys for both parties, and after dropping the child-stealing charges against Blake, Bonny began making plans for their wedding. She went down to the L.A. County Clerk's office on October 18 and picked up the marriage license.

Meanwhile, Blake quietly ordered his lawyers to draw up a petition for full custody.

---

11. Under a new California law, this section became moot and unenforceable after January 1, 2001.

7

On October 24, 2000, the *National Enquirer* carried a story with the headline: **Robert Blake, 67, in Bizarre Tug O' War Over Love Child,**[12] and thought the 600-word rant would otherwise have come up short, the pictures alone were worth it.

Beside a shot of a scowling, aged Robert Blake was a picture of Bonny in all her blowsy glory, hands on hips and her tummy visibly straining the waistline of her green knit skirt. A far more flattering portrait of the smiling mother and her newborn appeared nearer the bottom of the page with a cameo of Christian Brando at one side.

While there was no overt indication as to who planted the *Enquirer* story, the clues pointed away from Bonny. Both her own name ("Bonnie Lee") and her baby's name ("Kristian") were misspelled throughout the article, and she was clearly cast as the villain for sleeping with and then trying to force marriage on the unsuspecting Blake. Plus, the story related that Bonny had returned to Arkansas without her baby, but there was no mention of Blake's elaborate ruse to kidnap the child for his other daughter, Delinah.

After she read the article, Bonny dashed off an angry letter to Blake. "You talked to the *Enquirer,* letting them write that story to try to embarrass me," she accused.

The *Enquirer* story was merely a harbinger of things to

---

12. Though nearly five years after his trial, the front page was still dominated by the latest antics of O.J. Ironically, Blake's popularity had slid so far that many *Enquirer* readers didn't even know who he was.

come. What ought to have been of far greater concern to Bonny was the strange offer Blake made to her younger brother.

Bonny had introduced Joey Bakley to Blake during one of her many stays at the Beverly Garland when she flew in from Memphis to visit. Joey came up from San Diego to meet Bonny's newest celeb and Blake took a liking to the lad right away. He apparently saw some sort of outlaw romance in Joey's drugged existence, which he shared with his boyfriend, Francisco Gonzalez, just beyond the border in Tijuana. Blake called Joey one day in early October and asked him to meet him at a doughnut shop in the Valley. He had a job for him.

Joey and Francisco took the bus from Tijuana to Van Nuys the following day. When Robert saw Francisco, he grew nervous and insisted that Joey go across the street with him to a park.

Joey thought he was auditioning for an acting job, so he was on his best behavior. "Blake wanted to know more about my past," said Joey. "He was just feeling me out and talking about his own drug days. He was a cold, cocky little son of a bitch. I told him, 'I'm not perfect. I've had a few scrapes with the law.' I was busted a couple of times for drug trafficking and things, but that was a long time ago. I'm all right now."

Blake fixed him with a stare. "Did you ever do away with someone?"

Joey did a double take. "You mean, you want me to rub someone out for you?"

"And then he told me, 'Yeah, I do,'" Joey says of Blake. "I'll pay you $5,000 up front and more later."

Joey swallowed hard as he listened to Blake's plan. The target was a gay investment counselor who had fleeced Blake and two other friends before becoming an expatriate. Blake said that the man was older and would likely be attracted to a young stud like Joey. He lived on a yacht anchored off Rosarito Beach, twenty miles south of Tijuana. Blake gave Joey a small retainer and told him that if he was interested, he wanted him to buy a cell phone so that they'd have a single private line of communication between them.

Of course, when Bonny asked him to buy her a round-trip ticket to L.A. from Little Rock, he told her she had to pay for her own flight. Nor would he pay for a wedding ring. Bonny had to borrow money from her mother. Bonny rushed out before the ceremony and got them both platinum bands.

"Can you believe it?" she told her brother, Joey. "The cheapskate wants to do the right thing and marry me, but I've got to pay for the wedding bands."

Bonny wasn't going to be a complete pushover, though. She demanded Blake at least buy her an engagement ring. "Size 6," she said. "You can get it at a pawn shop or one of your flea markets. I don't care as long as it's real and from you."

But Blake even welshed on the engagement ring. He bought her a secondhand bauble set with an opal, not a diamond. Bonny made the best of it. She told her friends and family that it was just Robert's old-fashioned sentiment and not just that he was cheap. When the ring broke a short time after the wedding, however, she tried taping it up for a few days until she saw that it was a lost cause and quietly dumped it in the trash.

The couple was married on November 19, 2000—a chilly autumn Sunday. The ceremony was so private that friends, neighbors and relatives weren't even aware it had happened. They traded vows quickly in Blake's backyard with a nondenominational minister officiating.

"I announced their engagement and had pictures taken, and nobody used them because Bobby was cold at the time," said Dale Olson, Blake's longtime publicist. "The media, to a person, threw them away."

There was no honeymoon. They didn't even sleep in the same bed that night. Immediately after the wedding, Blake's bodyguard Caldwell rushed Bonny back to the Beverly Garland, where she spent the night by herself. "She spent a tearful, lonely wedding night alone," said Margerry.

The next morning, she took a plane back to Arkansas to finish out the final three months of her probation.

While it was Blake's second marriage, no one was sure how many times Bonny had been married. Counting on her fingers, her own sister didn't know how many times Bonny

had been to the altar. "I counted nine," said Margerry, until
a magazine reporter informed her of at least one more wedding documented in the recorder's office in Shelby County,
Tennessee. "Oh. Ten then."

Despite the travesty that wedding number eleven turned
out to be, Bonny was overjoyed. She was no longer a nobody
from New Jersey. She was Mrs. Robert Blake.

Like all those that came before, Bonny's marriage to
Blake wouldn't last, but it would end far worse than any of
those others. Within seven months of their November nup-
tials, Mrs. Robert Blake would be dead of an assassin's bullet. The fading film star who began his career in 1939 as one
of the last of the Little Rascals would become the prime
murder suspect.

Yet the events that were to follow did not result from de-
ceptions and double-dealing over the course of a few
months, or even a few years. Bonny and Blake were as star-
crossed as they came—dysfunctional lovers whose occasionally comic and frequently tragic relationship became a cautionary tale about romance gone horribly awry. And it began
decades before the two of them ever even met.

It began the day Robert Blake was born.

ACT II

Back Story

Children of the future age
Reading this indignant page,
Know that in a former time,
Love, sweet love, was thought a crime.

—Blake (William)

8

On September 18, 1933, Michael James Vijencio Gubitosi entered the world in the Newark working-class suburb of Nutley, New Jersey. Celebrated these days as the gentrified home town of Martha Stewart, Nutley was recalled quite differently by Blake in a 1970 interview: "I remember it as a sewer."

Mickey was the youngest of three, which included an older sister, Jovanny, and brother, James Jr. Blake said his mother had two abortions before having him, and the only reason he was born at all was that his parents couldn't afford a third.

"Poverty saved my life," he said. "This is gonna sound weird, but I believe I can remember hearing about it in the womb. I had dreams about it all through childhood, then again as an adult. I was in the womb, thinkin', 'Bro, when you get out there, you better hit the ground walkin' and talkin' 'cause it's gonna be *cold city*.' I have never forgotten this."

Decades later, when Blake returned to the old neighborhood, he asked around to see if his earliest memories had been real or imagined. "I hung out with the old people, eatin' pizza, drinkin' a little wine, listenin' to their tales. After a while, I heard the story. Then I heard it again and again. Twenty different people told me it was true."

According to Blake, Mickey Gubitosi was an unwanted child born to poverty. According to his cousins Rose Newick and Steve Visakay, it was worse than that. His uncle Sal fooled around with his mother behind his father James Gubitosi's back, and Mickey was the result. Before he was even born, James Gubitosi was silently identifying his younger son as, quite literally, a little bastard.

"I think that many people like me die in infancy," Blake said half a century later. "When you are left in a crib all night long freezing to death in your own urine or your own vomit and no one cares if you live or die, you die."

To hear Blake tell it, his father wasn't the only Gubitosi who had it in for him. Blake and his big brother had to sleep in the same bed for three years, and Blake learned early on to hate his guts. "He kicked my butt every chance he got— and that was *plenty*."

Throughout his adult career, Blake repeated the story of how his family was so poor that his father woke him before dawn each day so that he and his sister could sneak down the stairs of the Gubitosis' third-floor tenement and steal milk from the neighbors. "He'd give us one empty milk bottle and one filled with water, and we'd walk down a street early in the morning and take a little milk out of each bottle and pour in a little of the water so no one would suspect what was goin' on."

A poignant story, to be sure, but it didn't happen to Robert Blake, according to his cousins. "That happened to my father in 1939," said Steve Visakay. "He was taken out of school to pick rhubarb in the fields, and he stole milk off a truck. All that hard-luck stuff—that happened to my father, not to Robert."

While the Nutley branch of the Gubitosi family does not dispute that Robert might have been beaten by his father and brother, they question how much of Blake's oft-repeated abusive childhood was real and how much of it has been created over the years to make Blake's life sound more dramatic than it really was. "It was popular to say things like that on the Mike Douglas show," said Visakay. "Robert didn't steal milk. Our parents did. He wasn't poor. He left Nutley."

During the Depression, James Gubitosi Sr. was a blacksmith for the Works Progress Administration (WPA). Inside him, though, burned a desire for show business. "My father was a frustrated show nut," Blake told *TV Guide* in a 1976 interview. "He'd sit around the house all day long when he wasn't working and play Caruso records and sing with them."[13]

Always a dreamer, James Gubitosi took his children to picnics to dance and sing for spare change. Gubitosi called his kids the "Three Little Hillbillies," a vaudeville act for which he played bad backup guitar—one of his father's avocations that Blake adopted. As a group, the Hillbillies showed scant talent, but young Mickey displayed a precocious stage presence that his father recognized at once.

The Gubitosi children were such crowd pleasers that the next logical step was radio studios, where they won cash prizes and wound up on *Major Bowes' Amateur Hour*. Mickey even won a medal, which he treasured like a talisman. Almost before he could walk, he learned that performing well in public earned praise.

His father reckoned it would earn even more in California. He quit the WPA, and shortly after Mickey turned five, in October 1938, James Gubitosi piled his family and all their worldly goods into a 1928 Ford and drove 3,000 miles from Nutley to Los Angeles. "We were hungry, and it figured being hungry would be easier out here where it was warm," Blake recollected in one of his later fond remembrances.

The Gubitosis rented a bungalow in the L.A. suburb of Venice. His mother found work as a Baldwin Hills domestic and later as a seamstress, and his father became a part-time gardener when he wasn't chauffeuring his children to or from auditions. The cattle calls paid off when Mickey appeared as a $2.60-a-day extra in the popular *Our Gang* comedy shorts that had transformed child actors George "Spanky" McFarland, Carl "Alfalfa" Switzer, and Darla Hood into national celebrities. In 1938, MGM bought the sixteen-year-old series from its creator, Hal Roach, renamed it *The Little Rascals* and began auditioning for replacements

---

13. In 1985, Blake told the *Los Angeles Herald Examiner* that he hated his parents, but that his favorite performer was "Enrico Caruso in his prime," just like his father.

for the now-aging original cast. Mickey found a place immediately as a big-eyed, sad-faced waif who outwhined every
other member of the cast.

"The reason that MGM hired him for *Our Gang* was that
they could look at him and say, 'Cry,' and he'd cry, and not
many kids can do that unless they really want to cry," said
fellow Rascal Tommy "Butch" Bond.

Little Mickey became a little trouper, taking falls a grown
stuntman would have turned down. Once he nearly lost an
eye, and he constantly came out of rough-and-tumble scenes
banged up and bruised. He didn't seem to mind getting beat
up on camera, he later maintained, because that was how he
was treated at home.

"From the time I was an infant, my father beat me up,"
Blake asserted. "He tied me down. He locked me in closets.
I used to go to the studio with long pants on, and when I
changed my clothes, I'd be worried that somebody was
gonna see the welts on my legs. He was too smart to mess
up my face."

Blake's mother always stepped in just before her husband
did any permanent physical damage, according to Blake. "I
thought she was the good guy," he said. "And come to find
out, she was much worse than him because in a sense he was
helpless. He was clinically insane and should've been put
away. I was his caretaker. I was his punching bag. I was the
thing that kept him alive."

The one place where he could always be assured of praise
was on stage. He seemed to have been born without stage
fright. When another Rascal kept freezing up at his cue, little
Mickey chimed in with the required line—"Confidentially,
it stinks"—and all the adult faces hovering behind the cameras smiled at him.

"When I started being an extra, I mean, consciously I
could taste the love and the attention that you got when you
talked," Blake recalled. "I didn't know they were acting. I
didn't know that there was a difference between an extra and
an actor. All I knew is, when you talked, they paid attention
to you. And somebody'd come up and touch you physically
and give you a little hug and a little makeup, a little this and
a little that."

By 1941, the Gubitosi family was doing well enough to move from low-rent Venice to the slightly more upscale neighborhood of Palms, near Culver City. With the money that little Mickey was earning, James Gubitosi was able to invest in a small hardware store and get out of the gardening business. The following year, Blake appeared in *Rover's Big Chance,* his last *Little Rascals* film.

MGM's front office interviewed little Mickey for their personnel files that year, detailing his life and career for the studio publicity department. His idols of the moment were Mickey Rooney and Judy Garland, and not surprisingly his favorite movie was *Strike Up the Band* (1940), a Busby Berkeley extravaganza about a high school band that makes it big on radio. The stars of *Strike Up the Band* were Rooney and Garland.

On his eighth birthday, MGM threw him a party. It was the only party Blake claimed he ever got as a kid. Given Blake's later confessions about his father, what was surprising was the eight-year-old's selection of "Dad for a Day" as his favorite *Our Gang* role. In it, he played an adoring son of a strong, loving pop. He also told the MGM publicist that his family was very close. The one clue he gave about his real home life was his answer to the question "Do you govern your life by any rule?" Mickey's answer was one word: "Obedience."

Following his *Rascals* run, Blake appeared in more than seventy movies during the 1940s, beginning with the tear-jerking *Mokey* in 1942, in which MGM cast him as a runaway waif who wins the hearts of Donna Reed and Dan Dailey. Filming *Mokey* was "the best time of my entire life," he later told longtime pal Mario Roccuzzio. It was the first time he used the stage name Bobby Blake, and it stuck. Little Mickey Gubitosi disappeared forever from the children's section of the *Academy Players Directory*.

His final line in *Mokey* became a sentimental lifelong irony: "I finally got my own mother!" he says, throwing his arms around Donna Reed's neck.

Mokey was a Blake breakthrough. Never mind the tacky reviews, like this dismissive notice from *Variety:*

Bad judgment is evidenced by studio officials making this one unsuitable for the kid trade. During young Blake's runaway he waves a knife and talks about cutting off his head—certainly not good in a picture that might be shown to children of impressionable age.

Blake himself was hailed in the *Hollywood Reporter* with the headline:

Bobby Blake Great Little Star Trouper

And *Film Daily* raved: "Not often has a moppet been called upon to do such a man-sized job in a film."

Despite those mildly disappointing reviews, *Mokey* made money, which taught Bobby Blake a valuable early lesson about the difference between art and commerce. In his busy post-*Rascals* career, he went on to work virtually nonstop through the rest of the decade, beginning with *Andy Hardy's Double Life* (1943) and ending with the sweeping medieval costume drama *The Black Rose* (1950), shot on location in Europe. Because casting directors decided that his jet-black hair, ethnic features and olive complexion approximated that of a young Indian, B-movie mill Republic Studios turned him into "L'il Beaver" in dozens of low-budget *Red Ryder* films and serials. At one point, he was grinding out a new episode every ten days. Silent matinee idol Gordon "Wild Bill" Elliott starred in the first sixteen, and Allan "Rocky" Lane[14] then took over the role of the Western hero who first captured youngsters' imaginations through a syndicated newspaper comic strip.

Bobby also appeared in several mainstream feature films during the 1940s, including *The Horn Blows at Midnight* (1945), with Jack Benny, and *Humoresque* (1946), early romance novelist Fannie Hurst's melodramatic potboiler about a young violinist who rises to concert heights from the Lower East Side of New York.

---

14. In 1962, Lane achieved more lasting fame as the voice of TV's *Mister Ed.*

Starring John Garfield[15] and Joan Crawford, *Humoresque* was "mostly unadulterated schmaltz," according to *New York Times* film critic Bosley Crowther, even though vaunted New York playwright Clifford Odets wrote the screenplay. The plot revolved around a brash young violin virtuoso who rises in the music world with the help of a poor but encouraging mother. Along the way, a bored, wealthy, married matron of the arts with a taste for booze and boys (Joan Crawford) gives the violinist a hand, but art and sex don't mix well. Fireworks erupt and love ends badly—an oddly familiar story.

Blake played the virtuoso as a child, and in Garfield, the ex-Rascal found his first role model. Blake even bore a vague resemblance to Garfield, who immediately took the boy under his wing.

"I remember I had a real tough scene in the movie," Blake recalled. "I was out on a fire escape, but of course, it was the soundstage, and there was all this activity around. It was a tough scene, and I couldn't concentrate because of the crew moving around. Garfield just happened to be there, you know, sort of looking things over. He saw the trouble I was in, and he cleared the set. I mean, he cleared the entire soundstage. If you can imagine it, there was not a soul there but him and me. He just looked at me and said, 'Okay, kid, play the scene.'

"And so I went through it a couple of times, and it was fine. And he said to me, 'Just remember, you're an actor. None of these people would be working without you. Respect yourself, and respect your art.'

---

15. Born Jacob Julius Garfinkle, Garfield grew up in New York's Hell's Kitchen. Instead of turning to crime like many of his peers, he became an actor, signed with Warner's in 1938 and was typecast as a brooding young tough guy with a hair-trigger temper. After ten years as one of Warner's biggest stars, Garfield was blacklisted as a suspected Communist and his career was over. While estranged from his wife in 1952, he dropped dead of heart failure at a girlfriend's home. He was thirty-nine. His funeral was Hollywood's biggest since Rudolph Valentino's with thousands of female fans crowding the cemetery.

"I never had much in the way of upbringing, you know. If I could pick a father for myself, it would have been Garfield, and for my grandfather, Walter Huston."

Walter Huston's son John was the director who gave Blake his next shot at work. In *The Treasure of the Sierra Madre* (1948), Bobby landed a pivotal but uncredited role as the Mexican street urchin who sells Humphrey Bogart a winning lottery ticket, spurring the hapless Fred C. Dobbs on to a doomed search for gold. Blake didn't get the same paternal treatment from Bogart that he had from Garfield.

"He made a statement to me when he was in *The Treasure of Sierra Madre* that Bogart treated him mean," said Tommy Bond. "That hurts a kid's psyche."

At the same time, the bucolic home life young Mickey had described for his official MGM studio biography unraveled. As an adult, Blake rarely let an interview pass without adding new details. "My father was a tyrant who'd come in at three a.m. and beat the shit out of me because he couldn't get laid or whatever craziness was going on with him," he told *Playboy* in 1977. "My mother was nobody to turn to for mother love, for physical contact, for comfort, to dry your eyes or wipe your nose, that kind of thing."

Cold and distant, Elizabeth Gubitosi never embraced her youngest child. According to Blake, she stood by and did nothing as his father squandered little Mickey's earnings during an angry decade-long descent into alcoholism. Indeed, even in her declining years, well after she was estranged from her son, Elizabeth's other relatives called the tiny, dour-looking little woman "Old Stone Face" behind her back.

"She was a short little lady and she could have her temper tantrums like everybody else, but you never know what goes on behind closed doors," said Rose Gubitosi Newick, Blake's cousin. "My mother was just neurotic," Blake said.

The older he got, the more frequently and boldly he described his youth as one unending nightmare, punctuated with physical and emotional cruelty. "I was like most child actors," he told UPI's Vernon Scott. "I acted only because I was told to, and you can hardly consider what I did acting. I didn't like it. It was no kind of life. I had nothing going for me at school or at the studios—or at home. So when I was fourteen, I packed up and left home."

Elsewhere, he told interviewers variously that he left home when he was sixteen or seventeen, but he was clear on one point: his earnings went directly to support his family. His parents used much of their son's salary to invest in real estate during the late 1940s and early 1950s. Blake was especially incensed that the money received for his acting helped finance his older brother's college education. Years later, he tallied up his income from those years and calculated that he'd earned $16,000 from the time he first became a Little Rascal until the curtain came down on his child acting career in *The Black Rose*.

Of all his many relatives, only his uncle treated him well during his horrifying youth, according to Blake, and even that relationship came to a tragic end. "My uncle Louie, my father's brother, came back from World War II shot up and had fourteen operations after it was over," he recalled. "The whole time, he was sweet as God himself with me. The pain finally drove him to jump off a building."

That occurred on a Thursday afternoon in July 1947, when Blake was thirteen years old. His uncle leaped from the seventh floor of a department store at Eighth and Broadway in busy downtown Los Angeles. He glanced off a car, hit the pavement and died instantly. Louie's dramatic death was barely mentioned in the newspapers at the time, but it became fond and stagy grist for the imagination of a budding thespian who was already having trouble differentiating between reality and what played well with his audience. Blake invoked his uncle's spirit like a guardian angel.

Once, while racing his Triumph street bike along the winding crest of the Santa Monica Mountains on Mulholland Drive, Blake flew off the highway and hit the ground while his motorcycle remained hanging above him in a tree. He was revived by transmission fluid dripping on his face.

"It was like Louie upstairs was saying, 'Next time, I'm gonna drop the motherfucker *on* you,'" said Blake.

He gave up motorcycles for a while, but like most of his other addictions, only for a while. He eventually had to return to speed. He did keep his promise to Louie to ride more carefully in the future.

"Louie is the only one in my family who ever loved me," said Blake. "Not my father, not my mother, not my brother. They all hated me, little Mickey Gubitosi. Only Uncle Louie loved me. He's still with me, tellin' me I can make it. I talk to him for strength."

9

Bobby Blake had trouble the very first day he ever walked in a classroom. He was ten by then, never having had to attend school because MGM had always supplied him with a tutor. But how much a child actor studied was largely unregulated, and Blake's "instructor" turned out to be more of a baby-sitter than a teacher.

Blake also suffered from dyslexia, though the condition did not yet have a name and virtually nothing was known about it in the 1940s. Unless they were fortunate enough to have parents or a teacher who recognized their problem, dyslexics became dunces or delinquents. Thus, when Blake had to go to public school, he was barely able to read or write. Coupled with his general pugnacious attitude, the ridicule he was subjected to as the class dummy made the rest of his academic career a constant war. It didn't help that he was short, dark and clumsy, or that he'd become widely known as Red Ryder's sidekick. Any kid who'd ever been to a Saturday matinee knew who Blake was and L'il Beaver was a deadly nickname for a teenager.

"I couldn't understand why they were so hostile," recalled Blake. "In high school the only people I could associate with were the other outcasts—the other oddballs, so to speak. I spent most of my time hiding."

Others recalled Blake far differently. Norton Schultz, one of Blake's classmates at Hamilton High on L.A.'s Westside, recalled to the *National Enquirer* that Blake "was cocky and thought he was better than everyone else." Schultz recounted an incident in which Blake unzipped in the school's greenhouse and took a leak on a crop of radishes that students were raising for agriculture class.

"What the hell are you doing?" asked his teacher.

"What does it look like I'm doing?" shot back Blake.

Despite his defiance, Blake complained in later years that "Li'l Beaver" had a terrible time getting a date. Coeds preferred tall, blond football stars. Blake said he actually wept that he didn't have the fresh-faced farm boy looks of Van Johnson. "I kept telling myself if I really worked hard, I could make it all happen."

It didn't.

He claimed he was kicked out of Hamilton High twice, the first time for gambling on the football field and the second time for allegedly jumping out of a window. When Blake protested that he had been pushed, the vice principal called him a liar and suspended him, but a few weeks later Blake enrolled in another nearby high school.

"Every time they kicked me out of one school, someone else had to take me, whether they wanted me or not," said Blake. "It was the law."

Blake's hard-luck tales fell into a pattern after that, with someone else—usually an authority figure—invariably at fault. Robert had grave difficulty taking responsibility for his own failings, then and later. He liked to borrow a term from the world of insurance to describe his academic career, calling himself "the first assigned-risk student in L.A." In all, he claimed to have been "thrown out of five schools and one window," yet he still managed to graduate from Hamilton High in 1951.

He moved in with two older friends he later characterized as alcoholics and spent the next two years drinking and supporting himself as an occasional construction worker. "I was doin' a lot of physical work, 'cause when I was younger, I'd always been happiest that way," said Blake. "When I was unloadin' ninety-pound cement bags in the freight yards, I used to go home and fall into bed and I wouldn't give a fuck whether my father wanted to hit me in the head or not. I'd just fall asleep." For a time, he maintained, he lived off liquor store Twinkies because he was so strung out that he couldn't work up the nerve to eat in a restaurant.

Perhaps, but his cousins who came to California to visit

their successful relative in the early 1950s found everything normal. "I was over to his house for a week in the fifties and everything seemed fine to me," said Steve Visikay. "When I was a kid I idolized Bobby. I thought he was the coolest guy I ever saw. I saw him going out on a date and he had engineer boots, covered by dungarees, and a white T-shirt with a sports jacket. He had cigarettes rolled up in his shirt. He was the coolest guy I ever saw."

Yet to hear Robert tell it, his hellacious life was just beginning. When he joined the army in May 1953, Blake later maintained that it was not out of choice. He'd failed to register with Selective Service and was drafted. In the hometown newspaper clippings his mother sent home to New Jersey, however, Robert was hailed as a hero for volunteering to serve his country. There was no mention of the draft. Even in Beverly Hills, the parents he had come to revile proudly told the *Los Angeles Times* that their son "Li'l Beaver" had put on a uniform, but that they weren't too worried about him going overseas because his acting assignments had taken him all over the world to Europe and Africa.

Following boot camp at Fort Ord and sixteen weeks of light weapons infantry training that fall at Camp Roberts in central California, Blake was transferred to Fort Richardson, an experimental cold weather station in Anchorage, Alaska. There, while working for Special Services, he said, he learned how to play the guitar. He also discovered heroin. For the next three years Blake sampled whatever pill, powder or herb he could swallow, inhale or inject.

"There was nothing to do up there, so a bunch of us just fell into it," Blake recalled. "I was dealing, hustling. We'd score, sell. One day I'd be the dealer. The next day another guy would.

"I shot it for the next two years. You'd shoot dope because it made you feel better. You didn't feel good so you'd shoot dope and pretty soon you couldn't stand not to shoot it."

He told one interviewer that he met and fell in love with an officer's sixteen-year-old daughter. He told another she was an Eskimo girl. He told the *National Enquirer* in 1983 that the girl's name was Gloria, she lived off base, her father had wanted to press charges and Blake plotted to kill him. In Blake's febrile memory, the stalking unfolded like a scene from one of his movies: "For a full month, I watched this man's every move. I went to his house to learn his habits before he went to work at midnight. Across a dirt road from his house, there was an old broken-down trailer. I'd park a mile down the road and walk to the trailer to watch him, and as I watched, I planned his death."

Yet according to Blake's other accounts of the same story, the tryst resulted in his arrest for statutory rape.

"I could easily have ended up in Leavenworth," he told *Los Angeles Times* film critic Charles Champlin in 1992. In that version, he had already purchased an engagement ring for Gloria and a friendly priest narrowly averts a court martial by negotiating an agreement whereby Blake agrees to never see the girl again.

"I was escorted to the plane under guard by MPs and I flew home and was discharged with nothing bad on my record," he told Champlin with utter sincerity.

It was not the first or last time he got into trouble in the military however. He maintained he was busted for pulling a bayonet on six other soldiers, and was later sent to a mental ward for pushing a footlocker out of a third floor window.

"I did about a month in the hospital," he recalled. "They had me on some drugs and I began seeing a psychiatrist for the first time."

Finally, he was sentenced to three months and twenty-six days in the stockade, but not for rape, brandishing a bayonet, or throwing a footlocker out a window.

"I stole some things," he told Johnny Carson once on the *Tonight Show*. "I had to steal because I was cold."

His theft was a gas can that he took from the commanding officer's tent and took to his fellow enlisted men—a familiar Robin Hood theme that Blake liked to apply liberally to many of his misdeeds. Despite the black marks on his record, he claimed he only spent a month in the stockade before a priest showed up and had him sent to Special Services in Anchorage, where he learned to play the guitar.

"I wrote and directed musicals and put officers' wives in

the productions and then fucked 'em," until his honorable discharge in early 1956.

Once he returned to Hollywood, his life hit bottom. "I couldn't even get myself to go into a drugstore and buy a pack of razor blades to cut my wrists with," he said. "I was scunged. . . . I hated myself, hated everything, felt useless and worthless, had no friends, no love, no career, no education, no parents and no tomorrows. It all added up to nothing."

He worked briefly on the assembly line at Packard Bell, and kept his hand in Hollywood by doing stunt work, but he was still into drugs. "You could go to Tijuana with a pickup truck and come back with enough grass to last you the rest of your life, and it was easy to get, and there was tons of it. And pills were a piece of cake. I had drugstores that sold me pills by the handful, with no prescription."

At one point, he was running between Mexico, Vegas, and Hollywood, earning as much as $500 on a score.

"I had enough to eat, sleep, and have a car," Blake said. "I wasn't cool though. I wasn't really playing the role of the dope dealer."

Ultimately, Blake credited acting for weaning him off drugs. "I didn't have any dramatic, rolling-on-the-floor withdrawal symptoms. I just started studying acting—this friend said I should attend classes because I didn't have a chick and there were plenty of good-looking girls at the school.

"I started finding girls I had something in common with. The girls wanted me, not some dumb football player, because they were actresses and I'd learned something in all those years, after all: I was a damned good actor."

He met actress Virginia Leith, a contract player at 20th Century Fox throughout the 1950s, who introduced him both to acting classes and psychotherapy. "Blake worked like a bitch to be a decent person," she said. "He struggled with his demons. He was starved. He had no nourishment. No one was looking at him and saying he was talented. At five, he was paying all the bills for the family, and all they wanted to know was how much money he could make."

Blake's first shrink was of the touchy-feely variety, coming up with hokey lines like, "Coward, take a coward's hand

and together we'll beat this neurosis." Still, he was just the sort of doctor Blake needed. "I was at the end of the road, and we started back," recalled Blake. "He got me to acting again, studying acting for the first time. He said I had to face the demons I'd been running away from all my life, and he was right."

Blake also met actor Jeff Corey. Best remembered today as Wild Bill Hickok in *Little Big Man* (1970), Corey didn't work at all for several years in the early 1950s—a victim of the blacklist after he admitted to attending some communist cell meetings in the 1940s. He dug ditches and did carpentry work, keeping his hand in the theater by taking classes at UCLA.

But he was so good at apprenticing young actors that friends told him he ought to teach. Thirty people showed for the first session of the Jeff Corey Professional Actors Studio, and it quickly became an institution. For $10 a month, actors attended two classes a week. Besides Blake, luminaries such as James Dean, Jack Nicholson, Rita Moreno, Richard Chamberlain and Dean Stockwell were members at one time or another. The classes became so popular Corey had to extend the back of his garage another six feet so that his actors would have a stage.

As much as any psychologist, Corey changed Blake's direction. Despite years of floundering after his career as a child actor ended, Robert saw that he still had a long second act to get through before his life hit intermission. "I became absorbed, but even more important it made me feel as though I could be something, mean something," said Blake. "And it gave me hope that maybe I could change the way things are a little through acting."

He flew to New York at one point, where he auditioned for Lee Strasberg, the respected founder of the Actors Studio. In the era of James Dean and other rebels without causes, Blake had hopes of molding his own screen image in that of the famed young method actor. "Those were my James Dean days and I wanted the cycle and the leather jacket," he said. "It just seemed like it would be easier to be pretentious about it in New York."

Strasberg had a different view: Blake couldn't act. He

advised him to return to Hollywood and abandon any hope of a theatrical career. Robert was crushed, but not for long. After briefly knocking around Broadway, supporting himself as a box boy in a grocery store, he returned to Southern California.

Meanwhile, he continued his psychotherapy to rid himself of the destructive behavior that had plagued him since childhood. Blake himself later maintained that the therapist forced him to face the awful truths that had turned him into an angry addict.

"My dad [Blake's uncle Victor] said that Bobby was a nice boy until he was twelve or thirteen and then he found out through his mother that Sal was his real father," said Steve Visikay. "It made him crazy. He didn't get along with his mother or father after that because they'd lied to him. He didn't get along with anybody. He went wild and wasn't a nice boy after that. This is what my father told me, clear as day."

But Blake didn't remember it that way—at least for public consumption. Separating the facts of Blake's life from his fictions was proving more and more challenging. Before his very first therapy sessions, he'd already begun creating an autobiography that did not always square with the verifiable facts.

"I've heard that Robert likes to tell stories and that it's all bullshit," said former personal assistant Mark Canavi. "It's all, you know, image pandering. I think he thought it was good for his image to come off as an abused child, an unloved child, yada yada yada. So I don't know what the truth is. I heard from someone else that this abuse stuff is all nonsense because he was the breadwinner and he was treated like a king. He supported the whole damn family and they spoiled him."

The father he characterized as a demon, for example, committed suicide at forty-five, according to Blake, yet James Gubitosi's death certificate gave heart disease as cause of death at age fifty. It was clear in his will, however, that James Gubitosi died estranged from his family. He wrote: "I have intentionally omitted to provide for, and specifically direct that no part, share or interest in my estate go to, vest in or be taken by my children, Michael, James and Jovanny, and by my wife, Elizabeth. . . ."

Everything—his stamp collection, his 1949 Chevy two-door, his 12-gauge shotgun, even a treasured 1894 $20 gold piece—was sold to settle his debts. The rest went to his grandson[16] in hopes that his bitter rancor toward his immediate family might skip a generation.

"My father, when he died, didn't leave me a quarter,"[17] said Blake. "He didn't die—he *killed* himself. He left it all to his grandchildren. It turned out to be one guy, and he didn't leave nothing to me because he was crazy. I was his caretaker, and when I went off to the army, he killed himself."

A month before his father's death, and shortly after Blake's discharge from the army, James and Elizabeth Gubitosi divorced. Blake's mother was given the house in Beverly Hills while his father got their biggest investment: the Wishing Well Trailer Park in Torrance. It is interesting to note that James Gubitosi had adopted the same last name as his famous son when he died as James Blake on August 15, 1956.[18]

Meanwhile Blake—who appeared in three Hollywood releases that year (*Rumble on the Docks*, *Screaming Eagles* and *Three Violent People,* a Western that starred Charlton Heston and Anne Baxter)—did not attend his father's funeral. He later boasted that the only time he ever visited his father at Holy Cross Cemetery was to urinate on his grave.

---

16. Jovanny's son, Kirt Kip Austin, was James Gubitosi's first and only grandchild at the time of his death. By the time he received his final payment in 1979 at age twenty-four in accordance with his grandfather's will, Austin had received over $50,000.

17. The will did make provision to pay off a promissory note that Blake made his father sign before lending him the money for the down payment on his trailer park. Blake got $6,446.46 from James Gubitosi's estate.

18. Less than twenty-four hours later, Bela Lugosi died. The *Los Angeles Times* carried a two column obituary with Lugosi's photo. Blake's passing wasn't even noted in the newspaper.

10

The same year James Gubitosi shuffled off this mortal coil, Bonny Lee Bakley shuffled in.

The first child of Edward and Marjorie Lois Bakley was born on June 7, 1956, in Morristown, New Jersey. Edward gave his profession as tree surgeon, but his wife and children later said it was more accurate to call him the town drunk. He once offered to swap one of his kids for a quart of booze.

He was a mean drunk too. While Bonny was still in the womb, Ed Bakley would wallop her mother's swollen belly with his closed fist. The oldest of three children,[19] Bonny delicately maintained later in life that her father "got fresh with her," but her younger sister, Margerry, was more to the point. "The drunken bum molested my sister," she said.

Life with Father got worse, not better. At one point the Bakleys moved into a garage because they could not afford a house or an apartment. Bonny and her sister made pets out of the rats that lived with them.

When they weren't at each other's throats, both Edward and Marjorie yelled at their two daughters and son, Joey, calling them ugly, stupid children, according to Margerry. Bonny got so upset she would hyperventilate and pass out. It didn't keep her from getting battered.

Bonny was five when her grandmother bought Bonny her first Elvis Presley record. In the years that followed, no mat-

---

19. There were allegedly six Bakley children all told, but their parents gave up three for adoption, according to Margerry.

ter how bad things got, the little girl knew she could always rely on the King to make things right. He loved her tender, loved her sweet, and all his disciples in the pantheon of rock and roll did the same. Other girls might believe in Jesus and Sunday-go-to-meetin', but Bonny worshiped at the altar of *American Bandstand* every day after school.

In 1963, the Bakleys split up, and the children never saw their father again. He died ten years later in the drunk tank of the Morristown jail, allegedly beaten to death, though none of the children ever seemed to know how or why. Margerry always thought that he'd smarted off once too often to one of the jail deputies.

"I don't think so," said her uncle George Hall. "I think it was probably just cirrhosis of the liver."

Ed Bakley's widow went on to marry two more times, but Bonny wasn't around to see how those marriages turned out. Unlike her siblings, she was raised by her grandmother Margaret Hall. Margaret wasn't destitute but she was miserly. As far back as Margerry or Joey could remember, Grammy Hall never gave anything away. That was how she wound up with Bonny. While the child was still in diapers, Bonny's mother borrowed money once from her parents to bail Ed out of jail, and according to Margerry, Margaret demanded Bonny as collateral for the loan. After Bonny's father died and the loan went unpaid, Margaret demanded her daughter's firstborn and kept Bonny as her own from then on.

After Grampa Hall passed away, Bonny and Grammy Hall moved into a trailer in Hampton, in the rural northwest corner of New Jersey. Bonny grew up close to dirt-poor. Her grandmother had no money to buy her anything but second-hand clothes, and she was so frugal that she did not believe in wasting water. Bonny was rarely allowed to bathe or wash her hair, and subsequently she became the butt of jokes at school.

"Bonny, did you ever try to figure out why you're attracted only to famous people?" a friend once asked her years later.

"It's because I wanted to be that myself," she said, laying the blame for her obsession on all the girls who used to taunt her at school. "You think, 'I'll show them. I'll become a movie star,'" Bonny continued, adding with a sorrowful shake of the head, "But it's too hard."

The truth of the matter was Bonny had no talent. She couldn't sing. She couldn't dance. She couldn't play piano or paint or cook or tell a joke. Yet she was obsessed with show biz. She at least had good looks after developing a nice figure and a pretty smile while still in her preteens, but it turned out that show business required a lot of dedication and Bonny was just not equipped to give it. Show biz required focus. It required concentration. It required showing up. Bonny failed at all three. Her ambition far outstripped her willingness to work. And there was other outstripping going on in her life too, even before she was a teenager.

When Margerry was six, she went to visit her older sister at her grandmother's trailer. Bonny had just turned eleven. On one summer day Margerry and Bonny joined a third girl and went swimming at a nearby family-owned and -operated nudist colony. The manager, kindly old Mr. Johannson, had assured the girls that they would be allowed to wear suits, but he reneged after they arrived. It simply would not look good to the other patrons if an exception were made. It was sweltering. Bonny quickly made her decision. She talked the other two into doffing their suits and following her into Mr. Johannson's pool au naturel.

"I knew as a kid this was wrong," recalls Margerry, "but it was hot, it was summer and I never went back again. But I think that's where it all started for Bonny."

Unlike her kid sister, Bonny shed her natural shyness along with her clothing and showed no embarrassment. She was already developing breasts and brandishing them like trophies. Far from trying to cover herself at the approach of males, Bonny basked in their admiring looks.

Bonny continued to frequent the nudist colony. She'd grab her swimsuit, lie to her grandmother that she was going to the pool and ride over on her minibike, never once intending to wear the suit. "Her grandma was lovingly lenient," said George Hall. "If I'd been on the scene, I probably wouldn't have allowed her to do some of the things she did."

In 1970, George replaced their mobile home with a modest ranch-style home that he built on his mother's wooded lot. Bonny's status went up a notch, but not to any appreciable degree, given what was happening in the rest of Hampton. The New York metropolitan area had finally spread to western New Jersey, and more affluent city dwellers were building themselves weekend homes or big family dwellings where they could raise kids in a healthy, wholesome rural atmosphere. Bonny clashed with them immediately.

"She was never very happy in school," said George. "I guess the kids who moved in from the city used to tease her a lot."

Bonny found solace in nudism. By the time she turned eighteen, she proudly gave a local newspaper an interview about her introduction to nudism. Nowhere in the interview did she mention that she first learned about soft porn in the guise of the many sun-worship magazines that lay around the front office at the colony. Nor did she tell that classifieds in the back offered nude photos for sale as well as live nude modeling to interested photographers who could afford to pay stiff fees. For a girl with a good figure, it was easy money, and Bonny needed that money. She had to keep up on the admission prices for rock concerts.

"She did a lot of traveling, going to the shows to see all her stars," said her uncle George. "She picked up that wanderlust of hers when she was in her teens. She'd grab a bus for Atlantic City. She just had to be there. She had to go. There was no stopping her."

Bonny was twelve when she first saw Frankie Valli and the Four Seasons perform live. It was a concert in northern New Jersey, where the Four Seasons made their first record the year Bonny was born, and Bonny fell in love. She'd hear Frankie entreat "Sherry baby" with that piercing falsetto over *America Bandstand*, but listening to the pompadoured entertainer warble in person was a whole different experience. Bonny knew that he was singing to her! She stood in the audience and cried. Someday she would become Mrs. Frankie Valli.

"She decided right then and there she was gonna get him," said Paul Gawron.

The obsession went on for more than two decades, with Bonny finding ways to follow Frankie wherever he was booked around the U.S.A. Oldies show in Newark? Bonny was there. Lounge act in Vegas? Bonny stood outside his dressing room. Bally's main room in Atlantic City? Bonny bought a front-row seat.

But as time went on, Bonny lost heart.

"He prefers slim girls because he's slim," she sadly confessed to girlfriends, long after she'd progressed from svelte to zaftig. "He's married and has a child."

She paused and a twinkle appeared in her eye as she gave this last fact a bit more thought.

"But I understand he and his wife aren't getting along too well," she added with a smile.

11

In 1958, Robert made his big move. He was listed in the *Academy Players Directory* under the YOUNG LEADING MAN heading, along with such contemporaries as Warren Beatty, Theodore Bikel and Dennis Hopper. He found an agent who got him a three-picture deal as second lead with low-budget Allied Artists, a B-picture mill on Sunset Boulevard. His first picture for Allied Artists was a cheap war movie, *Battle Flame* (1958), tapping into the minor success he'd enjoyed as cannon fodder in the much higher-budget United Artists release *Pork Chop Hill* (1959), starring Gregory Peck. The second Allied Artists project was a prison film, *Revolt in the Big House* (1959), in which he portrayed a dupe in an attempted jailbreak. Its drive-in movie trailer screamed: "The Biggest, Toughest Thriller Of Them All! A raw, violent world of caged men unleashed! Killers and lifers blasting over the big wall!"

The third—*The Purple Gang* (1960)—gave Blake an opportunity to show his stuff. The neurotic "Honeyboy" Willard was a character Blake could really get into—a ruthless little hood whose Darwinian philosophy explained it all: "You get to the top by having more guts than the next guy."

The docudrama about Detroit's entry in the Capone bootlegging syndicate was a modest box office success, playing on a double bill with *The Atomic Submarine* (1959). More important, it got Blake noticed. *Los Angeles Times* reviewer Charles Stinson, described him as "a slight, dark, round-faced young man who is doing, without question, some of the finest-grained work to be seen among our younger film actors. He is intense, flexible, free of mannerism and capable of much insight and subtlety."

For the first time since his "Li'l Beaver" days, newspapers and movie magazines wanted to interview him. The fanfare gave him an opportunity to wax wise beyond his years. As he told the *Los Angeles Times*, he was now more interested in making "serious message films" than he was in selling popcorn.

As part of this seriousness, Blake returned to the stage. In 1961, he turned his alleged heroin habit to good use as lead junkie in the Gallery Theatre production of *The Connection*, where he earned $14 a week during its twenty-six-week run. Offstage, he began exploring the L.A. theater scene and, in March of that year, took in a new comedy at the Pasadena Playhouse. The play, *Make a Million*, starring Jackie Coogan, wasn't that good, but the actress who played the ingenue role of Julie Martin was. Blake had first seen her perform at the Equity Library Theater in New York, and this time he went backstage to introduce himself. Her name was Sondra Kerr.

"I nailed her then," Blake later told an interviewer, not without some pride.

Like Blake, she'd grown up in L.A., where she was infected early by the movies. Born to a Russian furniture salesman and his immigrant wife, Sondra Orans had walk-on roles in feature films as early as 1945, when she was still in grammar school. By the late 1950s, she'd changed her name and began appearing in a host of plays: *I Am a Camera*, *Bus Stop* and *Orpheus Descending*, as well as TV productions like *Annie Get Your Gun*.

Sondra liked that Blake was serious, brooding and a little dangerous. He liked that she was available, but still a woman with some class.

Meanwhile, though the stage may have satisfied Robert's actor's soul, the $14 a week didn't. When he was offered a role in *Town Without Pity* (1961), he quit *The Connection* and caught the next plane to Germany, where the United Artists film was being shot on location.

Starring Kirk Douglas and E. G. Marshall, *Town Without*

Pity[20] was based on the true story of the trial of four off-duty G.I.s who raped a young German teenager and faced the death penalty. As one of the rapists, Blake is the only soldier who shows enough remorse to leave his shirt behind so the naked victim could cover herself.

But Blake was not able to steal any scenes. *Town Without Pity* belonged to Douglas, who played the soldiers' defense attorney. In it, he wins the soldiers long prison sentences rather than execution by putting the victim's reputation on trial. The town turns on the young woman, who commits suicide as her four rapists are being shipped off to jail. In the end, the most memorable thing about *Town Without Pity* was the title song performed by Gene Pitney, which became a number-one hit.

After Blake returned to L.A., he married Sondra. She had already been married once at nineteen, but it didn't last. She envisioned herself as a serious actress first and a wife second while her first husband, a twenty-five-year-old Austrian scholar, thought it was going to be the other way around.

For an aspiring young Method actor like Robert Blake, Sondra seemed a much better match. They could, and did, play off of each other for the next twenty years, both on- and offstage. Sixteen months after their first date, they wed on November 25, 1962, in a tiny mountain town in the Tehachapis, fifty miles northeast of L.A.

"Most people we knew, though, and I believe rightly so, thought that we wouldn't last six months," Blake said from the perspective of fifteen years later. "I was nuts, she was nuts and we spent a lot of our time hiding from the world, driving around for days and days and living in a little dump.

"When we weren't doing that, we'd get into terrible sick fights and days of torturing each other with a lot of unhealthy

---

20. Originally teased as "The story of what four men did to a girl . . . and what the town did to them," some newspapers refused to carry the ads because of the inference of rape—a taboo subject in the early 1960s. The *Los Angeles Times* finally struck a compromise and accepted "The story of four men . . . and a girl . . . and what the town did to them."

dependency, because we weren't able to live our own lives. We were being consumed by our neurotic needs rather than by our love."

Domestic disturbance didn't dampen Blake's career, however. The following year, he got another break. He'd been doing episodes on TV since 1950, making guest appearances mostly on Westerns like *The Cisco Kid, Wagon Train* and the *Adventures of Wild Bill Hickok,* but he'd never done a regular series until actor Richard Boone saw him work on a couple episodes of *Have Gun, Will Travel.* It happened at the time that Boone decided to challenge TV's status quo.

In 1961, Federal Communications Commission chairman Newton Minow delivered his famous speech comparing television to "a vast wasteland," citing rigged game shows, formulaic sitcoms and violent Westerns to prove his point. As the early TV star of one such long-running Western series, *Have Gun, Will Travel,*[21] Boone had to agree. With the notable exception of *Playhouse 90*, prime-time television stank. But that didn't mean it had to, and Boone set out to prove otherwise.

Have Gun, Will Travel had already made him a millionaire,[22] so he decided to accept Minow's challenge. Boone— who had studied at the Actors Studio in New York with the likes of Marlon Brando, Karl Malden, Eva Marie Saint and Julie Harris—saw the program as a showcase for young talent as well as an attempt to deliver something more than predictable bilge to America's great masses.

He pulled together an ensemble group of the finest young stage actors he could find, began soliciting original dramatic scripts and imported distinguished playwright Clifford

---

21. Based on the odyssey of a hired gun in the Old West, the series ran from 1957 through 1963 on CBS, trailing only *Gunsmoke* and *Wagon Train* in the all-important Nielsen ratings.

22. By the time the show went into syndication, Boone had sold his interest for $50,000 a year to be paid over the next twenty years.

Odets[23] to coproduce and act as script editor for a fresh new anthology series.

But even a powerhouse like Boone could not sell the network brass on his repertory idea. The best offer he received from CBS, which had grown fat off the profits from *Have Gun, Will Travel*, was to air *The Richard Boone Show* on Sunday afternoons when nobody would watch and the whole thing could be quickly canceled.

No thanks, said Boone. He kept lobbying until NBC finally picked it up for prime time on the strength of Boone's hit-making appeal in *Have Gun, Will Travel*.

Young Robert Blake was intrigued enough to join. What initially drew him to *The Richard Boone Show* was Clifford Odets. The playwright, whom Blake first knew as the screenwriter of *Humoresque*, had abandoned Broadway in favor of the more popular audience represented by television. Don't wait for the common man to come to Broadway, Odets seemed to say. Take Broadway to the common man.

"Look, Clifford Odets could have stayed on Broadway, but he came out here to write movies like *The Big Knife* (1955)," said Blake. "I'm not comparing myself to Odets, but you've got to go where the audiences are." Unfortunately, a month before *The Richard Boone Show* made its September 1963 debut, Odets died.

Even without Odets' guiding hand, the program was a critical success. Though he did not appear in every episode (he was in twenty-six shows), Blake got top billing simply because the actors were listed in alphabetical order and Blake's name came first, even ahead of Richard Boone.

"It was like working with actors from New York, especially Bobby," said June Harding, one of the ten actors Boone signed to the show. "He was great to work with."

---

23. A former member of the American Communist Party who laced his plays with social commentary, Odets is best remembered for such plays as *Waiting for Lefty* (1935), *Golden Boy* (1937), *The Country Girl* (1950) and the screenplay for *The Sweet Smell of Success* (1957). Like John Garfield, another Blake role model, Odets was a cofounder of the gritty Group Theatre of New York, which championed the proletariat on and off Broadway.

Unlike many other television shows, on which actors read TelePrompTers and memorized nothing from the script, performers on *The Richard Boone Show* were expected to behave as if they were coming to the stage in Manhattan. Not only were they required to learn their own parts—they had to know everyone else's as well. The actors had to be on time and they had to come prepared, bringing a level of professionalism to their work many of them had never before experienced in television.

"I think a lot of us were used to the pretty faces, like the fellow who starred in *Ben Casey* (Vince Edwards) who didn't bother to do much more than face the camera and read his lines off a card," said Harding.

In an hour-long episode titled "Run Pony Run," Harding recalled Blake delivering a riveting performance as a junkie, drawing from his stage experience in *The Connection*. "It showed him heating the dope and getting ready for a fix," she remembered. "It was a very emotional scene."

That such a scene appeared on prime time in the early 1960s was a small miracle. It was a different era, when network censors worked overtime to protect American morality. Harding recalled one long scene where she and the others rehearsed all morning and then recorded it on tape, only to have it nixed by NBC's Standards and Practices division because Harding's jeans were cut too low and her navel appeared once during a close-up.

She thought Blake was terrific to work with offstage as well as on. "We shot at the lot at MGM, and I remember once I mentioned to him that there was a teapot on the set that I liked, so he stole it for me!" she said. "He was a big flirt, and he had a quality about him I really liked. He was very private, but not unfriendly. You could look in his eyes and see he had it all going on. You'd look in others' eyes and there wasn't anything there."

He still had some of the high school rebel in him too. He raised hell the day John F. Kennedy was assassinated because the network demanded that the show stay on schedule. While the rest of America sat in front of its TV sets, watching the horror unfold, the producers of *The Richard Boone Show* ordered the actors to keep on rehearsing. Blake hanged one of the producers in effigy.

"I had nothing but admiration for him and his work," said Harding.

For Blake, *The Richard Boone Show* turned out to be as much an object lesson in television economics as in performance art. NBC canceled Boone's high-minded attempt at quality TV in January 1964, long before the thirty original episodes had all aired—this despite praise as TV's best new dramatic program. Boone himself learned that his show had been canceled by reading about it in *Daily Variety*. NBC's media department hadn't shown him the courtesy of running the press release by him before shipping it out.

At least Boone didn't go away broke as well as broken-hearted. Under the terms of his contract, NBC was still obligated to pay him $20,000 a week on a deferred-payment basis. His actors, on the other hand, had been working for scale wages. Boone, who remained a friend until he died in 1981, offered this advice to Blake: "Don't let [show biz] get you. Don't die in front of the [TV camera] box."

Robert wasn't so naive as to invest his future in a TV series. He regarded *The Richard Boone Show* as a noble experiment, not a launchingpad for television work. His résumé began to include bigger roles in bigger films. The photo composite he now handed out to casting directors included a shot of him as a sailor in *PT 109* (1963), the World War II drama about Lieutenant John F. Kennedy (Cliff Robertson) leading his men in a daring escape from the Japanese in the South Pacific. The heading on the composite read, "A young leading man verging on stardom, currently making George Stevens' *The Greatest Story Ever Told*."

While it fell short of the promise in its title, *The Greatest Story Ever Told* (1965) did have the greatest cast ever sold. So many name actors took roles in the epic that they had to be listed alphabetically. Blake, playing Simon the Zealot, came between Carroll Baker and Pat Boone.

On Broadway that year, he played a very different role: a tortured, intemperate homosexual in the dark comedy *Harry, Noon and Night*, while back home in L.A., Sondra was giving birth to their first child, Noah Luther Blake, who was born on February 1, 1965. Delinah Raya Blake was born a year and half later, on August 23, 1966.

Blake next appeared in *This Property Is Condemned* (1966), a potboiler set during the Depression and adapted from a one-act play by Tennessee Williams.[24] The film's publicists described Blake as "a film newcomer from TV"— especially ironic given that the film's star was Natalie Wood, who was five years Blake's junior and, like him, a former child actor. That affinity made them quite close during the filming and for years after, clear up until Wood's untimely drowning in 1981. According to Natalie's biographer, Suzanne Finstad, the unique rigors of the child actor's life became a recurrent theme for both actors.

In 1966, the Blakes moved to the San Fernando Valley—not the hilly, green exclusive enclaves of the Valley, but the flatlands on Hatteras Avenue in Van Nuys, where convenience stores, fast-food franchises and gas stations crowded every corner that wasn't occupied by a post–World War II tract home. Robert Blake, at age 33, had been paying his dues for years. There were the marquee names, the well-paid and well-respected character actors, and then, like him, there were all the Screen Actors Guild regulars who slogged to and from auditions, always looking for their main chance, always scraping to get by. Blake grew weary of being a scrape-by actor, especially in light of his long, long, long apprenticeship. He took up boxing and weight lifting to relieve himself of his anger. He was due for a break.

It came in the person of Perry Edward Smith, a homicidal drifter who walked out of the pages of Truman Capote's best-selling *In Cold Blood* and onto the silver screen.

---

24. Williams hated the screenplay and demanded that his name be removed. One of the three screenwriters was a very young Francis Ford Coppola.

12

In a role that Columbia Pictures originally wanted to give to Steve McQueen, Blake finally found his career-defining character. He hounded director Richard Brooks for a full year before he landed the part and then spent another year preparing for the role—dredging up the worst of his past to put the Method that Lee Strasberg had denied him up on the screen. Blake credited Jeff Corey with making the difference.

"I went out and got *In Cold Blood* all by myself," he said. "After I got the job, I went to an agent and gave it to him to negotiate."

Even Truman Capote remarked on Blake's uncanny resemblance to the real-life killer, whose dwarfish legs and arms seemed out of proportion to the rest of his body. Blake gained sixty pounds for the role. Perry Smith, whose father played himself in the movie, was a guitar-plucking ex-con and social misfit who nearly died in a motorcycling accident and whose physical pain combined with childhood nightmares to transform him into an aspirin junkie.

The Columbia publicity machine made much of the misleading "fact" that *In Cold Blood* director Richard Brooks cast both lead roles with "unknowns": Blake as Smith and actor Scott Wilson as his fellow murderer, Dick Hitchcock. While twenty-five-year-old Wilson actually *did* launch his movie career with *In Cold Blood*, Blake, 33, was more of a Hollywood veteran than anyone else on the set with the exception of actor John Forsythe. Nevertheless, Blake was paid a paltry $200 a week to do the movie.

In Cold Blood was made for $2.5 million in black-and-white on location in Holcomb, Kansas, where the four members of the Clutter farm family were actually murdered. Cameramen had to shoot around bloodstains that remained in the furnace room of the Clutter farmhouse, where Smith and Hitchcock had killed the father, Herb Clutter. Both Brooks and Capote insisted on absolute realism as much as possible, just as Capote had in detailing the unfolding tragedy in his classic "nonfiction novel." Six members of the jury that found Perry Smith and Dick Hitchcock guilty also sat on the jury in the movie version, and the hangman who executed the two killers led Wilson and Blake[25] to the gallows.

Blake and Wilson got into character right off by being standoffish. Blake scowled when wholesome Holcomb folk approached to get his autograph. "It's for sure that Dick and Perry never knew the Clutters or anyone else here, so we don't figure we should hang around with them either," Wilson explained to *Life* magazine's Jane Howard.

"I don't get much out of doing a lot of research," Blake reflected on the Holcomb experience years later. "But in my life I end up playing a lot of real people, and a lot of people tell you: 'This is how he brushed his teeth.' Who cares? Whatever you want you can get out of your head or out of your heart or out of your soul. I am more interested in my contribution than a mimic."

In his Holcomb motel room, Blake taped a sign to his wall that read THE VIPER—THE STILLER HE LIES, THE MORE DEADLY HE BITES.

"I can't tell you what that means, but it has to do with my part," he told *Life*'s Howard. "All the time, I think how different Perry's life might have been if whatever talent he may have had for painting and music had been channeled

---

25. Prison officials gave Blake a bedsheet that Perry Smith used as a canvas in the weeks leading up to his execution. In pastels, Smith drew a sailboat on the open sea—a scene Blake had framed and put on his living room wall.

like mine—and how easily I could have turned out the way he did. But in his whole life, except when he was a tiny baby, there was never any sunshine."

Truman Capote, who flew to Kansas for the press junkets and part of the filming, had a more whimsical take on Perry Smith. "One day, when I was visiting him in death row, reminiscing about the day he and Dick were brought back to the Garden City courthouse to be tried, I told him how big the crowds were outside waiting for him. You know what he wanted to know? He asked me, 'Were any representatives of the cinema there?'"

All the emphasis on realism did not mean Brooks was opposed to illusion. He hired members of the Kansas City Chiefs as extras to make Wilson and Blake appear even shorter than they were. It worked so well that the five-foot-four-inch Blake complained years afterward that everyone in Hollywood thought he was a midget.

"People in the business didn't want to talk to me," he said. "Hell, they didn't want me to come to their damned offices. . . . *I* started to believe it!"

While universally praised, particularly by the New York Film Critics Association, the movie received no Oscars and fared only so-so at the box office. The already-angry young Blake became alternately arrogant and bitter. He plunged into depression, returned to therapy and didn't work for two more years.

"I guess we scored a point or two with *In Cold Blood*," he said. "The Supreme Court did outlaw capital punishment. Who's to say? Maybe we were the straw that broke the camel's back.

"But two whole years of my life went into that film. I came out of it not only broke but in debt. I'm not complaining. I'm a poor fella. It doesn't scare me. Everybody else in this country is in it too. But sometimes I ask myself, 'Robert, what the hell are you doin'?'"

He turned down $100,000 to play Angel in Sam Peckinpah's *The Wild Bunch* (the role went to Jaime Sanchez) and $125,000 to be Sergeant Angelo in *The Bridge at Remagen* (the role went to Ben Gazarra). Two years later, when director John Schlesinger asked Blake to fly to New York to audi-

tion for *Midnight Cowboy*, Blake refused and Dustin
Hoffman won the prized role of Ratso Rizzo.

Hoffman's success was a special thorn in Blake's side.
Both of them grew up in L.A., studied stage acting, went to
Santa Monica City College[26] around the same time, hung
around the Pasadena Playhouse, went to New York to ap-
prentice at the Actors Studio—and yet Hoffman seemed to
get all the breaks while Blake got the old heave-ho. Strasberg didn't send Dustin home to Hollywood with his tail
between his legs. He was accepted in the vaunted Actors
Studio, made it to Broadway in 1961 and stayed. He even
took over the lead of the homosexual in *Harry, Noon and
Night* after Blake played the role, to nice notices in the *New
York Times*.

But despite their many similarities, Hoffman managed to
parlay his Harry into an Obie-winning role in another play
the next season while Blake was back struggling for TV
roles in L.A. Hoffman took home Theatre World and Drama
Desk awards in New York, building toward that big break in
1967, when Mike Nichols saw him on Broadway and named
him as the title role in *The Graduate*. That same year Robert
became Perry Smith. British film critics named him one of
the ten best English-speaking actors in the world, but he
wasn't even nominated at Oscar time. Hoffman was,[27] and
though it would take four more nominations[28] before he finally won the prized golden statuette, Dustin's early career
struggles were well behind him.

Blake's just seemed to hang on and on.

When Blake returned to L.A. from Kansas, his old stage
buddy Strother Martin came to him for advice. He'd been

---

26. According to Blake, he also did one semester each at Los
Angeles City College and San Fernando Valley Junior College.

27. Rod Steiger won the 1967 Best Actor Oscar for his performance
as the Southern sheriff in *In the Heat of the Night*. The other nominees
that year were Warren Beatty in *Bonnie and Clyde*, Paul Newman in
Cool Hand Luke and Spencer Tracy in *Guess Who's Coming to Dinner?*

28. Hoffman was nominated for *Midnight Cowboy* (1969) and *Lenny*
(1974) before he finally won Best Actor in 1979 for *Kramer vs. Kramer*.

studying for his part in *Cool Hand Luke* (1967), a small but potentially significant role of the prison captain. Martin had been struggling with a line in the script. Every time he spoke it aloud, it sounded forced. Everyone said Robert had an uncanny way with phrasing. How would he handle it?

Blake told Martin to pause every few syllables and spit, just the way a Southern straw boss might. The result was one of the most memorable lines ever uttered in film history—a line that made Martin's career: "What we have here is a failure to communicate."

But while Blake could quickly analyze and solve other actors' problems, he seemed cursed when he tried to solve his own. The same year Dustin Hoffman starred as Ratso Rizzo in *Midnight Cowboy*, Blake played the title role in *Tell Them Willie Boy Is Here*. He had to hustle once more like a SAG unknown just to land that job. When director Abe Polonsky proposed Blake for the role, Universal production chief Jennings Lang vetoed the idea. He didn't want a brooding, temperamental actor with an explosive reputation. Lang wouldn't even meet with Blake.

Robert took a chance, picked up the phone and called Lang, faking Polonsky's high-pitched nasal voice over the phone: "Jennings, this is Abe. I have Robert Blake here in my office. Now listen. I'm prepared to blow this whole picture unless you have the decency to at least talk to this young man."

They met. Blake was uncharacteristically solicitous of the blustery Lang, biting his tongue like the stoic Indian he was about to play on the screen. He got the job. The *New York Times* would call his portrayal of Willie Boy "very much a John Garfield part—tight, taut, antihero." Blake immersed himself in the role in what was becoming a familiar pattern. He lost twenty-five pounds and acquired a deep tan. He learned to speak Cahuilla, the nearly extinct tongue of the Indian he was about to portray.

"He lived out there, on the desert, in meditation, for three to five days at a time over a two-month period—and he didn't even have the part at the time!" said Polonsky.

During filming, the cast and crew headed out to the Mojave in the middle of summer, when daytime temperatures reach 110 degrees. While the rest of the company ate in relative comfort beneath a tent, Blake took his lunch out to a flat rock in the desert and ate alone. When Polonsky invited him in where it was cooler, Blake looked at him without cracking a smile and said menacingly:

"Indian no eat with white man."

The Method could be a toxic way to live, as Blake was warned more than once by family and friends alike.

"He was so in a bubble all his own," said Virginia Leith. "You have to have somebody who can relate to you. You cannot just be in a bubble. You just can't."

"I think I went too far in *In Cold Blood,*" Blake admitted to the *New York Times.* "I kind of bent my head permanently by playing an obviously neurotic, inhibited, very sick guy. It was very, very hard on my wife and children, living with Perry Smith for two years. But I finally got shed of him—it took some doin'—and now they like Willie Boy considerably better, and so do I."

Blake tied with Alan Arkin, Peter O'Toole and the infernal Dustin Hoffman as runner-up in that year's New York Film Critics Association voting for Best Actor.[29] When it came to paychecks and promotion, however, he was still second tier. As the sheriff who tracks down Willie Boy, Robert Redford received $250,000 to Blake's $50,000, and far more media attention. In the theater marquees, newspaper ads and film posters, Redford's name and photo dominated. Blake might have been Willie Boy, but in the eyes of America, he was an also-ran.

"Those ads hurt," he said. "There's this blond, freckled god Redford up there on the billboards. And *I'm* Willie Boy. I went out there in that desert and traced that Indian's path over three hundred miles. I ripped that part out of the rocks.

---

29. The award that year went to Jon Voight, whose Joe Buck to Dustin Hoffman's Ratso Rizzo in *Midnight Cowboy* also won them both Oscar nominations, though the Oscar itself went to John Wayne. Blake wasn't nominated.

But it doesn't matter. Ain't nobody sees that picture without knowing who Willie Boy was—or who he is."

Once again, short, dour Robert Blake was upstaged by the Van Johnson clone, the captain of the football team, the guy who gets the girl. Though he tried to brush it off as the hand that he was dealt, his words dripped with resentment.

"It's not his fault," said Blake. "Robert Redford was born way ahead of where I'll end up."

13

One day near the release date for *Willie Boy*, Bobby Blake read about the passing of another Bobby. Almost from his uncredited debut in *Lost Angel* (1944), Bobby Driscoll had been a star—the first child actor Walt Disney put under exclusive contract. He epitomized "cute" in Disney classics like *Song of the South* (1946) and *Treasure Island* (1950), and immortalized himself as the voice of *Peter Pan* (1953). He owned his own star on Hollywood Boulevard and won a special juvenile Oscar in 1949 for his precocious performance in the non-Disney thriller *The Window*.

By the mid-1950s, though, Driscoll was no longer adorable. Disney dropped him from its roster, and he made his last movie, *The Party Crashers*, with Connie Stevens in 1958. He became as unemployable as Blake had once been, and like Blake, he moved to Broadway to learn stagecraft. He told fellow child actor Jackie Cooper that he wanted to show that he was a legitimate actor and not just a screen hack.

In March 1968, a decomposed body was found in a New York tenement building. Cause of death was ascribed to a heroin overdose. The body went unidentified and unclaimed and was buried in a pauper's grave. A year passed before fingerprints identified the John Doe as Bobby Driscoll.

Driscoll was not the only kid actor whose untimely death Robert read about. Rivaling Blake as the cutest Rascal on the set back in his MGM days was Spanky's little pal, Scotty Beckett. He was the Rascal who wore his ball cap sideways and had the biggest, most innocent eyes. Like Blake, Scotty also graduated to movies once he was ousted from *Our Gang*. His most memorable turn was as young Al in *The Al Jolson Story* (1946).

Scotty became less and less innocent the older he grew. In 1960, police arrested him for beating his stepdaughter with a crutch. In 1963, at age thirty-three, he was again arrested for assault with a deadly weapon. Soon thereafter, he made his first suicide attempt. He was admitted into rehab after an attempt at slashing his wrists, but was soon back on drugs. On May 10, 1968, Scotty overdosed on barbiturates and died at the Royal Palms Hotel in Los Angeles. He was thirty-eight.

Another famous Rascal had already reached an untimely end. On January 21, 1959, Carl "Alfalfa" Switzer known to a whole new generation of children who were then watching TV reruns of *Our Gang* comedies, died at age thirty-one. A professional hunting guide named Moses S. (Bud) Stiltz shot and killed Switzer over a disputed $50 debt. Because Switzer had been drinking and threatening at the time of the incident, the Los Angeles County Coroner ruled Switzer's death justifiable homicide.

Like all the other Rascals—including Blake—he had never seen a dime in residuals from the thousands of reruns of his comedies or the exploitation of his familiar freckled face and his untamable iron cow lick. His childhood was owned by King World Productions.[30]

Years later, when Blake put up lobby cards and posters around the house from his Rascal and "Red Ryder" days, he told *Los Angeles Times* film critic Charles Champlin that these child star tragedies haunted him:

"I think of all the Rascals and all the pals I had when we were kid actors together. Scotty Beckett, all of them. Dead too young. Suicides. ODs. Just worn-out and defeated by life. I'm here. Sometimes I'm not sure why or how, but I'm here.

---

30. On the strength of its *Little Rascals* library, King World went on to produce and distribute such syndicated TV hits as *Inside Edition*, *American Journal* and the most successful talk show in TV history, *The Oprah Winfrey Show*.

"Alfalfa and Bobby Driscoll and Scotty Beckett and others are dead because they had no backup, no support. I think I survived because I was too dumb to die. You figure it."

He certainly was too belligerent to work with. Despite the triumphant upturn in his career following *In Cold Blood* and *Willie Boy*, Blake continued to have career trouble—and usually of his own making. That same Method intensity that made his screen presence so riveting created a temperamental monster when he was off the set. "If you fight with me, I will fight you forever," Blake told one interviewer, summing up his philosophy. "I like to fight—that's healthy. But if you mess with me, I'll kill you."

His difficult reputation stayed with him throughout his adult career. In 1970, during an appearance on the nationally televised *Dick Cavett Show*, Blake slammed Bishop Fulton Sheen and the Catholic Church, further alienating both the public and producers who might have considered hiring him.

"I knocked him out of the box," bragged Blake. "He'd been going on about how he used to go into Harlem with a bag of food—beans, I think—for the Puerto Ricans.

"So I turned to Rex Reed, who was also on the show, and said, 'You know more about fancy clothes than I do. How much would you say those loafers he's wearing cost?' Reed said, 'Oh, $60, I'd guess, give or take a few dollars.' The bishop clammed up after that."

Nor was his home life domestic bliss. As far back as Noah Blake could remember, his parents were either screaming at each other or at war with the neighbors. Growing up in their tract house on Hatteras Street and, later, a cracker box on Farmdale Avenue that Blake bought in 1972 with a $30,000 Cal-Vet loan was like growing up in a bunker. "Both my parents, I think, required a lot of attention and required a lot of spotlight time," said Noah. "And I don't think there was just a lot of room for the children."

The Method never switched off for Blake. He remained the same tough guy at home that he was on the set. "He definitely wore that mantle," recalled Noah, who uses none of the "dese" and "dat" New Jerseyisms that his famous father laced through his speech both in public and private throughout his life.

In the early 1970s, when Noah and Delinah were still very young, Robert angrily told an interviewer: "My kids, I must tell you—they think it's a joke. They don't respond to [prejudice] the way I do or the way Sondra does. They're much more secure than we are, so they find it for the most part funny. I think that my little girl has been rejected from time to time because of what she is [a mix of Robert's Neapolitan blood and Sondra's Russian ancestry], but she didn't know it."

Robert's fatherly advice to the youthful Noah and Delinah was unequivocal. When people behave badly, don't try to understand them. Shun them. Defeat them. Bring them *down*. Bigots and bullies deserve nothing less than total revenge. He once pointed at a hated neighbor's house and announced: "I tell [Noah and Delinah] very specifically that those people are assholes. They think they're better than we are because they're born with blue eyes and blond hair and they come from the same culture as President Nixon."

Blake's angry persona cost him one of the title roles in *Little Fauss and Big Halsey* (1970). Instead Michael J. Pollard got the part opposite Robert Redford, which was probably a blessing in disguise. Not only did the story about a mismatched pair of motorcycle racers flop at the box office, it would also have been Blake's excuse to renew his recurrent harangue about Redford's good looks and how Blake had been wretchedly handicapped since birth because he was short, dark and Italian.

Blake signed on to play the title role in *Corky* (1972), an oddball hot rod movie that featured cameos of real-life racing legends Richard Petty, Bobby Allison and Cale Yarborough. Not unlike the Rascals of his youth who spiraled into madness and an early death as adults, Blake's character is a frustrated stock car driver on the edge who goes completely berserk by movie's end, gunning down scores of innocents.

While principal photography wrapped in November 1970 at the Peach Bowl Raceway in Atlanta, audiences didn't get to see *Corky* for another two years because director Bruce Geller and MGM warred over the final shoot-out scene. Executives at the dying studio kept ordering the film back to the cutting room to rid it of gratuitous violence while Geller pleaded that there was no other way that the dissembling character Blake portrayed would have behaved. The result was a film edited by committee, that the studio refused to promote.

Once again, a performance critics praised ("Blake comes across very effectively in a challenging role," wrote *Variety*'s Art Murphy) got short shrift at the box office. When *Corky* finally did arrive in theaters, the movie was stillborn and closed in a week.

Blake was also set to play the lead in *My Old Man's Place* (1972) about a returning war veteran, but that job also fell through. Blake disagreed with director Edwin Sherin, who wanted to tap into the psychological conflicts facing a soldier coming back to his home town after a tour of duty in Vietnam. "I think it's about the fact that all the things wrong with this world should be burned down, destroyed and shoved aside to make room for new and better things," Blake told him.

In January 1972, the trades announced that Blake would star in *Electra Glide in Blue* (1973),[31] a period piece envisioned as the police flipside of *Easy Rider* (1969), capturing both the optimism and hopelessness of the Vietnam era.

Blake's character, John Wintergreen, was a short, idealistic motorcycle cop[32] who dreamed of being promoted to Homicide only to be disillusioned and done in by corruption following his investigation of the mysterious murder of a desert hermit.

"I directed *Electra Glide in Blue*, wrote three quarters of it, cast it, did everything," said Blake. "Didn't put my name any place on it. Put another guy's name on it. He never was near show business, film, anything like that, before or since."

The director was rock musician James William Guercio,

---

31. The title refers to the type of motorcycle used by the Arizona highway patrol.

32. One of the promotion lines lifted from Wintergreen's dialogue reads: "Did you know that me and Alan Ladd were exactly the same height?"

a twenty-eight-year-old wunderkind who was once one of Frank Zappa's Mothers of Invention. Later Guercio would produce a string of hugely successful LPs for the band Chicago[33] and one hit album from Blood, Sweat and Tears.

"I laid out the movie like an album," said Guercio. "Fast scene, slow scene, funny scene."

The result, according to *Time* magazine film critic Jay Cocks, was "an eclectic, impersonal exercise; a market research report on fads, trends, styles."

Nevertheless, *Electra Glide in Blue* became *the* big hit of the 1973 Cannes Film Festival. "Guercio showed up like the new DeMille, with jodhpurs and a crop, just like Cecil," said Blake's veteran publicist Dale Olson.

Despite his gripes about Guercio's direction, Blake sensed his movie-star career, which had derailed so often since *In Cold Blood*, was now back on track.

Blake turned down a $125,000 offer from Dino DeLaurentiis because he wanted to see what would happen following the release of *Electra Glide*. With the film's remarkable reception at Cannes, it finally looked like Blake was going to the major leagues. But when the advertising campaign opened, it was the comic element rather than the tragedy[34] that the studio played up:

He's A Good Cop. On A Big Bike. On A Bad Road.

Electra Glide was not a hit, but it did fair business at the box office. And though it was the darling of international film critics at Cannes, the movie was shut out of the Oscars, garnering not even a single nomination.[35]

"I might be getting to the popcorn-eating audience," said

---

33.   Guercio cast Chicago band members in bit parts throughout *Electra Glide in Blue*.

34.   In the film's climax, lavishly filmed in Monument Valley, John Wintergreen is brutally and senselessly murdered by a carload of Mansonesque hippies.

35.   Blake did get a Golden Globe nomination for *Electra Glide* and wore a denim tuxedo to the awards.

Blake. "This is the first time I wasn't neurotic or crazy. It's been a long, hard row. United Artists gave me another light, warm one, *Busting*. So I'm waiting. If the two do well, maybe I'll have a chance to—fail."

Blake moved on to *Busting* (1974), an odd buddy picture about two cynical L.A. vice cops at odds with their superiors, the system and a local crime lord. The young producers, Robert Chartoff and Irwin Winkler, originally paired Elliott Gould with actor Ron Leibman, but Leibman withdrew in March 1973 due to "irreconcilable artistic differences" and their second choice was Robert Blake. Blake developed similar artistic differences with Winkler and Chartoff, but instead of settling them amicably, he slammed them in the press as "Winkum and Blinkum"—know-nothings who "probably think the movie's got a message. Ha! Know what the message is? Make money!"

Blake hated the script. He hated the director. He hated everything but his costar, underscoring his admiration for Gould by demeaning other peers like Richard Benjamin and Bruce Dern. He would *never* have agreed to do the picture with either of them. Gould's praise for Blake was equally sycophantic: "Bobby represented L.A. and I represented New York. Between us, we got it all."

Blake prepared for *Busting* by hanging out with real vice cops, but he did not like what he saw them doing on the streets of L.A. "We'd go into gay bars and I'd see some homosexual friends," said Blake. "I'd say, 'Hey, these are my friends! What are you guys gonna do to them? What kind of job is this?' I don't think they know either. I think they hide behind their badges, just like crooks hide behind their guns, except the cops got the law on their side."

By the time *Busting* was in the film can, Blake was spewing all over the film's premise, making sure that anyone who might have wandered into a theater to see it was warned ahead of time not to waste their money. "I don't know what vice is," he said. "The sky is falling and they're running in a $5 hooker who's just trying to earn a living. If you want to find vice, you should go to Washington."

Film critics were far less critical, regarding it as a good, solid, old-fashioned B flick. *Time* called *Busting* "a pointedly low-down movie about low life," while *New York Times* critic Vincent Canby planted his tongue deep in his cheek and called it "a cool, intelligent variation on a kind of movie that by this time can be most easily identified by the license numbers on the cars in its chase sequences."

The Gay Activists Alliance didn't see it that way. Both during shooting and after the film's release, they staged protests, and in his inimitable blunt fashion, Blake had to agree with them. It was a gay-bashing film that deserved to die. And die it did, once again underscoring Blake's remarkable propensity for sabotaging his own success.

"I was number two in line for *Lenny*,[36] number two in line for *The Godfather*,"[37] said Blake. "I was becoming Mr. Second String Charley around town. Instead of just sayin', 'Well, fuck the movies, I'll do a play or go on television,' I kept thinking, 'No, I gotta be a *movie actor.*'"

The following year, he did it again, effectively killing any chance he had of portraying Broadway impresario Billy Rose in *Funny Lady* (1975), the widely anticipated sequel to *Funny Girl* (1968). With both a disposition and a stature comparable to those of the diminutive Rose, Blake was perfect for the part and would have had it if he hadn't lost his temper with Barbra Streisand. "I had the part," said Blake. "I threw the script in her lap and said, 'I'm sick of fucking with this thing. I've tested for it twice. If you can't make up your mind, go fuck yourself,' and walked out."

The role went instead to tall, laconic James Caan, who was exactly wrong as Billy Rose.[38] Blake cursed his lousy luck, only belatedly coming to understand that it wasn't so

36. The title role of the 1974 biopic on the life of comedian Lenny Bruce went to Dustin Hoffman, who won an Oscar nomination for his efforts.
37. Al Pacino won the role of Michael Corleone in all three *Godfather* films, and in so doing not only garnering Oscar nominations but establishing a lifelong movie star career.
38. The producers sent Blake a case of expensive champagne as a consolation prize, so Blake took it to a nearby bridge, where he and son, Noah, popped open each bottle and poured it into the Los Angeles River.

much luck as it was career suicide. "All that movie work I did before didn't amount to much," he said. "When each of those movies was over, I just dropped out of sight again. Then, by accident, I got on the Carson show and had the first degree of public success I ever had, except for a few good reviews."

Beginning with his debut appearance on February 19, 1970, Blake went on to make nearly one hundred appearances on the *Tonight Show* over the next fifteen years. "I had a high Q rating," said Blake. "You know what that means? It means they like you and want to see more of you on television."

His pulp-fiction persona, vomiting vilification on everyone from the studio executives to his own parents, whom he blamed for all of the horror in his life, became an instant hit with the late-night TV crowd. Blake was asked to return to Johnny Carson's couch again and again.

"You know, on different nights I kept going back to do the Carson show, and gradually I came around to the view that my whole life was very funny. Before, I tended to view it as very tragic—all that stuff I went through as a child actor and all. When I did *In Cold Blood* and *Willie Boy*, I pulled a lot of heavy tragedy out of my early life. But Carson saw it all as funny, and gradually he convinced me too."

By the time *Electra Glide in Blue* and *Busting* were released, newspaper and broadcast reporters weren't even calling him an actor anymore. They referred to him as a "TV talk-show personality."

14

Robert Blake's reception on the *Tonight Show* with Johnny Carson ought to have taught him a thing or two about fame, but the lessons didn't sink in until years later. In the early 1970s, Blake's unguarded angst bubbled over with every appearance, and late-night America fell under his spell, not unlike the daytime audiences of today who empathize with the jilted, the angry and the just plain pathetic who guest on the Jenny Jones, Jerry Springer, Rikki Lake, Sally Jesse Raphael and Montel Williams circuit.

The major difference between Blake and these sad sacks was that he was a movie star—or very close to it—who alternately blubbered to Johnny Carson over his abused childhood and snarled about the authority figures in suits who made his singularly blessed life so damned difficult.

"It was almost like the guy in *Network*, you know?" Blake recalled some twenty years after his *Tonight Show* debut. "The crazier he got the more famous he got."

On May 19, 1972, Blake discussed his uncontrollable temper and how he'd gotten himself into repeated trouble by being blunt. His remarkable lack of diplomacy was a theme Johnny would return to again and again over the next thirteen years, playing it for laughs but frequently with long-term negative consequences for Blake. "They hired me on that show, and when I did really start coming apart, they loved it," Blake later lamented. "It was terrible. You are supposed to fall apart in your front room, not in front of millions of people."

Like every other actor who sat at the right hand of

Johnny, Blake shamelessly plugged his movies and TV appearances, but Robert's unique appeal among the mostly forgettable *Tonight Show* guests was his naked angst. He treated Carson's couch as if it were a psychiatrist's. In fact, Blake's therapist actually advised him to let it all hang out on Carson. Telling the world what patients usually reserved for the safety of private group therapy would be cathartic, Blake was told.

"The *Tonight Show* made him interesting," recalled Ed McMahon. "You know, what happens in our business is that somebody can be a great actor, but if they start to get interesting, they have a whole different following. That's what made Sinatra so great. He was the greatest singer alive, but he was also interesting. Blake was not only in a series, but he was an interesting guy in a series. A lot of guys have series, but not a lot of guys are interesting."

The result of Blake's TV therapy sessions was regular public confessions of his childhood abuse: his time in and out of jails; twelve-step programs and juvenile hall; his stockade episode in the army; his fall from Catholic grace and his slapstick experiences as an altar boy. "One of my first failures in show business was as an altar boy," he said. "I couldn't make it. I didn't understand Latin and I ate all the wafers."

He turned grief and confusion into one-liners, talking about running away from home, from booze, from drugs, from family and finally, from himself. His neurotic guest shots became such a staple of late night that they were ritualized, beginning with his token retrieval of a cigarette from a box atop Johnny's desk. Through two commercial breaks, Blake would finger and nurse the cigarette, but never light it as he babbled on about his inner demons.

In one appearance he'd be off tobacco for good, chewing Nicorette gum. A few months later, he'd be back on. Same with alcohol, prescription drugs, fast women. His onstage pronouncements about licking his addictions turned to mush offstage, but the *Tonight Show* audience never heard that part. They obeyed the APPLAUSE signs when he soberly recounted how he'd beaten demon rum, smack, nicotine, Valium, etc.

Blake's guest shots were as much antic as angst-ridden. He later likened his performances on Carson's stage to those of a trained monkey. He played "Home on the Range" on a handsaw and "When the Moon Comes over the Mountains" on a balloon. Carson drafted him into skits as a Mighty Carson Art Player and encouraged him to play the fool. He was such a hit that the producers had him guest-host the show at one point. Since his Rascal days, Blake had never really tried to be funny, and he was pretty good at it.

"I don't ever want to go back to that maudlin way of thinking again, because, after all, you can deal with big themes and the universal elements with comedy," he rationalized. "Kubrick did it in *Dr. Strangelove*. Look what Bogart and Hepburn did in *The African Queen*. Through his entire career, Charles Chaplin used tragedy in a comedic and human way. I'd like to do that."

Robert yukked it up with Johnny over his shyness during a nude scene in *Willie Boy*; his fury over the lack of promotion for *Electra Glide in Blue*; and his contempt for the Motion Picture Academy and its movie-rating system. He was publicly bereft over the passing of comedian Wally Cox and elated over meeting Carol Burnett for the first time. He waxed nostalgic about *Our Gang* and came close to tears in describing a pilgrimage he made to Italy to visit his one-hundred-twenty-year-old great-grandfather.

Whenever he was invited back, Blake wore high-heel boots to disguise his diminutive stature, elevating himself to the level of Ed McMahon's chin. He never wore a suit and tie like Johnny, defiantly leaving his shirt open as if he'd just dropped by for a few moments instead of spending hours in makeup and rehearsal in the *Tonight Show* green room. To the NBC audience, Blake passed himself off as a recovered heroin addict, a recovering child actor and an iconoclastic enemy of the studio system.

"I made a reputation for myself telling lies on the *Tonight Show*," Blake said years later to *Entertainment Tonight*. "The whole story about drugs is my fault. The whole story that I beat up everybody at Universal is my fault. [MCA/Universal chairman] Lew Wasserman hugs me when I see him. I made a fortune for Universal."

For Blake, the *Tonight Show* was an object lesson in show biz symbiosis. Carson used Blake to entertain his audience just as Blake used Carson to advertise his movies, TV projects and public persona. If Robert was actually ever as manic depressive as he advertised, the *Tonight Show* audience never got a glimpse of his depression. Even on the dullest of evenings, Robert Blake was always wacky and wild—and good for some big laughs:

- Blake on Thanksgiving: "I'm thankful I'm not dead, that I haven't gone to the bone orchard."
- Blake on prison: "I don't want to go to the penitentiary. If I ever went to prison they would carry me out 'cause I would either kill somebody or they would kill me. Oh yeah. Definitely. It would happen. Somebody would try to make me their girlfriend or their mother."
- Blake on bending over for the "suits": "They'd do it to me again if they could find a place on my asshole where there ain't no scar tissue."
- Blake on finding the right woman: "I need to go out with a woman about eighty or ninety years old and then go to bed with her granddaughter."

"It's the bursting bubbles," said Ed McMahon. "I am a big fan of W. C. Fields. He burst balloons and was not afraid to take on the establishment, and Blake represented that in our time."

Robert knew better than to get too serious for a network audience. Mawkish was okay if it ended in a punch line, but genuine discourse on genuine problems was verboten. Carson had a long history of shutting people off instantly if they displeased him. Long after he'd become a staple of the show, Blake's worst fear remained that he might not get asked to come back.

"It's not a talk show," said Blake. "It's some other kind of show. I mean, he has such energy. You got like six minutes to do your thing and you better fucking do it and you better be good or they'll go to the commercial after two minutes, and when they come back, you'll be over in the recovery room with Spanky [Ed McMahon] there."

McMahon took Blake's contempt and liked it. "He had a great line for me one night, when he said to Johnny: 'Yeah, you and your pal, Wimpy.' And then he looked over at me. I think he said it came from *Popeye*. Johnny loved him and I loved him. He was just his own man. He was not the last angry man, but he had an edge of anger about himself."

Johnny Carson taught Robert the importance of publicity. All the fine work that he had done through the 1960s, from *The Connection* and *The Richard Boone Show* through *In Cold Blood* and *Willie Boy* was seen by a fraction of its potential audience because of a lack of public exposure. It was not enough to perform well, to communicate viscerally with the audience and to crystallize the deepest human emotions in an electrifying moment on stage or screen. First of all, you had to get the audience's attention. Even Shakespeare had to play to the cheap seats.

Blake learned to manipulate the media as never before. He began a lasting relationship with *Los Angeles Times* film critic Charles Champlin, who managed a lengthy profile of the actor every two or three years, almost as if he was serializing Blake's life. Similarly, Blake kept up positive relations with the potential publicity machinery at *People* magazine, *TV Guide* and even the *National Enquirer.* He studied his audience and catered to it: Robert Blake, blue-collar little guy who fights the good fight against the powers that be. Never mind that he grew up very whitebread in the midst of the world's most glamorous business.

Despite his newfound notoriety as a Carson regular, he and his family still led a very blue-collar existence. Blake purposely lived in a déclassé section of North Hollywood and drove an eleven-year-old car to work. He wore black T-shirts and threadbare Levi's to the studio, and his kids wore clothes from Sears and went to public schools. He no longer had to live out on the flat plain of the San Fernando Valley anymore, and in fact, he soon wouldn't. Affluence would catch up with Blake in a big way.

Robert Blake owed his biggest debt to Johnny Carson. "*Baretta* came out of that," he said. "It came out of Carson."

15

While swimming off the Central Pier in Atlantic City during the summer of 1974, Bonny Lee Bakley and a boyfriend drifted out too far and began screaming for help. The sea was rough and a riptide had them in its grip. Fortunately, lifeguards arrived in the nick of time and pulled them both ashore. Bonny made the most of the moment, carrying on breathlessly about how she nearly drowned.

The next day the *Atlantic City Press* carried a short article about the dramatic rescue—one of many that occur each year in the southern New Jersey resort city. The boyfriend didn't give it a second thought. But Bonny was thrilled. It was the first official Bonny news clipping. She saved it, and every scrap of newspaper, magazine article, press release or advertisement that came thereafter.

"She took her portfolio with her everywhere," said her uncle George Hall. "Bonny was always going off to New York, showing her photos and what-not to producers and agents. She was wild about the show business. All that little girl ever wanted was to get noticed."

Bonny had almost a heroic determination to actually *be* one of those *American Bandstand* girls she'd seen sidle up so often to a Frankie (Avalon, Sinatra, or Valli—any would do). But she wasn't simply interested in sidling. She wanted to land herself a pop star like a live tuna. She did not outgrow her Frankie fantasy; it outgrew her. Her whole existence was given over to her obsession. She would make her dreams come true or else.

She dropped out of Northern Regional High School in her

sophomore year, reversed her first and middle names so that her "stage name" became Leebonny Bakley and traveled to nearby Union City, New Jersey, to earn a certificate suitable for framing from the Barbizon School for Modeling.

She'd never given up on nudism either. "She used to tell me they had all these orgy parties out there and everything when I was still a little kid," said her brother, Joey. "Sounded so good, I wanted to go too."

She modeled in nudist magazines, preached sun worship and entered nude beauty pageants, which she maintained she lost only because she had strap marks from her bikini. She was leggy, bosomy, blond and cute, though she could never be accused of being beautiful. She began advertising in the back pages of nudist publications, offering to model in the buff, and had many takers. Her photo sessions taught her a valuable lesson in economics. She earned more money in a single shoot than she would have taken home from selling fries beneath the Golden Arches in a month. Easy money.

Along the way, she married and divorced in short order. Through her mail-order modeling business she met Evangelos Paulakis, a young Greek national who wanted a green card so he could remain in the U.S. He was cute and offered to pay, so Bonny married him in a ceremony at the Spruce Run Lutheran Church in Glen Gardner, New Jersey.

"She was late to her own wedding," said Joey. "She showed up in this old Lincoln Continental limo she was driving back then, with this yellow light on the top, brakes squealing, her jumping out in her dress and running up the church steps. When the minister came to the part where he asks if there's anyone who objects, all of us on her side of the aisle—my mom, my sister, me—we all busted out laughing."

Within weeks, she discovered that she'd taken on a husband who had many of the same problems as her late father.

"He had sessions where he was drinking and Bonny didn't like that too well," said Uncle George. Her sister, Margerry, put it far less delicately. "The asshole beat her, so she had him deported," she said.

During her estrangement from Paulakis before she had him shipped back to Athens, she began a practice that turned into a lifelong habit: she taped his phone calls. Years later, when police discovered the hundreds of hours of phone conversations that Bonny had secretly taped, with everyone from Jerry Lee Lewis to Robert Blake, they found at least two cassettes labeled EVANGELOS.

Following her first experience as a married woman, two things became crystal clear to Bonny about men: they thought with their genitals and could never be counted on to support a woman.

She continued her groupie ways. In the summer of 1976, Bonny made a pilgrimage to Graceland, home of Elvis Presley. She milled outside the famous treble clef wrought iron gates until she figured nobody was watching and then climbed over the brick wall that surrounded the mansion grounds. She then scaled one of the trees on the front lawn for a better look inside the second floor of the faux plantation residence. She knew that was where Elvis' bedroom was located. That was when George[39] the security guard spotted her, and under much protest, Bonny became one more in Graceland's daily allotment of fans tossed off the grounds before she had a chance to meet the King.[40] She was still able to cross the street to one of the Elvis emporia that specialized in Presley memorabilia, however, and purchase a phony photo of herself standing next to Elvis—a treasure that she added to her growing Leebonny portfolio.

"That girl lit out everywhere first time she could climb in a car and go," said Uncle George.

Bonny hooked up with her cousin Peggy and headed out to California and took in all the scenery in between. She could never stay in one spot for too long—a peripatetic pattern that remained with her throughout her life.

In the meantime Barbizon did less for Bonny's career than did her early experience as a nudist. In Manhattan, a

---

39. Like the "Evangelos" tapes, police also found an early tape of George among Bonny's collection.

40. Elvis died a year later, on Aug. 16, 1977, before Bonny could get back to Memphis for a second shot at Graceland.

serious young actress had to make the necessary connections to break into the business by auditioning for extra work on soap operas and making casting calls for commercials. The problem was, she couldn't act. As Leebonny, she maintained on her résumé that she had been accepted at the Lee Strasberg Acting School in New York. She discovered that she got far more attention with her clothes off than on.

She placed ads in magazines and took nude modeling jobs. Over the years Bonny crossed the line from tasteful nudity to full-out porn. In June 1977, *Hustler,* the groundbreaking men's magazine that became the first nationally distributed periodical to "go pink" by featuring centerfolds with female labia in living color, gave the world its newest regular feature: "Beaver Hunt." Among the young women honored in this first-ever below-the-beltline talent search was a girl from Clinton, New Jersey, by the name of Marjorie Carlyon whose happy combination of hooters and howdee! haunches immediately won the hearts and groins of thousands of men, young and old all across this great land.

It was Bonny, of course, achieving national exposure by using her mother's name. In a text box accompanying the photo spread, the demure young woman made a modest offer to perform at stag parties. Back home in Clinton, the neighbors came calling with the magazine in hand, demanding to know if in fact that was Mrs. Carlyon displaying herself in a notorious national skin magazine. No, she said huffily. "Bonny and I look alike."

The notoriety was not welcome. Not long thereafter, Mrs. Carlyon sold the house and moved to Tennessee. "Honestly, that girl has no shame," she said. "How she can show her face in public is beyond me. But she considers it a feather in her cap!"

By that time, Bonny had moved to Tennessee herself.

16

At a New York gathering of the nation's TV critics in November 1974, ABC-TV president Fred Pierce announced that he'd just offered actor Robert Blake his first weekly series since *The Richard Boone Show,* replacing New York stage actor Tony Musante in the network's low-rated cop show *Toma.* Based on a real-life Newark detective who relied heavily on disguises, the show had actually been canceled after twenty-two episodes, but showed such a resurgence in summer reruns that ABC decided to resurrect it. The only problem was Musante had gotten his fill of the weekly series sausage factory and wanted out.

At the same time, on the strength of his Carson show appearances, Blake contacted Jerry Levy, a talent agent he'd known since the late 1950s, when he landed his Allied Artists contract. Blake told him he was desperate for work and gave him two months to find him something—anything. Blake had been so unnerved by the failures of *Electra Glide* and *Busting* that he thought he was dying. He checked himself into Cedars Sinai Hospital for two weeks of tests, only to find out that he was fine physically. "I wound up in a fucking hospital, staring at the walls and asking, 'What's the matter?'" Blake recalled. "I had reached the end of a period of tremendous hope and energy—and tremendous mistakes that I made—in the film industry."

Levy switched him to TV. In a deal similar to the Allied Artists three-picture deal, the agent garnered Blake a contract to make four movies-of-the-week with Universal Studios, the biggest sausage factory of them all. When ABC programming chief Michael Eisner heard about the deal, he offered Universal and Blake a twelve-show guarantee if Blake would step into an existing detective series called *Toma*. The headache of transforming *Toma* into *Baretta* was handed to writer-producer Stephen J. Cannell, who was given five days to refashion *Toma* into a pilot script.

"Blake didn't even want to take a meeting," said Cannell. "He hated it. 'I'm not going to do some other guy's cast-off show.'"

But Robert came around. He and Sondra came up with the Baretta character (excluding his pet cockatoo, which was Cannell's idea), though their nitpicking turned the five days Cannell had to complete the pilot script into five weeks. Every time Cannell thought he was finished, Blake tossed his pages back. Cannell was annoyed, but had to marvel at Blake's insight. "He would be shredding my stuff and coming up with something better," said Cannell. "He was shrewd and smart."

Blake recalled *Baretta*'s genesis as an opportunity to bring the ambiguity of real life to the fakery of TV police drama.

"I hate cop shows," said Blake. "I hate precinct stations. I hate good guys and bad guys. I mean, as a viewer I like to watch them, but they wouldn't be comfortable for me to do. We're doing a show about the kind of people that you find living downtown. The old people who have no reason to live. The religious people who hang around on the corners shouting messages.

"When they came to me to do this show, I said, 'Let's do what's comfortable for me. I'm comfortable on the streets, working like a social worker. I've played characters on the other side of the law all my life. This character has just moved over one degree. The thing you got to show is that all crime is relative.'"

On Blake's orders, Cannell did away with Toma's wife, parents and children, renamed the show *Baretta* and built it around a character who was part macho cop, part sensitive guy—part Edward G. Robinson[41] and part John Garfield, both of whom Blake characterized as among his most influential role models when he was growing up.

Cannell changed Toma's name to Tony Baretta and moved him from Newark to the seedy King Edward Hotel on downtown L.A.'s Skid Row, where the program was actually shot. When he wasn't disguised as a bag lady or a Mafia hit man, Baretta wore an apple cap[42] from the 1930s, put lifts in his shoes to make himself appear taller and worked with a yellow-crested cockatoo named Fred riding on his shoulder.

Once Cannell finished the pilot script, however, he quit. He'd been working simultaneously on *The Rockford Files*, where James Garner was solicitous of his writers. Acting more like a big brother than a star, Garner would bring Cannell coffee and a sweet roll in the morning whenever Cannell showed up on the set. "So I was going from Garner, who said that he thought he had the best writers in Hollywood working for him, to Robert, where I got my head handed to me," recalled Cannell. "I agreed to do *Rockford* full-time."

Once Blake had the basic characters and story line down, he was merciless about honing scripts to his high yet oftimes quixotic standards. In addition, he insulted directors, accused crew members of incompetence and generally made the shooting of every episode a living hell. When he couldn't get his way with tantrums, he turned to flattery.

"He's so damned talented and could be so charming and professional even though he changed everything," said Jo Swerling, one *Baretta* producer.

"He is absolutely impossible to work for," another *Ba-*

---

41. Blake claimed to have punched out a director on a movie he made with Robinson, but the only one ever released in which both appeared was *A Woman in the Window* (1944), directed by the legendary Fritz Lang. Blake was ten years old at the time.

42. In one of his first wars with "the suits," Blake insisted on wearing the hat, even though Universal wardrobe and supervising executives insisted that a cop would not go around downtown L.A. looking like one of the Bowery boys. Blake won.

retta producer, Bob Lewin, once told *TV Guide*. "He runs roughshod over his writers, ignores his directors and turns everything into a war—him against the world. When I was producing the show, I'd call people to work for us and they'd say, 'What do I need that for?' The word was out. He's poison."

"He and I have a love/hate relationship," said the late Roy Huggins, yet another *Baretta* producer. "I love him and he hates me."

With predictable regularity, Blake would stop in the middle of a scene, announce to everyone that his dialogue was "crap" and tell his writers to shove their pages up their asses. Then he'd dictate his own dialogue, all while expensive union camera crews twiddled their thumbs. His comments ran from "They threw me another dead rat and want me to make it into Thanksgiving dinner" to "The script is another shit pile, but somewhere in there let's hope for a pony."

"I don't give a damn about hurt feelings," said Blake. "I'm interested in maintaining quality, not relationships. All I care about is what goes on in front of that camera—what people actually see on their screens. Without that, none of us has a job."

Swerling saw Blake's perfectionism as a need to buck authority as much as a need to maintain high professional standards. "It wasn't that he always disliked the script," said Swerling. "It was that he saw the script as an order. It was telling him what he was supposed to say and what he was supposed to do, so he was compulsive about changing it. He could not stand authority, even if it was just a script."

In the beginning, Fred the cockatoo received nearly as much fan mail as Blake—one of many sore points with the actor. According to the Universal Studios publicity machine, Fred was portrayed by a Chinese-speaking cockatoo named Layla, whose owner earned $1,000 a week during production. The much pampered Layla even had a stunt double dubbed "Weird Harold."[43] On particularly touchy days,

---

43. Over the three-year run of *Baretta,* three different birds played Fred. The last Fred, who was actually named "Fred," won a Patsy Award

en Blake joked about wringing the bird's neck, there were
se on the set who believed him.

The year *Baretta* was launched as a midseason replace-
nt turned out to be a banner year for Italians on TV. Barry
wman starred in *Petrocelli* on NBC, Peter Falk was in his
rth year as Lieutenant Columbo and Blake created his
st enduring persona in Tony Baretta. Along with Al Pac-
and his *Baretta* predecessor, Tony Musante, Blake was
ored in 1975 by the Federated Italo-Americans of South-
California "for their portrayals of Italian-Americans in
itive and sympathetic roles."

Not everyone agreed. Novelist and priest Andrew M.
eley, who was then program director at the National
inion Research Center, singled out *Baretta* among other
ian TV cops for being "cocky, arrogant and quick with
ir fists."

"Is the machismo of an Italian cop much of an improve-
nt on the Capone gangsters who lost all the big ones to
ot Ness?" asked Greeley.

The national PTA and the American Medical Association
o weighed in, threatening to boycott *Baretta*'s sponsors if
weekly body count didn't drop dramatically. Blake's an-
er was to take out a full-page ad in *Daily Variety* that read:
on't forget to watch the murder and mayhem on *Baretta*
ore the AMA takes it off the air."[44]

When Blake had contracted to do *Baretta*, he decided to
ke it real—so real that he frightened half the people on
set and alienated the rest. In one episode, the script called
Tony Baretta to push a mobster up against a wall. Instead,

---

his work and retired to San Diego Walk Animal Park, where he was
fly birdnapped in the autumn of 1990. Within two days, the thirty-
r-old cockatoo was found and returned to his roost without further
dent.

44. Blake also used trade paper ads to publicly slam his enemies in
industry. When director William Friedkin refused to take his calls
r considering him for the lead in *The Sorcerer* (1977), Blake took
an ad in both *Variety* and the *Hollywood Reporter* reading: "Put *The
cerer* where the sun never shines. Peace & Love, Robert Blake."

Blake leaped on the hapless actor and jammed his face
a toilet and flushed. When ABC's Standards and Practi
censors killed the scene because they did not beli
America was ready for flushing toilets in prime time, Bl
replayed the scene by pushing the hapless actor's face i
sink.

"It's like being the coach of a football team," Blake o
explained. "If the team is shitty, the coach has gotta go cr
to get 'em stoked up. And if the team is great, he lays b
and cools it. If I bring in a writer I know is good and he d
shitty work for *Baretta*, I go crazy. If a director's no goo
fire him. Or try to make him better. I do the same thing
actors. If one of 'em comes on the set and treats *Baretta*
it's just another job, he gets my foot up his ass."

From the very first episode Robert taught other actors
example, delving deep into his years of Method acting.
pilot opens with Tony Baretta squiring his girl to an Ita
restaurant in the back of a rented limo because this is
night that he is going to ask her to marry him. But Bar
has made an enemy in the local Mafia don, and as the cou
steps from the limo to the restaurant, a hit man drives by
sprays them both with gunfire. Baretta is seriously woun
but lives. His fiancée dies.

Throughout the week of filming, during rehearsal and
stage as well as on-, Blake treated the actor who played
Mafia don like scum, refusing to eat with him, speak w
him or even share the same makeup room with him. W
one of the producers finally asked Blake what was upsett
him about the actor, whom everyone else got along w
quite well, Blake turned to him and snarled: "That son c
bitch killed my fiancée!"

"It wasn't that he couldn't get out of character mod
said Swerling. "It was that he wouldn't."

Blake cited the higher standards demanded of stagecr
and moviemaking that he was raised on. "Because I'm n
in an environment that gives rise to mediocre work fr
mediocre people, I've *become* a madman."

By the second season, Blake reluctantly bowed to pub
pressure. He did agree to begin toning down the violen
But again, it wasn't his fault. It was the writers and the p

cers and the pace of putting out a weekly series that made
s character violent. "We're getting rid of a lot of shooting
d hatred that we were doing on the show last year," he
id. "A lot of stuff last year I nearly strangled on. We didn't
ve the time to rewrite it."

Yet he was not above threatening violence offscreen to get
s way. The producers were nominally the final word on the
t, but Blake wielded nearly absolute power.

"I did an episode of *Baretta*," recalled actor Ed Begley
"I played a guy who worked with trained dogs, and it
arred me and Christina Raines. Christina was late to work
.e day, so Blake fired her and replaced her with Karen Val-
tine. He said, 'I've been doing this since I was a young
an and there's no excuse for being late. We don't do that.'"

The following day, Blake fired a second actor. He wasn't
te, but the guy still managed to piss Blake off.

"I came back a third day and somebody didn't like the
g, so he got fired too," said Begley.

The wars with the "suits," as Blake called the executives
ABC and MCA/Universal, persisted. He even grumbled
out blowing up MCA's so-called "Black Tower" head-
arters—a landmark fifteen-story building on Lankershim
ulevard just off the Hollywood Freeway. *Baretta* always
nt overbudget and usually because of Blake. When the
torious tightwads at MCA tried to rein him in, Blake went
llistic.

"I did tell one guy on the fifteenth floor that I was gonna
row him out the window, and I threatened to punch people
the set more than once," said Blake. "Every time they
t dirty, I got dirtier. I'd go on the *Tonight Show* and tell
e whole world how full of shit Universal was, until when-
er they heard I was goin' on with Johnny Carson, they'd
t paranoid, and that's a mild word for it."

He used the Carson show as a pulpit to publicly humiliate
e executives who held the purse strings, sometimes by
me. Single-handedly, he made the standard Brooks Broth-
s business suit worn by most MCA executives a symbol of
hite male chauvinistic oppression. He'd phone the brass at
ree a.m. just to harangue them and pulled stunts like hav-
g his psychiatrist call in sick for him, saying that he would

not be able to get out of bed until his producers were ax
In 1976, he took Universal to court and threatened to q
Baretta if the "suits with their gray flannel hearts and doubl
knit brains" didn't back off.

Jo Swerling occasionally wore slacks and a tie to the s
dio, but that all changed when he went to work on *Baret*
"When I saw how Robert reacted to them, I thought, '
better not look at me as a suit,'" said Swerling. "He resen
them [MCA and ABC executives]. Didn't think they contr
uted anything except bad ideas. So I changed my wardro
and because of Robert, it has continued all these years
wear jeans, a black golf shirt and gray shoes that look l
slippers."

Robert was finally a rebel with a cause, and with a lot
power to boot. When a director told him he had to chew
food with his mouth closed during a scene, he belch
When he was ordered to keep his gun in a shoulder holst
he stuck it in his underwear. He was the kid pissing in
radishes back at Hamilton High, but this time the vice prin
pal had no power to threaten him with expulsion.

Sometimes he went too far.

"There was a scene on a bus in which Baretta is disguis
as a bag lady," recalled Swerling. "He's sitting at the ba
of the bus. It's not a tight shot and there's no dialogue."

Even so, there was a microphone to catch the ambi
sound, and while the director wasn't listening, Blake wh
pered: "I just want all of you to know that the director
the show is a complete asshole."

The following day, ABC network executives joined t
producers to watch the dailies, and there was Blake's voi
booming over the sound system.

"Robert, whatever possessed you to do that?" demand
one of the producers. "My God, man, you called the pc
man an asshole on tape in a room full of people."

"Ah, I call everyone an asshole," Blake replied.

Blake reluctantly apologized, but it did not mark the e
of his frequently ill-conceived practical jokes.

And yet nearly everything Blake did during his impulsi
fits of pique and perfectionism made the end product bett

s insistence on the best in everything—acting, writing, hting, timing, continuity—took *Baretta* to another level.

"I knew we'd fall short, but you've got to set yourself trageous goals," Blake said.

His own offbeat character and those of the streetwise mp Rooster (Michael D. Roberts), the burned-out ex-cop rned desk clerk Billy Truman (Tom Ewell) and a gravelly-iced informant named Fats (Chino Williams) make *Ba-tta* continue to hold up nearly thirty years after it first went the air. When sized up next to dated chestnuts from the me era like *Mannix, Adam-12* and *The Streets of San Fran-sco,* there is simply no comparison.

"I wanted to dislike what he was doing because of all ese vast changes that were occurring," said Begley. "He as doing jobs not in his job description. I was taken aback it all. But it was impossible to dislike him because it was tter."

His audience was eclectic. Men liked him because he was e classic antiauthoritarian antihero. Women liked him be-use he was cute.

"Blake has a very strong appeal to women," said Swer-g. "He was a cop they could like."

Not necessarily on the set, however.

"He didn't like to take any kind of orders or direction om women," observed Barbara Zuanich Friedman, a for-er NBC publicist who was occasionally assigned to *Ba-tta.* "Anything we had going on, I had to tell a guy, who uld then tell him. There were very uncomfortable mo-ents, which made me feel like I was worth about ten nts."

He went over big on college campuses. Harvard Univer-y made Blake its Hasty Pudding "Man of the Year." But bert was ambivalent about his fame from the outset and mained so for the next three seasons. To those who criti-zed him for stepping down from motion pictures to televi-on, Blake had this answer: "I spent a lot of years trying to ake important films. I'm not a politician, not a brain sur-on. But I am concerned about affecting my environment. d like to make some changes, some contributions."

A weekly series gave him a voice he never had in the

movies. "Let me tell you: One episode of *Baretta* about
tarded people, about how they should be allowed to rem
in society if they can take care of themselves, and I get h
dreds, thousands of letters from people," he said. "I get
ters of commendation from institutions. I'm not just fool
myself. People want to listen. They want to change thin
fix things up."

He was subversive about promoting his own soc
agenda, suggesting story lines he knew network cens
would veto, and then he'd savage them in public. He as
to have Tony Baretta track a heroin shipment from the stre
of L.A. back to government agencies like the DEA and C
which allowed the drugs to be imported, but was told
story was too ambitious and too political.

"I also wanted to do a story about an openly homosex
cop, but when I proposed that one, suddenly they stop
returning my phone calls," Blake complained.

Despite his gripes, life had finally become comparativ
comfortable. When he began his *Baretta* run, Blake wor
from one of the rows of bungalows out on the Universal
where everyone from Jack Benny to Cary Grant once had
office. Inside, he had a chair and a desk, and he decora
his walls with *Playboy* foldouts and the kind of angry
scenities better suited to a boy's bathroom stall in jun
high. *Eat my fucking ass. This show sucks. Blow me, s
face.* Etc.

But after *Baretta* became a hit[45] and Blake reaped a f
of the goodies accorded stars, both his material demands a
his accommodations changed, even though his attitude
not. "He had his walls knocked out to make his dress
room twice as large," said actor Kevin Dobson, who star
in *Knot's Landing* at Universal in the same era as *Bare*
"It ruined negotiations for all the rest of us. Mr. Blue Col
my ass."

And then, of course, there was the money. For the first

45. Even the *Baretta* theme song, "Keep Your Eye on the Sparr
was a winner, with Sammy Davis Jr. scoring a top-forty hit.

years of his career, he was used to getting paid spit. Su
denly, he was pulling down $35,000 a week. "More mon
in one week than I ever made in any damn movie," he sai
In addition, he signed on as the national pitchman for S'
motor oil additive—another lucrative gig while it lasted
Blake finally moved his family out of the tract house
North Hollywood and into a sprawling ranch house in t
gated community of Hidden Hills at the opposite end of t'
San Fernando Valley. They had horses and wide-op
spaces, all the familial pleasures that money could buy.

"When I finish this round, I will have a million dolla
and I will stop working," he told Virginia Leith, one of ma
old friends for whom he arranged guest shots on *Barett*
"This lifestyle is not any good for me. I like a much simp'
life."

But while he was hot, he stayed in the spotlight eve
chance he got. He kept up his monthly guest appearances (
the *Tonight Show,* started making similar stops at the *Me'*
Griffin Show and was asked to sit in several times on *Holl'*
wood Squares. "I've always wondered at actors who agr
to do something and then punish everybody around the
because they feel they shouldn't be doing it," said Canne'
Robert Blake, who rationalized his role as *Baretta* but a
ways believed that TV was beneath him, was just such a
actor.

"He was tightly wrapped," said Cannell. "He was pro
to emotional explosions: you know he was unhappy doi
the show. And he was wonderful! He won an Emmy doi
it. Best actor on television."

Indeed, the midseason replacement that ABC had toss
into the breach won Blake top honors in 1975 as actor in
series during the twenty-seventh Annual Emmy Awards.
accepting the award, Blake quipped that his son and daught

---

46. In 1977, the Federal Trade Commission sued STP Corporati
for falsely advertising that its product could improve gas mileage. T
following year, STP paid a $700,000 settlement. Blake's TV comm
cials ended around the same time.

nought he'd won for his work as a Little Rascal, which was
nen a rerun staple of daytime kids' TV. But he couldn't help
arping a little about the country's social condition too. He
ryptically complained to the audience that people in the
hettos of America weren't "getting theirs." Backstage, he
xplained to reporters that he meant that he felt bad for Viet-
am refugees trying to make it in America.

"Sure, I was excited and surprised," Blake told the gath-
red press. "I never won nothing in this town. Not even a
raffic ticket. I was very moved. I mean, I knew all about
hose awards. I know that they're not fair. But I don't know
nuch in life that is. I really don't."

After three seasons, despite the show's early popularity,
atings began to slip, and Blake could no longer get along
vith anybody. In April 1977, before ABC or Universal could
o it, he unilaterally pulled the plug on *Baretta*.

"I want to quit a winner and not overstay my welcome,"
3lake announced in his resignation press release. Leaving
fter three straight Peoples' Choice Awards as TV's best dra-
natic actor was the right thing to do. "If Humphrey Bogart
vere on TV every week, they'd get sick of him too."

17

In November 1977, six months after her *Hustler* magazine spread, Bonny married her twenty-seven-year-old first cousin Paul Gawron.

It occurred to Gawron that might cause problems because Bonny's mother was Paul's aunt, but he didn't care.

"I thought she was real good-looking," said Gawron.

In more recent years, since televangelists Kenneth Copeland and Creflo Dollar converted Paul to born-again Christianity, he has scoured his well-thumbed Bible, searching for a prohibition against cousins marrying. He has been unable to find one, and he reasons that if both God and the states of New Jersey and Tennessee say that it's all right, then he committed neither felony nor sin by taking twenty-one-year-old Bonny as his wife.

"That marriage never went over well with the rest of the family," said Bonny's uncle George Hall. "He was abusive with his remarks and physically too at times. Why would you put up with this? I guess she thought a lot of him, but he never acted very normal to me. He broke her nose one time. He was insulting in public and used very foul language. That's something a girl shouldn't have to put up with."

Paul's temper evolved in the New Jersey foster-care system, to which he and his sister had been abandoned most of their lives. Paul was never sure whether his mother just didn't want him or couldn't afford to raise him. Either way, he had institutional orderlies and foster families as parents. When he and Bonny found each other, they already had the ingular trait in common: their own mothers didn't want hem.

Paul admitted to being an irresponsible hothead when he vas younger. Bonny liked that in a man. She had developed knack for picking men with a violent streak and then pro-oking them. Once, Bonny told her mother, she taunted a roup of truck drivers into gang-banging her at a Pennsylva-ia truck stop. She continued to traffic with tough guys the est of her life—a habit she inherited from both her es-ranged mother and Grammy Hall.

"I thought her grandma was mean," said Gawron. "She idn't like herself, I think, 'cause she was so huge. And hort. I swear, if you pushed her, she'd roll, and I'm not rying to be mean—that's just how she was. She was a pig, nd I think she hated herself for being like that, and she took t out on anybody that got near her."

During their earliest days together, Paul lived in a trailer n a driveway next to Grammy Hall's. She didn't want him iving in her house. Bonny, though, stayed inside Grammy's .ouse—a living arrangement not conducive to warm marital elationships, thus angering Paul even more.

While she and Paul were still living in Washington, New ersey, Bonny had her first child, Glenn Gawron, in Septem-er 1979. Holly was born two years later.

"Both kids turned out normal," said Uncle George. "I'm urprised."

What began the same as many another American family uickly became bizarre, given Bonny's unique profession nd her obsession with stalking celebrities. Though Paul fa-hered three of Bonny's four children, he never paid for their upport. From the beginning, it was understood that Paul vould stay at home and care for the children while Bonny it the road as the breadwinner—a veritable Willie Loman f porn.

"Her whole life she started taking those two- or three-veek trips constantly," said Paul. "She'd be home for a veek, gone two. Home for a week, then gone. And even vhen she was home she was just in the bedroom sleeping all lay."

Her family didn't seem to mind her unique career path.

In addition to looking after the children, Paul had to co]
and address lurid letters that he then sent to hundreds of m(
who answered Bonny's ads. For a fee, he sent out expli(
photos of his wife, accompanied with her written assuranc
of sexual gratification.

The business took its toll on domestic bliss. In answer
the question, "Did you love her?" Paul answered: "I dor
know. I don't know. At one time, maybe, you know. I stay(
with her 'cause I wasn't leaving my kids. I didn't stay wi
her; I stayed with the kids."

While Paul raised Glenn and Holly, Bonny used the san
tried and true methods to dupe the gullible all over the cou
try. The first ploy revolved around a broken-down car: s]
would gladly come to visit if the victim would just ser
enough money to pay for repairs and gas. Next, she wou
measure the distance between the victim's address and h
own, mark the halfway point on the map, and telegram tl
victim: her car had again broken down at a town near tl
halfway point. Could he send more money or, better yet,
credit card? Bonny played out the string as far as it wou
go, until they eventually wised up that she was never goi
to show. Only with the rarest of marks would she actual
rendezvous.

In her warped way, Bonny did try halfheartedly to sep
rate the merely struggling from the truly destitute. "On
send money if you can afford to," she wrote in her ear
correspondence. If the idiot could afford to, she figure
Well, what the hell? He's a grown-up. He's got money
burn. If not on me, then on what? Cigars? Roulette? Booz(
At least dirty pictures and a little postal porn won't give tl
stupid sonofabitch cirrhosis of the liver.

Of course, men stopped answering her ads when the
found out that they'd been had, but Bonny didn't worry. S]
simply began adopting aliases and sometimes revisited tl
same marks she'd already burned. She borrowed the nam
and Social Security numbers of every female she knew, fro
her childhood friends to Judy Howell, her sister, Margerr
and their acquaintances as well.

"She actually gave one of my girlfriends a middle name
says Margerry, who discovered the deception when she to(

e woman to her neighborhood Social Security office. They
und that Bonny had obtained an identification card, adding
e middle name "Crystal." Margerry's girlfriend had no
iddle name, but she liked "Crystal" so much that she de-
ded to keep it as her own.

And so Bonny's scheming went on, year in and year out,
ith Paul as her partner. He could be slow on the uptake, but
e was oddly obedient. His youthful temper slowly waned,
pecially with Bonny holding the purse strings. With the
sence of his hotheadedness, he lost much of his self-
nfidence.

Once, a pair of muggers attacked Bonny and made off
ith her purse, which contained her glasses, camera and
50 in cash. Paul stood by, frozen, until Bonny shrieked at
m, "Don't just stand there! Go after them!"

He did, returning a while later with lumps on his head
d no purse.

That incident became a metaphor for his ineffectuality in
eir marriage. She'd get herself in trouble and shout for
lp, and loyal Paul would belatedly ride to the rescue, usu-
ly falling off his horse in the process. Paul became more
a low-rent butler than a husband. Finally one of Bonny's
ctims showed up at Grammy Hall's front door: a "mail-
der guy" who had traveled all the way from Alaska to see
onny. She went out with him over Paul's protests, and Paul
as left to fume in his trailer. The next day, he quit her scam
protest and went to work as a pipe grinder—"hard, dirty,
w-paying work," as he described it, but honest.

Paul did not last long. It was too hard, too dirty and too
w-paying. By 1979, he'd quit both the pipe-grinding job
d his marriage to Bonny, though he humbly returned to
r mail-order scam after he realized what an easy way it
as to earn a living.

"You place the ad, you have the mailbox and the stuff
arts pouring in," said Harland Braun, the L.A. attorney
ho would have occasion to put Bonny's business beneath a
icroscope in the years ahead. "You know which guys are
e targets. You could sort of sense it. And then you go after
em to get some money, and think it's a thrill."

Gawron and his ex-wife remained partners and occasional

lovers for the next twenty years. He grew used to her sleeping with other men—sometimes right in the next room. Years later, when he found Jesus on the tube courtesy of Bonny's stolen cable TV box, he warned her of perdition. They discussed the insidious ways of Satan, but when the conversation got too serious, Bonny either fell into her patented little-girl giggles or retired to her room to get some more sleep. "I was giving her the Word as I learned it, you know," he said. "Unfortunately, maybe I didn't know enough to get through to her. And maybe it's just that people won't believe what they don't see."

Paul remained illogically loyal, given the manner in which Bonny treated him, and he cared for their children each time Bonny left on one of her celebrity road trips. She could be gone for weeks, sometimes for months. She remembered her responsibilities, though. She sent money home to pay the rent. Paul maintained that he resented being strung along with just enough money to feed the kids and keep the electricity turned on while Bonny moved around the country, but he never made any serious attempt to leave.

By 1980, Bonny had raised the business to a new level, invoking her charms to persuade oldsters to include her name on their life insurance policies or in their wills. In one case Philip Wright Worcester, a Pasadena man, altered his last will and testament on June 28, 1980, to include the paragraph: "All the rest, residue and remainder of my estate, of whatsoever kind and nature wherever situate, I hereby give, devise and bequeath to my fiancée, Bonny Lee Bakley. . . ."

This naturally came as a rude surprise to Worcester's two grown children, Stephen Worcester and his sister, Linda Sue Merlo. The new will said that they received an inheritance only in the event that Bonny died first. Worcester also named Bonny his executrix.

By now Bonny's business had become a family affair. Bonny lassoed her younger sister, Margerry, in briefly after Margerry divorced, became a single mother, and needed an income. Bonny taught her how to string someone along on the phone, alternately cooing, giggling and talking dirty. Margerry quit after a year, but admitted much later that even she was floored at how easy it was to separate a horny male of almost any age and background from his greenbacks.

Bonny also took frequent vacations, usually to places like Atlantic City, when Frankie Valli or some other golden-oldies rocker came to play one of the new casinos. Bonny might have kept up this pleasant porn/celeb stalking routine forever if not for the lure of show business. In 1982, still believing she could sing, she was thrilled to be asked by her accountant, astrologer and Palisades Park record producer Robert Stuhr to be both his bride and one of the headliners on a future "Tribute to Elvis" record album. In short order she got a Mexican mail-order divorce from Gawron. Six weeks later, she was saying, "I do."

<u>18</u>

In a broad-ranging interview for *Playboy* that ran three months after he quit *Baretta*, Robert Blake aired his views on everything from the death penalty (against) to homosexuality (live and let live) to abortion (the guy should have as much say-so as the girl). He also had this to say about homicide:

> I don't believe in killing at any time under any circumstances. I don't believe in killing old folks by taking the tubes out of their arms and I don't believe in killing babies before they get a chance to fight back. If we believe there's more divinity in a human being than in a chair, there's *no* circumstance that allows for killing. Now, I can conceive of *me* killing somebody, but that's because I'm a human being, not God, and I'd hope that somebody would stop me from doing it. All I'm saying is that it's wrong and that I feel strongly about it.

When *Baretta* ended, Blake imagined his audience must be as sick of the self-righteous little cop and his obnoxious bird as Blake was, and said so in his rote, reaming the television industry.

"A series is the asshole of the industry," he said. "It's the worst job on the fucking planet for an actor to do the same shit every day. It's like eating a beautiful shrimp dinner and then throwing it up so you can eat it again tomorrow."

But if he wasn't interested in doing a series, then what? Movies, that's what.

"I got a very strong hard-on to do a certain two or three films, and I'm gonna do 'em," he told *Playboy*. "And you can take that to the fuckin'‟bank and collect interest on it."

For the remainder of the decade, Blake collected no interest and wound up withdrawing a lot more cash than he deposited in the bank. His belligerent public attitude began catching up with him.

"I was like the guy in the bar who starts fighting people without knowing why," he said. "I insulted producers all over the place."

His first post-*Baretta* project was *The Hamster of Happiness*,[47] a pet film project that Blake purchased at a bargain price. Based on a screenplay written in 1969 by celebrated script doctor Charles Eastman (*Little Fauss and Big Halsey*), much of Hollywood had known about *Hamster* for years, but nobody bought it. Blake waited until Eastman was down on his luck and made him an offer by literally sending his business manager to knock on Eastman's door and pull several thousand dollars in cash out of his pockets to tempt him. Eastman negotiated the price up to $14,000, but only then did he learn who'd purchased it.

Once Blake owned the script, he called upon *Electra Glide*'s James William Guercio—this time to produce, while star cinematographer Haskell Wexler manned the cameras and Hal Ashby, the quixotic creator of cult classics like *Shampoo* and *Harold and Maude*, directed. A so-called "backyard film," *Hamster* should have been a hit. With a $7 million budget, it was shot cheaply on location without the usual expense of sets, studio overhead or union crews. While he tried mightily to capture Eastman's bleak humor on screen, his intent misfired. *Hamster* was a sad comedy about a pair of born Texas losers—Dinette Dusty and Loyal Muke—who marry during a drinking binge and hit the road

---

47. When it was finally released in 1981, it was retitled *Second-Hand Hearts*.

for California together with three of Dusty's unruly young-sters in tow. The movie gave Blake a chance to showcase the whimsical comic side he'd honed on Carson and finally begun to develop during the final season of *Baretta*. With its gritty, quirky characters, the story of *Hamster* also demonstrated the strength of family, even in tough times, and ended on an upbeat note, unlike most of Blake's previous movies.

"To me, the family unit is the most important thing in the world, and civilization is doing irreparable, incurable damage to itself by destroying the family," he preached at film journalists who made the trek to El Paso, Texas, where most of *Hamster* was shot. "As bread is the staple of the diet, so the family unit is the staple of society."

With family in mind, he gave Sondra a strong supporting role, even though it was not the female lead. The Dinette Dusty role went to actress Barbara Harris, a darling of movie critics who fought with Blake and Ashby through most of the filming. The off-camera angst found its way into the on-camera footage, and Ashby took months to edit. Even after that, *Hamster* took another two years getting to theaters.

In the meantime, Blake tried to be funny again—this time with Dyan Cannon, cast as a rich-bitch nutcase on the run from her husband. She catches a ride from New York to L.A. with redneck trucker Blake, hence the title *Coast to Coast* (1980). The result was supposed to be a romantic comedy but it was neither romantic nor much of a comedy.

Blake hated it. In a replay of some of his most vitriolic *Baretta* moments, he denounced the director, the producers and especially his costar on the *Tonight Show*, excoriating Cannon and the film at every opportunity.[48] Even Johnny Carson, who had grown to expect the unexpected gibe from his most volcanic regular guest, was surprised. "You made sure that nobody would go to see it," he told Blake in a post–*Coast to Coast* appearance on the *Tonight Show*.

---

48. Instead of cringing at Blake's remarks, *Coast to Coast* producer Steve Tisch maintained that the actor was using reverse psychology to promote the film. "He's a great salesman. . . . Is there such a thing as bad publicity?"

Reviewers tended to agree with Blake, slamming Cannon's performance, yet saving a compliment for Blake in a movie with few positives. "Blake . . . gives a very good, low-key performance," said *Daily Variety*. "An actor who seems incapable of any phony behavior on the screen."

When *Hamster* finally came out a year later, critics were not nearly so kind. The *New York Times'* Vincent Canby suggested that Blake must have "overdosed on old Wallace Beery movies." *New York* magazine's David Denby said, "Flabby now,[49] Blake shouts his way through the part in a high squeal, eyes darting anxiously. His hysteria seems like an acting-class exercise, yet it goes on for two hours." Most vicious of all, the reviewer for the *New Republic* wrote, "Robert Blake is notably loathsome in any case, but that case is helped along here by his painfully self-conscious groping to do things right."

The reaction at the picture's premiere during the Montreal World Film Festival ought to have been warning enough to Guercio, Ashby and Blake that they were in for a bumpy ride when dozens stood up and walked out before the movie was half over. When *Hamster of Happiness* finally went into wide release, the domestic box office totaled less than $10,000. The movie finished near the top of *Rolling Stone* magazine's list of the biggest bombs of 1981.

Robert retrenched, buying a second home near Jackson Hole, Wyoming, where he went to lick his wounds. "I've got a million bucks in the bank, so even if I make a lot of mistakes in the next five or six years I can go on feeding the family," he said. "I've spent twenty years in therapy unraveling the mess my life has been and I keep reaching plateaus—little plateaus, but they're something."

Reluctantly, Blake returned to TV. He worked with his wife in a series of four NBC movies-of-the-week, portraying a fictional L.A. sleuth named Joe Dancer. Written by crime drama neophyte Robert Crais,[50] the drama featuring Joe

---

49. Blake responded to his critics by taking up weightlifting and going on a diet of three onions and six raw eggs a day.

50. Cutting his teeth in the late 1970s on *Hill Street Blues*, *Quincy* and *Cagney & Lacey*, Crais went on to write a series of bestselling Joe

Dancer was to be nothing less than "the best show ever produced for television," according to Blake, in part because he was its executive producer as well as its star.

Critics viewed Joe Dancer differently. According to one, the private eye was "part John Garfield, part Dick Powell and part Humphrey Bogart," but wound up being "all Robert Blake—and that was just the problem. [He] fluctuated between casual brutality, forced humor and self-conscious pathos."

Though six scripts were written, only four Joe Dancer movies were produced and only three ever aired. *The Big Black Pill*, the first in the series, sounded more like a ripoff of Raymond Chandler's *The Big Sleep* than the best show ever produced for TV. In the movie, Dancer is offered big money to chase down the black sheep of a powerful family. Thugs thump Joe before each commercial break, but he still manages to track his quarry down to a small town. Seconds after Joe finds his boy, an assassin guns the black sheep down and Joe gets the blame. Will Joe find the real killer before the eleven o'clock news?

The best part of the Joe Dancer movies turned out to be Sondra Blake, who played Blake's emaciated girlfriend. "My perception of Sondra was that she was a really good actress," said Stephen Cannell. "She was good at playing strange, downbeat women: hookers, street people with a drug problem. She was very skinny and looked malnourished. She was sweet and quiet—the polar opposite of Robert. They seemed to have an okay relationship."

Blake was keenly aware that Sondra had placed her career on hold to raise a family, and all along he had lobbied mightily to include her in his productions as frequently as possible. During *Baretta,* he almost walked off the set after ABC objected to casting Sondra as a call girl when all the other call girls in that particular episode were at least ten years younger.

---

mystery novels featuring Elvis Cole, an offbeat private investigator with an uncanny resemblance to Joe Dancer.

"We tried to explain our reservations, but he took that as an attack on his wife," recalled *Baretta* producer Jo Swerling. "We got ABC to back off and give in to him and he was not wrong in insisting she do it. She brought it off."

Blake no longer had the juice he had with *Baretta*, and Joe Dancer's weak Nielsen numbers did not translate into a network offer.

Life on the home front had also worsened since *Baretta*. Not for the first time, the Blakes' rocky fifteen-year marriage seemed headed for divorce. When Blake won the 1976 Golden Globe for best TV actor, he sent his wife to the ceremony to pick it up. She cracked up the audience with her acceptance speech: "Bob is home barfing his brains out. It's his way of handling success."

What entertained on stage was a strain at home. Sondra was not joking about her notoriously neurotic husband's remarkable propensity for self-destruction, and it finally drove her away.

In the 1976 movie-of-the-week *Helter Skelter,* Sondra played call girl Ronnie Howard, a witness for the prosecution in the gruesome 1969 Manson Family murders trial. During filming, according to gossip published at the time, Sondra began an affair with actor Steve Railsback, who starred as the demented Charles Manson. For a husband so irrationally controlling that he shrieked at his wife for even hugging another man, it was a declaration of war.

"I don't want somebody to kiss her," he said. "I just don't want them to. It's not a matter of trust or that it's going to phase two. My closest friends—when they walk in the house and they give her a hug and say, 'Ah, Sondra, it's lovely to see you'—it gets my jealousy going."

While Blake whined on the *Tonight Show* about losing his wife, the tabloids reported years later that in private Blake responded to her purported philandering by prying her jaws open and shoving a gun in her mouth. Blake's own alleged philandering on and off the set had never been reported at all.

"She seems to have a better capacity for my involvements with other people, or a better capacity to handle her problems with it—whichever the case, I don't know," Blake told

Daily Variety reporter Will Tusher. "I think she's as possessive as I am, but she's not as jealous."

Blake admitted to freakish rages during the early years of his marriage to Sondra when he used to force her into his car and drive her over the back roads of Southern California sometimes for days at a time.

"I needed her so much for so many things, for so many neurotic things because of my own weaknesses," he said. "I would just spend twenty-four hours a day with her. Slowly the sick part of the love or the dependency part of the love diminished and was replaced by easier kinds of love that are easier to cope with, easier to live with."

"He wanted to be with Sondra," said Virginia Leith, Blake's old friend from the fifties who had first introduced him to psychotherapy. "Sondra was a real classy woman. She was not common. But I think he had a hard time getting it up for that classy kind of woman, so I think he needed cheap women."

In August 1977, Sondra filed for divorce. A month later, Blake gave a weepy interview to *People* magazine, lamenting the regret he felt at the collapse of his marriage. "Fame cost me my family," he said. "Now I'm sleeping with a stranger called success."

Two decades later, Railsback told LAPD detectives investigating the Bakley homicide that Robert didn't limit his threats to Sondra. Blake had also threatened to put out a "hit" on Railsback during this period. Railsback told the police that he was so terrified of Blake's murderous intent that he stopped dating Sondra.

Following his very public campaign to win her back, Robert and Sondra reconciled and their divorce was dismissed. Yet their happy reunion was only temporary. The pressures following his decision to quit *Baretta* led Blake to hit the bottle and take pills to get up, pills to go to sleep. As he later described in an *Entertainment Tonight* interview, he and Sondra finally came apart during the filming of Blake's TV remake of the Steinbeck classic *Of Mice and Men* (1981).

Down in Texas, at the end of *Of Mice and Men*, I did something that really clicked later. I had to kill

Lenny [a retarded character who is Blake's partner in the story], and I wanted it to be really tough to do. Did I think about choking my wife? My kids? No—I imagined strangling Mickey Gubitosi from *The Little Rascals*. I played the scene imagining killing myself as a little kid.

We finished up and I drove into the mountains around Death Valley. My company was the horses I rode and the wild burros I talked to. After three weeks, I knew I had to come back down and get strong enough to do what I had to do—change a lotta my life.

So I came back. I went into intensive therapy, stopped all the sleeping pills and booze, went through the divorce . . . and I started calling people, explaining the nervous breakdown. I went to all three networks, apologizing for all the harm I'd done. Some people wouldn't see me. Others did, and said, 'Too bad you were so rotten. I don't care.' Most people just listened and said, 'Okay, I'll watch; see what you do.' The bottom line is I didn't have one job offer for one and a half years.

The Blakes separated for the final time on April Fool's Day 1982, due to "unfortunate and irreconcilable differences and difficulties." Seven months later, on October 28, Blake made their divorce final by suing Sondra for custody of the kids.

According to the tabloids, he once again reverted to strong-arm tactics to get his point across to Sondra. After she moved out, he tracked her down and had her call Noah and Delinah, who were then sixteen and fourteen, respectively. Blake reportedly forced his soon-to-be ex-wife to tell both teenagers that she didn't love them and wanted them to live with their father. What she did not say during that brief conversation was that Blake was holding a gun to her head as she spoke.

Blake retained custody of both children as well as most of the community property. Sondra wound up with cash and property worth about $300,000. Blake sold off the family's horse ranch in Hidden Hills and moved into his Mata Hari

Ranch in Studio City with Noah and Delinah. For public consumption, he once again went on Carson and sadly told *People* that he had found the capacity to carry on. "I took the kids and went off to a ranch—just took the van out into the wilderness or rode my horses," he said.

Meanwhile, Sondra found solace in a support group of celebrities' ex-wives. Dubbed LADIES (Life After Divorce Is Eventually Sane) by its founder, Marilyn Funt, the group apparently became the inspiration for the hit comedy *The First Wives Club* (1996). LADIES charter members included such famous exes as Mrs. Michael Landon, Mrs. Gavin Mac-Leod, Mrs. Ken Berry and Mrs. Glen Campbell. According to Marilyn, the second of *Candid Camera* founder Allen Funt's three wives, LADIES was about getting better, and not necessarily about getting even.

"Being the wife of a famous man is a unique category," she said. "[The media] makes us look like a bunch of bitter women who have been dumped. But none of us are wallowing or sitting around. We're not against men and we're not against marriage."

Sondra Blake certainly wasn't wallowing. She mustered up the courage to hire high-profile feminist attorney Gloria Allred to win her children back. Psychological testing was ordered for the whole family in an effort to determine which parent would act in the best interests of which child. By the time the frequently delayed matter finally came to court, however, both children were over eighteen and opted to continue living with Robert. In a round of woe-is-me interviews, Blake mined mounds of publicity from his troubles.

"A few years ago I was a big star with millions in the bank, a big house in the hills, horses and land," Blake lamented. "Now I'm in some cracker house in the Valley, trying to fix my own car! I'm struggling."

He wasn't struggling too much. Richard Boone had taught him well about bleeding the networks and the studios while one was hot, because there would not always be that gravy train. Blake's *Baretta* legacy included hiring a veteran Hollywood business manager, who diversified his portfolio and invested his earnings wisely. The suits he so hated at Universal had paid him well, and he managed to hold on to most of it.

He was a millionaire in his real estate holdings alone. In addition to the Mata Hari Ranch on Dilling Street, at the time of his divorce Blake owned the Second Street property that housed Santa Monica's Gold's Gym plus an interest in a horse ranch in Hidden Hills beyond the one that he and Sondra sold. The value of the horse ranch alone was put at $800,000. Blake also held interests in Shaker Productions, Inc., Lukor Inc., Of Mice and Men Inc., Mickey Productions, Inc., the DeSoto partnership, the Bedford Royale partnership, Eli Kai apartments and Delinah Enterprises—a wholly owned subsidiary of Breezy Productions. He could well afford to turn down acting jobs for a while. If he tried fixing his own car beneath the car port of his Mata Hari Ranch, it wasn't out of necessity. He could just as easily have torched it, caught a cab to the nearest new car dealership and bought himself another.

He couldn't do the same with his career.

19

"e was at a sold-out show at the Hartford Convention Cen-
with Chuck Berry and Chubby Checker, and during the
w I was up by the stage area and saw this long-haired girl
nding there," recalled J. W. Whitten, Jerry Lee Lewis'
mer road manager, of a date in the summer of 1984. "She
d she'd love to meet Jerry—never met a celebrity before.
d I said, 'Well, I'll see what he's doing after the show. If
u hang around, I'll ask him.' So she hung."

J. W. was as good as his word. He had Jerry give the girl
uick nod following his set. Then J. W. took her back to
et Chubby Checker, Joe Green and some of the others in
 oldies show. Her eyes glazed and her mouth parted,
ming a small O that remained that way until she reluc-
tly left the backstage area. J. W. hovered nearby in case
 fainted dead away and needed someone to carry her out.

"After that, she started showing up at shows all the time,
vays by herself," said J. W. "I started talking to her. She
ver bothered anybody. She was very quiet. Wasn't what
u'd call a looker: a little chunky and she *always* had a bad
r day. She dressed kind of old-timey, like she got her
thes from a thrift store. I never asked her her last name. I
vays called her Bonny."

That oldies show in Connecticut did much more than sat-
y the star lust of a twenty-eight-year-old groupie. Whitten
1 unintentionally altered the course of Bonny Lee
kley's professional life. She was sick of trekking across
 Hudson River from Jersey just to mingle with the pervs
1 talent agents of Broadway so she could audition for a

"modeling" job or some nothing part in the background
a TV show.

She'd hustled to be an extra on the soaps and wormed
way into crowd scenes such as the one in *Chapter T*
(1979). You couldn't even tell it was Bonny walking arou
Manhattan with the thousands of other people in the cro
scenes. Her singing career wasn't advancing much eith
Bob Stuhr, who had briefly been her husband on the v
that he would make her a star, kept promising he'd rec
an LP with her, but he never came through.

But when she saw the Killer's face smiling back at h
Bonny understood what she must do. She concluded that
fact that they had both married their first cousins put th
on the same wavelength. She even thanked her mother
giving her "Lee" as a middle name. That was one m
thing she had in common with Jerry.

Before the year was out, she packed up Paul and the ki
loaded them in the van along with her porn inventory a
headed for Memphis.

"She was what you'd call a professional groupie," s
J. W. "We met a lot of professional groupies on the ro
There was an older woman one time who had an antic
business, and she sold it just so she could follow Je
around. She'd hop a plane to Vegas or L.A., but she even
ally ran out of money. They all did, except Bonny. She v
always there. We'd look out there after the show and th
she'd be. I don't know how she did it."

Bonny had been to Memphis before, of course, chas
after the King. But once the King died, it made perfect se
to get close to the Killer instead. Jerry Lee lived just acr
the Mississippi border in a rock 'n' roll compound in DeS
County. That became Bonny's primary target once she'd
up housekeeping in Memphis. She aimed to get herself ins
uated behind those walls and not get tossed out this time
way she once had at Graceland. Bonny had learned a th
or two about celebrity stalking since those early days, a
one of the finer points involved cozying up to business as
ciates and family. That was how she came to be best frie
with Linda Gail Lewis, Jerry's kid sister, and Judy How
secretary to Jerry's current wife.

She met Judy at the Vapors Supper Club in Vegas, where
ry Lee was a regular. As a regular in his Memphis entou-
ge, Howell noticed the diffident blonde who showed up
ght after night, staring at Jerry Lee from a distance as if he
re a Greek god. Bonny finally cornered Howell in the la-
es' room one night and asked if she could introduce her.

"Sure!" said Howell, and though she never got as close
Lewis as she would have liked, Bonny made a lifelong
end in Judy.

"I'd never been inside a bar until I was thirty-three," said
dy, who wound up working for Jerry Lee's organization
ough her musician brother. "I ran into Bonny at Dad's
ace out on Brooks Road and Hernando's Hideaway, where
rry Lee and my brother both played. We just hit it off.
ople don't know that sweet, generous side of Bonny. They
t know this awful woman who preys on old men. That's
t Bonny. That's not the Bonny I knew, and I knew her
out as well as anyone."

The Bonny that Judy came to know had great legs and
rked briefly as a stripper until she developed a bad back
d started going to chiropractors. That Bonny came to look
e someone's frumpy housewife trying desperately to
etty herself up at the makeup counter at Wal-Mart, and
she ever seemed to think about was getting close to the
ller.

A short time after she'd settled in Memphis, Bonny
oudly took her little sister one night to meet Jerry. There,
e more naive Margerry Bakley learned a painful lesson
out proper groupie etiquette.

"I didn't know how to behave around stars," said Mar-
rry. "I didn't know the difference between Jerry Lewis
d Jerry Lee Lewis, and I didn't know that when you are
ound Jerry, you're supposed to shut up and listen. So he
mes in and everyone hushes, but I just kept on chattering
d he just came over and slapped me in the face. He cold-
cked me. It broke up the party and we all had to leave."

She said Lewis apologized to her many times thereafter,
t the incident taught her firsthand the importance of star
ference. It was a fact of groupie life that Bonny seemed to
derstand intuitively. Stars basked. Fans worshiped.

"Whenever Bonny showed up, Jerry Lee was usually
vorcing somebody or didn't have a wife at the time," s
J. W. Whitten. "He was nice to her, as he is any fan.
really adored him. I let her have her photo shot with I
once. You can tell by looking at it that he's looking off so
where else and she's just smiling so big, posing nearby,
that picture meant so much to her."

Bonny bought a 1979 Lincoln Continental that had b
run into the ground by its previous owner and kept break
down. Still, it didn't have a dent and it shined up real go
It was just the sort of boulevard boat that would mak
lasting impression on a star of Jerry Lee's stature. She dr
it to his gigs, hoping someone would notice. Someone
His name was Sam.

"He was this aging semiretired gangster," reca
Margerry. "He was one of those guys who say 'nigger'
and 'nigger' that."

Sam drove a Jaguar and lived in a mansion in the qu
wooded fringe just outside Memphis. Hanging from the tr
surrounding his fenced property was an array of voice mo
tors and video cameras. Sam knew who was coming up
long driveway long before they ever got near his house.
was seventy-four when he and Bonny met. Old, mean,
tive and rich, Sam was a charter member of the real Me
phis mafia, but what actual drug dealing he did at his age
small potatoes, according to Margerry. Sam was an emeri
hood. His forte in his dotage was laundering other mobst
money through his construction business.

"Life was exciting with Sam," Margerry reminisced. "
had a machine gun alongside his bed and sold rebuilt airc
to the Contras."

Margerry recalled Sam giving Bonny an ultimatum a
they'd been out on a few dates: either give up her obsess
for Jerry Lee or give up Sam. For a time, as much a
pained her to do so, Bonny gave up—or at least pretene
to give up—Jerry Lee. She even began taking fertility dr
in an effort to seal her undying love for Sam with a cland
tine pregnancy. Sam had neglected to reveal to his yo
lover that he'd had a vasectomy many years earlier.

Once they were an item around town, Sam's ardor be

cool. "And yet, the colder Sam got, the more she was
o him," said Margerry. "Bonny was like that: the colder
nebody got, the more she wanted him, but when they
nted her, she didn't want them. Sam knew he could get
re by being cold than being hot."

When Grammy Hall died in 1985, it nearly broke Bon-
's heart. She remembered one of the last trips they'd taken
ether, from New Jersey to Atlanta, where Bonny signed
to become a member of the Screen Actors Guild. She'd
d joining SAG and the American Federation of Television
d Radio Artists in New York, but the Manhattan chapters
the two actors' guilds required a résumé, credits and some
mal theatrical training before they'd let someone become
nember. Bonny learned from other struggling young ac-
sses that all the Georgia chapters of SAG and AFTRA
manded was a membership fee and a written application
t nobody ever bothered to check up on.

Paul remembered that trip as being very much like all
others he'd made over the years with Bonny and her
andmother: "She sat in the backseat and bitched the whole
y. All she cared about was money. Gimme, gimme,
nme."

Not so Bonny. She was generous to a fault.

"I've seen her help people that she didn't know that
ll," said Uncle George. "Take my brother-in-law, for in-
nce. He was pretty distant. She didn't know him well at
. But he lost his leg in an operation in the hospital and he
eded cable and didn't have any money to get it, so she just
ve him $400.

"She had girlfriends and such, and she'd give them her
othes. She'd take friends and relatives out to dinner, take
m on trips. If she had $1 in her pocket, fifty cents of it
s yours."

Without exception, Bonny's biggest disappointments
ppened when she fell in love. As long as she kept the male
the species at bay, Bonny felt she was on safe ground.
sides, mail-order porn was the only thing that could be
unted upon to support her family.

"We all knew what she did for a living," said Judy. "I

made calls for her for about a year. She paid me $25 hour."

The business had grown sophisticated enough that Bon was now buying mailing lists from porn publicatio "She'd send out form letters," said Judy. "She *never* g her phone number, but they would write and give her *th* number. Then she'd send photos and ask them to send $ so she could drive to meet them, but she'd never go."

She made Judy call the victims back and come up v some excuse, asking for more money at the same time. felt sorry for them," Judy said. "They were guys in their twenties and thirties. She did take advantage. She did ha talent. You've got to admire the woman. There were e some women who wrote her. Bonny was open to sex, kinds of sex. She got $150 from a woman in Pennsylva once, but it turned out Bonny didn't get to meet her beca she was two or three days late for their meeting. Bonny always late."

For all of her shrewd scamming, Bonny had little to sh for her years of porn. She planned nothing long-ra Someone had to watch out for her well-being, so Judy t on the responsibility.

"She wanted to get out of doing mail order, so I sugges she get into real estate," said Judy, who had enjoyed sc success in buying houses for little or nothing down and t renting them out to pay the mortgage. Judy rode the ris market and, after a few years, sold for a profit, plowing equity into yet another property. She told Bonny she co do the same thing and sold her one of her first houses. W Bonny's mother moved to Memphis, she got in on the estate game too, and soon they owned several properties tween them.

Bonny and Paul moved into one of the houses, but w the neighbors found out what Bonny did for a living, t wouldn't let their kids play with hers.

"She hid nothing from anyone," said Judy. "Her life an open book. She'd just grin and go on, until she was alc That's when she cried."

20

By 1982, Robert Blake had spread enough hubris aroun[d] Hollywood to guarantee that no studio, production house [or] network would touch him. On November 13 of that yea[r] when he hosted *Saturday Night Live,* the writers spoofe[d] Blake's prickly persona in an opening sketch that feature[d] Merv Griffin in a send-up of Griffin's talk show.

"With us is one of your favorite stars," Merv bega[n]. "He's controversial, he's exciting, he's not afraid to spea[k] his mind—and I can't wait to hear what's on his mind to[night]! Would you welcome the Wild Man of Hollywoo[d] Robert Blake!"

To wit, Robert immediately unloaded on Hollywood va[cuity]. "From now on, I don't do *anything* unless it's g[ot] meaning—and dat's da name of dat tune," he said.

As if offstage, *SNL* regulars Joe Piscopo and Julia Loui[s]-Dreyfus watched Blake's bathos on a TV monitor with u[n]-disguised contempt.

"It's amazing he gets away with it," said Louis-Dreyfu[s]. "I mean, here's a guy who grew up in Hollywood and y[et] he talks with this tough Brooklyn accent."

"I'll tell you, Julia, nobody buys it," said Piscopo. "Th[e] guy's like a professional BS artist."

After Blake dumped some more on the "suits," Loui[s]-Dreyfus continued: "What a bag of wind."

"I know!" said Piscopo. "A couple of years ago Blak[e] was just like this washed-up actor. He goes on a bunch [of] talk shows, does the tough guy routine and gets a series."

"Right. And did you ever notice Robert did a number of the *Baretta* episodes in drag? I mean, just think about it."

"Yeah, I wonder what he was trying to tell us," said Piscopo. "I *know* what he was trying to tell us: the guy's a wussy! *That's* what he was trying to tell us!"

At that moment Blake materialized beside Piscopo, flexing his biceps and demanding to know why they were making fun of him. Piscopo, himself a Jersey muscle man, got right back in Blake's face.

"You don't need us to make a fool out of you, Bob. You do a pretty good job yourself. Tough guy!"

"Oh? You don't think I'm tough?" asked Blake. "You want me to show you how tough I am, you with your big mouth. You want me to show you? Watch this!"

With that, Blake punched Julia in the gut. As she gasped for breath, Blake continued addressing Joe. "Watch yourself, Piscopo, because *you're next*!"

Joe turned to the camera and spoke soberly. "Ladies and gentlemen, what you've just seen is a trick ending. It's called 'breaking reality.' Right now I'd like to introduce to you the Breaking Reality Players. Please welcome Robert Blake."

"Thank you very much," said Blake, who then thanked Merv and Julia.

"She had a small part, but it was a very important part," said Blake. "Because while we are poking fun up here, we also wanted to make a point, a very serious and a very dramatic point about battered women. And if we here have stopped just one guy, just one of you Joes out there from gettin' out of line, why, as artists I feel like we've all done our job. And once again, thank you very much, Julia, for a job well done!"

At which point, Julia kicked Blake in the testicles.

Poking fun at his reputation may have given Blake some satisfaction, but it didn't land him many job offers. If anyone in Hollywood held the record for burning his bridges, it had to be Bob. Even his closest friends commented on Blake's knack for shooting himself in the foot.

"Certain actors in this town have had roller-coaster careers," said Oscar nominee and Blake contemporary Sally Kirkland. "I will include myself: I am very hot and then the

phone doesn't ring at all and then I am hot again. So m
heart goes out to any actor that is as incredibly talented :
Robert who doesn't get to work all the time."

With *Blood Feud* (1983), the story of the rivalry betwee
Bobby Kennedy and Teamsters boss Jimmy Hoffa, 20th Cen
tury Fox gave Blake a chance at a TV miniseries. There wa
a condition, however. Blake's salary remained in an escro
account until the project was finished. According to his u
usual contract, he received his money only after Fox chai
man Harris Katleman personally approved of his conduct
and off camera as "fully professional."

Robert had lost his *Baretta* bargaining power by 1982 an
had to agree to Katleman's terms. However, not only did I
play Hoffa in a "fully professional" manner; Robert's bra
vura performance got him his biggest raves since *In Co
Blood*. Blake himself later maintained that *In Cold Bloc*
and *Blood Feud* represented his best work.

"Jimmy Hoffa was a modern-day Ahab," he said. "I
fought his way to the top of the Teamsters and couldn't l
go once he got there. That's why the Kennedys could ri
his back into the White House in 1960. And that's why I
ended up dead in some swamp or dump or incinerator, whe
he was trying to take over the union again after getting o
of jail.

"I understand a guy who went out and got arrested eig
teen times in one day to get his union going. Jimmy was
street fighter, not a politician. Of course he did business wi
the Mob. But everybody did that—the FBI, other labor lea
ers. But the Kennedys didn't go after them. They went aft
the one guy whose anger would put them on the front pag
Jimmy played right into the Kennedys' hands. Jimmy wa
programmed to self-destruct. Bobby Kennedy was too."

Blake knew a thing or two about self-destruction. He co
tinued making sporadic appearances on the *Tonight Sho*
with Johnny Carson, still carping about the vagaries of Ho
lywood. He remained proud of his independence, shunnin
agents and managers or any other kind of career plannin;
He claimed he believed in serendipity.

"You try to plan things, and they fall through," Blak
said. "Then something like the Carson show can con

through without your planning on it and change things completely. Listen, getting up in the morning is a risk. So I think career planning is bullshit. You want to worry about your career? You should worry about doing the best job that you can. The only real calling card you've got is your work. Not your agent and not the great excuses you can make. Just your work. To be honest with you, I don't know what advice to give except never do any bad work. Let every piece of film you print be worth printing, and you'll be OK."

During the early 1980s political activism had also gripped Robert. In 1981 he joined Jackson Browne's No Nukes movement and tried to shut down the Diablo Canyon nuclear power plant by demonstrating with the Abalone Alliance.[51] He regularly sounded off on behalf of Cesar Chavez's United Farm Workers, advocated gay rights and called himself a feminist. Since the mid-1970s, when he first gained a national forum via the *Tonight Show*, he had used his celebrity to promote personal causes and vice versa. There was nothing like a good cause to generate publicity, especially when one found oneself at the bottom of the roller coaster.

The cause for which he had always been an outspoken advocate was battered and abused children, going so far as to solicit Senator Ted Kennedy to draft a children's bill of rights. The headline on an April 24, 1977, interview in the *Los Angeles Herald-Examiner* read:

Actor Robert Blake Embarks on a
Crusade to Save the Children

"Kids ain't got no rights in this country," Blake ranted to *People* magazine. "There has to be a bill of rights to give kids legal recourse and a birthright of three hot meals a day

---

51. After boasting during the demonstration that "that big fat sheriff ain't gonna get me," Blake was forced to apologize to San Luis Obispo County sheriff George Whiting when it turned out that Whiting was neither fat nor attempting to get Blake. Whiting concentrated instead on the 1,100 demonstrators who tried to blockade Diablo Canyon. They were jailed while Blake, who did not join the blockade, remained free.

from the time they're born. Every kid has to have the rig
to complain, the right to some peace in this world, son
guidance, some freedom."

That same year, when he was still riding his *Baretta* hig
Blake traveled to Washington, D.C., to speak on behalf
the nation's youth. He told the House Select Committee c
Narcotics Abuse and Control that a minor's use of grass le
to heroin, while alcohol did not.

"As a former juvenile delinquent, heavy narcotics use
dealer and grower, I'm familiar with the severe drawbac
of marijuana for the young people of America," Blake to
Joseph Nellis, the committee's chief counsel. "For the 6
percent to 70 percent of our young who have the beginnin;
of severe emotional problems, marijuana can be devastatin
If a kid is having trouble with his parents, with school
with society in general, he's going to seek escape from h
problem—and he'll try whatever's handy."

Robert didn't want Noah, Delinah or any other child s
duced by drugs. But in arguing *against* legalizing marijuan
he wound up arguing *for* underage drinking. "Every time
kid gets drunk to avoid his problems, he wakes up sick, hun,
over, horribly sober and keenly aware that his problems a
still there," he reasoned. "With a little luck, these setbac
encourage him to seek help from counselors, guidance cli
ics, public facilities, private therapists, his parents, his re
gious leaders, whatever. None of these advantages applies
marijuana."

Baretta's words antagonized PTA and AA meetings fro
coast to coast. When the nation's parents bitterly assaile
him for endorsing booze over pot, Robert reeled. How ha
he managed to garble his own message?

As a shrewd and cynical child of Hollywood, he was a
ways aware of the presence and power of the media, and sa
every public appearance as an opportunity to promote h
public image as a bad boy with a heart of gold. At times h
carried his passion for the underprivileged to extremes.

In 1983, Stephen Cannell's fifteen-year-old son died tra;
ically in a freak accident at the beach, suffocating in a sar
tunnel. Blake was among dozens who came to Cannell
house to offer condolences during a memorial for the boy.

"Robert went into the kitchen and took a plate of food at the front gate," Cannell recalled. "He had adopted this five-foot-two black guy he called Fats because he was, well, fat. About as wide as he was tall. A little later, Robert comes to me and says, 'Listen, Fats is sitting out in the car. Can I bring him in?' I say, 'Sure.' He brings him in, and it turns out Fats is this street person from First and Broadway. He talks like: 'How doin', boy?'

"So I had this racist friend, and Fats sits next to him at the bar and asks, 'So, muthafucka, what a muthafucka like you do?' And my friend answers, 'I'm an executive at an oil company in charge of research and development.' Fats gets indignant and says, 'Oh. *You* the muthafucka costin' me all my money, you muthafuck. So why don't you jus' swing on my dick, Tarzan!'

"To which my friend answers, 'As we say at the club: fuck thee.'"

For all of his compassion for street people, Blake had none for his own brother or mother. At every opportunity, on Carson or in print, Robert blasted his older brother, James, as a mean-spirited predatory homosexual. "I never heard that he was gay," said Blake's cousin Rose Newick. "James was nice and quiet, didn't talk about anything." In fact, the older brother Blake regularly skewered as an effete, jealous faggot was married, responsible and concerned enough about his aged mother to care for Elizabeth Gubitosi when she had grown too feeble to live on her own.

Robert also lambasted his mother regularly. Following her husband's death in 1956, Elizabeth Gubitosi had sold the family home in Beverly Hills and moved back to Nutley. She took an apartment near the very intersection of Bloomfield and Romano, where Robert had been born. For the next twenty-five years she worked on the assembly line at Hoffmann-La Roche Laboratories, stuffing cotton balls into the mouths of aspirin bottles. Known to her family as Lee (or behind her back as "Old Stoneface") the miserable little woman with the sour, drawn face rarely had visitors.

"She would never, ever smile," said Rose. "Once in a blue moon she would laugh. She was a very serious, serious person. If you look at all the pictures of her, you'd never see her smile. She never had any interests and she didn't really talk about Robert. But if one of us would say, 'Oh, Robert did this and Robert did that,' she would say, 'Oh, that bastard.' They had no love for each other. You could tell that."

"She kept to herself, never went on vacation, never went anyplace," echoed Steve Visakay. "Yeah, she was angry and bitter. She was not a happy-go-lucky person, to put it mildly."

Blake never called or visited until she fell into her final illness. After Rose contacted him, Blake phoned his mother and implored her to "hang in there," but once she was well enough to leave the hospital, he never called again.

"When she got sick and went to Mountainside Hospital, James was the one who cleared out her whole apartment and took her back to Long Island and put her in a home. He buried her."

The funeral was at the Holy Family Church in Nutley. Blake refused to attend.

"I think it's sad that Robert makes it seem that everybody picked on him," said Rose. "I think it's just to make people feel sorry for him."

The one family member he did not curse was his sister, Jovanny Austin. In 1984, when the fifty-two-year-old exercise and fitness instructor developed liver and colon cancer, Blake invited her and his niece to come stay with him. On February 28, 1985, Jovanny Austin died at Robert's Studio City home. Her daughter, Noreen, then 29, moved in and lived with Robert and her cousins for a while. Whenever Blake was asked how many children he had, he answered, "Three."

21

In 1985, Blake took his last shot at series TV. As Father Noah "Hardstep" Rivers, he traded in *Baretta*'s cockatoo for a priest's collar. It was a role for which he claimed he'd been in training since childhood, when he was both a real-life altar boy and also played one in MGM's *Going My Way* (1944).

As usual, he fought initially with company executives. He invested some of his own money into *Father of Hell Town*, a two-hour $2.5 million NBC movie of the week that he envisioned as a pilot for a weekly foray into an inner-city parish in downtown Los Angeles. NBC programming chief Brandon Tartikoff ran the idea by his prime-time brain trust. They didn't like it.

"Robert, I got some real mixed reviews," said Tartikoff. "Some scenes are Frank Capra, some are *Baretta* and they never hang together. We should never have given you the authority and we overstepped ourselves."

Blake bit his tongue for a change and pleaded for an audience with NBC chairman Grant Tinker, but forbearance had never been Blake's strong suit. Going to anybody hat in hand grated on him. Prior to his meeting with Tinker, he muttered in disgust: "Peck's Bad Boy is dead. I'm fuckin' Little Lord Fauntleroy."

Blake groveled all the same. Tinker would not make *Hell Town* a midseason replacement, going up against ABC's top-rated *Dynasty* the way that Blake had wanted, but the NBC chairman did give it a green light for the fall.

The gritty feel of L.A. at its seediest permeated the NBC series as completely as it had in *Baretta*. *Hell Town* was shot on location on skid row as well as in an earthquake-condemned church in East L.A. In addition to starring in the series, Blake also worked as executive producer. He said years later that the dual pressure of acting and producing drove him to sleeping pills, junk food and the brink of suicide. "I would get in the limo to go to the *Hell Town* location every morning, and I'd be so uptight I could hardly breathe," he said in a 1992 interview.

The hope was that Father Hardstep would work the same ratings miracle as Michael Landon, who had put his own God drama on NBC that year and immediately garnered a 35 share. *Highway to Heaven,* in which Landon portrayed a guardian angel, shot to the top of the Nielsens and stayed there. That didn't happen for *Hell Town.* As acerbic *Los Angeles Times* TV critic Howard Rosenberg prophesized in his review, "Blake doesn't have a prayer in *Hell Town.*"

"Doing a series is like humping a gorilla," Blake observed. "You gotta keep on humping until the gorilla says stop, 'cause like in the beginning, it might even feel good, and when it starts feeling bad and you wanna stop, gorilla says, 'I ain't finished yet.' And you gotta keep going and you gotta keep going."

Despite mixed reviews and fair ratings, *Hell Town* inexorably moved Blake toward the nervous breakdown he so richly deserved. He could no longer be the jack-of-all-trades that he'd been during *Baretta.* Starring and producing while making nice with Columbia, NBC Standards and Practices and network suits eventually did him in. After sixteen episodes, the *Hell Town* plug was pulled.

"On episode sixteen I literally could not go on," Blake said later. "It was like I couldn't hear myself talkin'. My ears were ringing. It was like I turned into a five-year-old or something. I was looking down to find where my marks were and trying to think of what I had to say, you know, like a kid who was in front of the camera for the first time. That's what I felt like.

"So I walked away and I said, 'You know what? You can take all of show business and just put it in gerbil heaven for the foreseeable future because I don't wanna die.' And all I really knew is that I didn't want to die."

After walking off the set and getting *Hell Town* canceled, Blake lay on a pile of fur blankets on his living room floor for days. He remembered circling endlessly through the house, mumbling like a mental patient. Noah went away to Michigan to study jazz drumming that year, and Delinah had graduated from high school and begun college. Blake found himself increasingly alone.

"After the divorce, my dad didn't date much," said Noah.

Others maintained that whatever he lacked in actual dates Blake more than made up for in sexual harassment. He was a relentless flirt, pursuing women who were decades younger. Anne, a young woman who grew up to be a screenwriter and asked that she not be identified by her last name, recalled Blake approaching her once while she was still in high school, just a few years older than Delinah. "He drove up and motioned to me to come over to his car," she said. "I knew who he was from television and I wouldn't get in. He was really creepy."

During *Hell Town*, Blake's dark caprice with women showed itself again in a disturbing incident documented at the time in *TV Guide*. Darlene Chehardy, who later became a New Orleans publicist, befriended Blake on the *Hell Town* set, where she was breaking in as a young actress. Blake alternately teased that she must have slept with someone to get hired and confided in her about his enduring emotional problems. At first, he unburdened his tortured soul during private walks away from the rest of the cast, but then friendship turned tawdry. Once, she walked off the set when he informed her that he was coming to her house "for dinner and a massage," according to Chehardy. A short time later, after she returned, Blake "pushed me into a closet," she said. "I couldn't believe it."

He grabbed her and, according to Chehardy, said, "I want you. I just have to hold somebody. Help me make it through this day." Again, she left the set, but two weeks later, when she refused yet another offer of a romantic midnight dinner: "I got a call. 'The word has come down. He doesn't want you on the set.'" She had been fired.

Meanwhile, Sondra struggled to make ends meet without Blake opening doors for her in Hollywood. She couldn't get any more TV work after *Joe Dancer*. She continued her stage work, however, and opened in *Blind Faith* at Theatre West on November 22, 1985. In a wicked bit of irony, the black comedy about lying, deceit and priestly politics garnered good reviews three weeks before the crash of *Hell Town*. The final line of the play is: "Welcome to the Church."

Following Blake's *Hell Town* debacle, there seemed little doubt that the slow slide that began after he quit *Baretta* was now a free fall. Robert had nothing but regrets over his career in the very medium that had brought him his greatest fame.

"Doing a series is probably the most singular destructive thing I ever did in my life," he said in reflection. "Doing *Baretta* was almost like putting a gun in my mouth and blowing my head off. Nobody does *In Cold Blood* and *Electra Glide in Blue* and *Tell Them Willie Boy Is Here* and goes and does a series. You do a series on the way up or you do a series when you are on the way down. I would rather go downtown and stand on the street corner and do *Cyrano* with a beer can in front of me with people dropping quarters than do a series. I got money now. My kids are grown-up. I could sit in this front room until hell freezes over. I don't have to work."

He made his final appearance on the *Tonight Show* on November 14, 1985, bitterly denouncing the same cast of "straight" Establishment officials whom he always seemed to blame for his failures.

After explaining to the audience how their own laughter is "sweetened" with a laugh track, Johnny brought out his first guest, but it was not Robert Blake. It was Eura Irwin, an eighty-one-year-old newspaper delivery woman who had been married at fourteen and begun delivering newspapers when she was seventy-three.

When Blake came on two commercial breaks later, Johnny gave him a few minutes to plug *Hell Town* and to announce to the world that he had recently fallen in love with a married woman, but then Johnny moved on to the next guest. The old days when Blake could wax on interminably were gone. Johnny waited for a commercial, pushed

Blake over on the couch and brought on consumer advocate David Horowitz to talk about hamburgers and home safety for infants.

"He and Johnny had chemistry, but it finally ran its course," said former *Tonight Show* publicist Charlie Barrett. "You reach a point with some guests, it just kind of ends."

"I hate all those years that I did the *Tonight Show* and all that shit," Blake said a decade later for the magazine *Detour*. "It was so sad and so sick, up there making a fool of myself, carrying on. But if the phone rang, I would go. I did it once a month for twenty fucking years, and the crazier I got, the more they liked it."

At one point, Blake went on the show a couple of times and sang as he played the saw—a far, far cry from Method acting. He played it for pathos and he played it for laughs, but he played it.

"If I'd have cut my throat on camera, they'd have said, 'Tune in tomorrow night and watch him bleed.' I got nothing out of that except a really shitty image. Like I was my father's fucking monkey, I was their monkey," he groused. "Toward the end, I was falling apart. They should have been decent people and said, 'Robert, don't do this show.' They used me. It was kind of sad."

Blake began his descent into anonymity. Scripts were offered to him, but they were *Baretta* retreads. Now that he'd failed as a priest, it was back to the old tried-and-true: cop shows.

"Everybody said, 'Take them. Go to work,'" Blake recalled. "I said, 'I don't want to go back and be leaping from building to building.' The reason I quit was I realized how terribly, terribly abusive I always had been to my career."

His blood pressure shot through the ceiling. He took pills to go to sleep and drank coffee by the pot to get himself up in the morning. He went to the doctor for energy shots. He was told they were B-12 injections, but he didn't believe that for a second.

"I knew they weren't B-12 and so did the doctor," he said. "I was taking uppers."

On the other hand, he became as incensed as the old Robert Blake when anyone suggested that he might have a drug

Bonny Lee Bakley, celebrity stalker, small-time grifter, and Internet porn entrepreneur. (Photo courtesy of Dawn Dupré.)

A five-year-old Blake (far left) as "Mickey" in Hal Roach's *Our Gang* series. Blake appeared in the long-running serial from 1939 through 1944. (Copyright © John Springer Collection/Corbis.)

Young Bobby Blake as "Little Beaver" in the *Red Ryder* series, which starred Allan Lane. (Copyright 1947 Republic Pictures. Photo courtesy of Irv Letofsky.)

Blake as a young Mexican boy selling lottery tickets to Bogart's "Fred C. Dobbs," went uncredited in the movie classic *The Treasure of the Sierra Madre*. (Copyright 1947 Warner Bros. Pictures Distributing Corporation. Photo courtesy of Irv Letofsky.)

Blake as "Sidney" in the film version of the Tennessee Williams play *This Property Is Condemned*, which starred Natalie Wood and Robert Redford. (Copyright © 1966 Paramount Pictures Corporation. Photo courtesy of Irv Letofsky.)

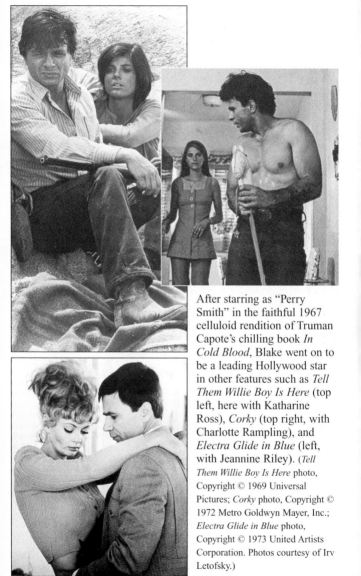

After starring as "Perry Smith" in the faithful 1967 celluloid rendition of Truman Capote's chilling book *In Cold Blood*, Blake went on to be a leading Hollywood star in other features such as *Tell Them Willie Boy Is Here* (top left, here with Katharine Ross), *Corky* (top right, with Charlotte Rampling), and *Electra Glide in Blue* (left, with Jeannine Riley). (*Tell Them Willie Boy Is Here* photo, Copyright © 1969 Universal Pictures; *Corky* photo, Copyright © 1972 Metro Goldwyn Mayer, Inc.; *Electra Glide in Blue* photo, Copyright © 1973 United Artists Corporation. Photos courtesy of Irv Letofsky.)

Blake, with Elliott Gould, in the 1974 detective film *Busting*. (Copyright © 1973 United Artists Corporation. Photo courtesy of Irv Letofsky.)

Blake in his defining role: Detective Tony Baretta—pictured with Fred the cockatoo, Meg Foster (standing), and Elizabeth Cheshire. (Copyright © Universal Pictures. Photo courtesy of Irv Letofsky.)

Robert Blake in later years, caught during a peaceful moment. (Copyright © Cristina Salvador.)

Robert and Bonny Lee Bakley, with Will Jordan (seated, left) and Chuck McCann (standing). (Photo courtesy of Paul Gawron.)

The car in which Bonny Lee Bakley was murdered on May 4, 2001. (Reuters/Los Angeles County Superior Court/Handout. Copyright © Reuters New-Media Inc./Corbis.)

Evidence photographs released by the court on May 1, 2002, included this 9mm Walther P-38 found near the crime scene the night Bakley was killed. (Reuters/Los Angeles County Superior Court/Handout. Copyright © Reuters NewMedia Inc./Corbis.)

Blake at Bonny Lee Bakley's funeral, holding their daughter, Rosie Lenore Sophie Blake. Blake's daughter from a previous marriage, Delinah, stands to the left. (AFP Photo/AP Pool/Damian Dovarganes. Copyright © AFP/Corbis.)

Officer Gary Brennan (left), Chief Bernard Parks (center), and head homicide investigator Captain Jim Tatreau (right) of the Los Angeles Police Department field questions from reporters after Blake's arrest on April 18, 2002. (AFP Photo/Vince Bucci. Copyright © AFP/Corbis.)

Attorney Harland Braun talks to the press after Blake's arraignment.
(Reuters/Jim Ruymen. Copyright © Reuters NewMedia Inc./Corbis.)

Blake family lawyer, Cary Goldstein, faces questions after Blake pleaded not guilty to the charge of murdering Bakley. (AFP Photo/Lee Celano. Copyright © AFP/Corbis.)

habit. "I haven't been near street drugs since I was in my twenties, and anybody who says I have is a tin-horned gob of snot and their mother is Komodo scum who eats on all fours, and if they wanna do anything about it, I'm easy to find and I ain't a bit bashful," he told Pat O'Brien during an interview for *Entertainment Tonight*.

His social activism blossomed as his career tanked. On March 1, 1986, the Great Peace March for Global Disarmament began—an 8½-month trek from Griffith Park to Washington, D.C., with Robert Blake in the vanguard. Although he walked less than half the 3,235 miles, he was credited with keeping it alive, long after others had written it off as folly.

"There were originally 1,200 people, but when we got out to the Mojave, our corporate underwriting disappeared," recalled Jerry Rubin, one of the March organizers. "The next day, 700 headed for Greyhound and 500 stayed behind. We all held hands for about a half an hour and then Blake starts singing "Amazing Grace" and everybody followed him looking up at the sky and spiraling into this tight circle, cheering. We were about to just call it all off and probably would have if it hadn't been for him. He rallied us. Two weeks later, we'd made it across the desert and there was no stopping us, but I know it wouldn't have happened without Robert."

Blake himself made it only as far as Colorado before turning back, but he kept up the causes. In February 1987, he was arrested during a protest at a nuclear test site in Mercury, Nevada. In October 1987, he spoke at a gay-lesbian civil rights rally in Washington. He was arrested again at the Nevada test site in March 1988. He joined the Hollywood boycott of table grapes in support of Cesar Chavez's United Farm Workers, and he spoke out against gang warfare, dyslexia and, of course, child abuse.

He also did much soul searching in the late eighties, musing on the three parts of his personality—the abused young Mickey, rebellious Bobby, and Robert Blake, the "junkyard dog" of the *Tonight Show*. He decided the Brentwood therapist he'd been seeing for over thirty years was a fraud who only wanted his money. By the time he fired him, Blake claimed that he was paying him $150,000 a year.

"I pulled him up over the desk once, toward the end, and was thinking about biting his throat out."

Or, as he more dramatically described the moment for the *National Enquirer*:

> I saw his glasses tilted, his face getting red and swelling up. He started coughing. Frothy bubbles were leaking from his mouth and his eyes were bulging. The next thing I knew, I was in my car. It hit me—"I killed him. I'm a murderer!" I sat there thinking, "My life is over. I'll be in prison and my kids will never see me again."
>
> I was still sitting there frozen two hours later when the therapist walked out of the building and I realized I didn't actually kill him. To this day I don't remember everything that happened in that office.

In 1989, he entered an "adults abused as children" program, which included hypnosis, and he began to get in touch with his inner child.

22

Other gentlemen may have known Bonny Lee Bakley and her flimflamming ways better than the late DeMart C. Besly, but none of them wrote a book about it. On the very first page of "Ubiquitous Bonny, Mistress of Sham," Besly delivered this sad assessment of his curious four-year odyssey: "I was a lonely widower, a world-traveled retired military man, seeking a young lady to share my home in the hope of developing a meaningful relationship."

He thought he'd found his dream girl in Bonny. She was just thirty-two when the Montana widower married her at a casino chapel in Elko, Nevada, on December 7, 1988. Besly was eighty-one, making it a genuine May-December marriage. Despite the fact that Bonny and Besly had known each other for years through letters or phone calls, they'd met face-to-face for the first time just a few days earlier.

Bonny was all smiles—everything that Besly had hoped for in the twilight of his years, right up until the moment they both said, "I do." Besly sealed their sacred vows by handing Bonny a roll of nickels to play the slot machines, and she disappeared.

"She had been my blushing bride for less than an hour when she suddenly vanished on that Pearl Harbor Day of infamy, and I have not seen her since," he wrote.

The saga of "Ubiquitous Bonny" actually began in February 1984, when Besly's wife of forty-four years succumbed to cancer. He had little kind to say about her. For the nineteen years before she died, Mrs. Besly had been as frigid as a Rocky Mountain winter. In addition, she had other faults, according to Besly. She was grasping, defiant, scheming, ignorant, evasive, hysterical and materialistic.

Even so, he became lonely following her death. In his long lifetime Besly had been a cowboy, a logger, a sailor and sheriff of Darby, Montana (pop. 942), but never lucky in love. Now he hoped to change that.

Six months after his wife's death, he visited an adult bookstore on the pretense that he was looking for a raunchy Christmas card to send to an old navy buddy. He found the card, but he also found *The Love Club,* a swinger's publication with an ad that read:

Beautiful girl, 23, brown eyes, five foot five, 120 pounds, very lonely. In desperate need to find someone to write to and talk on the phone and meet with soon. I'm in a hurry to meet a man to stay with. So please, no matter what your age or how far away you live, I'm free to travel. Are you? I promise to answer your letter the same day I receive it. Clinton, N.J.

Accompanied by a photo of an attractive young minx with shoulder-length blond hair, the ad had been appearing regularly for five years in the same publication. But Besly didn't know that. All he knew was that the portrait revealed a nude in platform shoes, squatting so that the thatch of black fur twixt her thighs belied the authenticity of the blond atop her head.

He waited a week, but couldn't resist answering the ad. He was seventy-six, and he had enough retirement money socked away that he no longer had to work.

His first tip that something was awry ought to have been the fact that Bonny did not answer his letter the same day, as promised. She didn't even answer it the same month. Weeks passed before he finally received what appeared to be a form follow-up reply signed, "Love always, Leebonny."

The letter sounded like free-flowing dictation from a semiliterate female Jack Kerouac, recounting her adventures on the road with a pickup artist and a gang of hippie gypsies. There was no pitch for money, but Leebonny admonished him to "write back soon."

He didn't. He knew a scam when he saw one.

The following week, a second letter arrived. This one was from a Miss Sandra Gawron. It too rambled, but this time the writer claimed she was Leebonny's sister and that she had nude photos of herself for sale. She also threw in an aside that she had once slept with actor Robert Urich, though she spelled his name "Urick." To prove she and the actor were an item, she enclosed a photo of her standing beside him. Only much later did Besly learn that Bonny had the photo shot while on the set as an extra in *Turk 182!* (1985), a stunningly bad action film about a New York City firefighter (Urich) and his younger brother (Timothy Hutton) who take on city hall.

"She would entice," said attorney Jonathan Kirsch, who represented Besly's niece when she inherited "Ubiquitous Bonny" upon Besly's death. "If you were a lonely guy and you had an opportunity to correspond with someone who advertised herself as a beautiful young woman who was in a little bit of distress, and you could help her out for not much money, what you got in return was the gratitude of a beautiful young woman.

"But then she would play that out by raising the temperatures of the letters so that she was inducing the man who wrote to her to give her more and more money in exchange for more and more explicit correspondence and more and more explicit photographs."

Besly took the bait. He sent $10 for the photos and got back a pair of crotch shots, along with a Christmas card and a promise that she would call. By now he knew that Leebonny and Sandra Gawron were one and the same. He just didn't know how many other aliases Bonny had.

Some time after New Year's 1985, Bonny phoned. She was giggly and effervescent. While Besly thought they were just doing a little get-acquainted chatter, Bonny was taking notes at the other end, detailing his likes and dislikes, hobbies, tastes, pastimes and net worth. Then she asked if Montana was anywhere near Kentucky or Kansas City.

"Good God, I thought. Didn't this girl ever go to school?" wrote Besly.

When she wrote again, the pitch for money was stronger.

She needed $300 to pay off her sister's debts before she could catch a bus to Montana. Besly didn't answer and filed the letter away.

Three years passed, and Besly came across Bonny's ad in *Select*, another swinger magazine. She was also featured in *Swinger's Bulletin* and *Swingin' Women*. The name on the ad this time was Florence Paulakis, but the address, the style and even the come-on photo were unmistakably Bonny's. Besly answered the ad and letters flowed anew.

> Hi. How nice to hear from you again. I really loved your letter. And of course thank you again for buying something and helping me to save for that car I want so badly. You are really such a help to me. Not just because of you helping me save for a car, but because every time I receive a letter from you it really makes me happy. I just love to receive letters from you. . . .

The letters went from folksy to fellatio in just a few paragraphs, describing in lurid detail just how many different ways she was prepared to make her correspondent achieve pleasure.

"She was a really gifted pornographer," said Kirsch. "She's signaling to her victim that she'll play this sexual game any way they want to play it; that whatever their sexual predilections are, wherever, whatever direction they want to go in, she'll go, which is the essence of pornography. Pornography caters to the private sexual fantasies of the one who consumes it, so it's a highly specialized and focused and targeted kind of literature."

The letters might have been nothing more than the postal equivalent of phone sex, but Bonny had something else in mind. When she showed up at the Darby bus station, she was shorter, more shabby and dumpier than her photos had led Besly to believe. At 140 pounds, the five-foot-three-inch Bonny did not match the sexpot image of her crotch shots. Her clothes were strictly Salvation Army and her cardboard luggage was cracked. Her toiletries consisted of towels stolen from the Ramada Inn and tiny bars of soap lifted from motels and hotels across America. Instead of discouraging him, however, the real Bonny gave him hope. Besly was not so naive as to believe that a babe was going to marry him, but a down-on-her-heels bimbo like Bonny just might.

He took her back to his cabin. Years earlier, Besly had bought a red fox fur coat for his late wife, and he gave it to Bonny on the condition that she pose for him. She disappeared into the bathroom to strip and came out in the living room with only the coat wrapped around her. She let Besly run through an entire roll of film without displaying much more flesh than a thigh and a breast. Besly got excited. He had his speech prepared.

"I've been wondering when you were going to boldly tear my zipper open and attack my manhood as you so graphically described in your typed letter of December 9, 1988, when I responded to your ad in *Select* in which you advertised, 'Men please write. I need some loving and good sex to go with it. Let's meet soon. I'll answer all.'"

According to Besly, Bonny never blinked. She drilled him with a cold, steady gaze and said: "I never have sex with anyone unless I'm either engaged or married because I don't trust men."

Continuing to play coy, Bonny behaved like a dumb blonde. When Besly remarked to her that the Alcan Highway went right past his front door, he found himself having to explain the difference between North and South America, the location of the Arctic Circle and its proximity to Montana.

"Gee, you sure know a lot," she said with her trademark girlish giggle. "I still don't get it. I've never met anyone like you before. You're intelligent. You should get on that *Jeopardy!* show."

She later mistook the Snake River gorge for the Grand Canyon. "Bonny seemed to have absolutely no concept of geography and doesn't seem to know where she is half the time," wrote Besly.

But the time eventually came during her Darby sojourn when she began asking for money—over and over. The list of reasons was endless:

• My car broke down. I need $300 to repair it.
• I want to take a trip to see my mother.

- I need bus fare.
- I want some plastic surgery done.
- I need new contact lenses.

Eventually even Bonny tired of asking and obediently followed when Besly told her to pack up because they were going to Elko, Nevada, to get married.

"There were always plausible reasons why she needed money, and she was trying to get these guys to think of themselves as her sugar daddy, not just someone paying for dirty pictures," said Jonathan Kirsch.

Targeting male fantasies has a long literary tradition. The famed diarist Anaïs Nin and Pauline Reage, author of *The Story of O,* both earned their livings that way, according to Kirsch. "The way that bread-and-butter money was made during the 1930s and into the 1940s and 1950s was to write pornography for rich patrons," he said.

But Reage and Nin's elegant erotica paled beside Bonny's down-home variety, which carried lines like, "I am what is known as a trisexual in that I will try anything."

"Nin's pornography is not very nasty stuff compared to what we're used to nowadays," said Kirsch. "Our sensibilities are brutalized after so much. What you see now is so explicit. But that's what I find fascinating about 'Ubiquitous Bonny,' because that's what, in essence, this is: erotica. And it's also what it has sunk to."

During Bonny's career, porn had evolved to a point where customers could literally select their category. "I mean, you can actually go and pick, you know—S and M or interracial or different kinds of sexual practices and sexual casting," said Kirsch.

Bonny's specialty was personalization. At the same time that she catered to private sexual fantasies, she studied her client's entire personality. "She had this psychological insight making it seem less like the postal equivalent of phone sex and more like a relationship," said Kirsch. "It's one thing to say to somebody, 'I'll send you dirty pictures and dirty letters if you send me money.' That forces the person on the other end of that bargain to admit that they're paying for sexual gratification in the most impersonal sort of way.

It's quite another thing to say, 'You're going to help me. I'll be grateful to you. You'll be my benefactor and my savior,' escalating to actually standing in front of a minister and getting married. It was the ultimate sham."

After Bonny disappeared, Besly waited around Elko for a day in hopes that she'd just gotten lost. She didn't know the difference between North and South America, so it stood to reason that she might not know the difference between North and South Elko. He finally accepted the truth and returned home to Montana. There he discovered that in addition to leaving him at the altar, Bonny had also stolen his gun and his late wife's jewelry.

A week after she'd left him, Bonny called from a Memphis dance hall, where Jerry Lee Lewis could be heard playing in the background. She hollered, "I love you!" in the phone, then hung up. The following week, Besly got a Christmas card, again vowing her love and asking Besly to send her his military separation papers so that she could get a medical care card from the V.A.

After that, Besly heard from her regularly. Between promises of coming back to Montana, she talked about affairs and three-ways and lesbian love fests. She asked him to buy her "one of those vibrators that squirts liquid like a man coming in me." Accompanying the letter was an advertisement that featured a smiling orangutan holding one of the squirting devices. Like a few others he'd met in his long life, Bonny would "fuck a snake if someone would hold its head," observed Besly.

She also boasted regularly in her letters about her Hollywood contacts. She'd moved beyond Robert Urich and now claimed to have been a guest at actress Sandy Duncan's birthday party, where she met Lenny Bruce's mother and hung out with screenwriters and comedians like Chuck McCann and Will Jordan. Once, after a particularly poignant letter, Besly broke down and sent her $1,000 to buy a car, convincing himself that the only reason he was doing it was to string her along. But in his heart, he always held out hope that she'd come to her senses and return to him.

"She abandoned him," said Kirsch. "She ran away from him. She was continuing to milk him for money and finan-

cial support for another year until he finally kind of smart-
ened up, woke up to how he had been victimized and
arranged to be divorced."

On October 5, 1989, Besly dissolved the marriage.

Bonny kept the cards and letters coming, and called
sometimes several times a week. She stepped up the pace
around Christmastime, hoping that the sentiment of the season might break Besly down and he'd send her a few bucks
for the holidays.

"So it was part of the continuing exploitation," said
Kirsch. "The marriage was the next step in drawing this guy
closer and inducing him to support her financially. He
thought that she was sparing herself what she might have
regarded as the unpleasant task of actually being his sexual
companion or his wife, but she didn't cut him off completely."

Another year passed before Besly's next shock. When he
received his 1990 property tax bill, he was stunned to see
Bonny's name as well as his own. A further check at the
county recorder's office revealed that Bonny had forged his
signature and put herself on the deed. It had been notarized
by a Memphis used-car dealer whom Bonny later admitted
she'd been "shacked up with at the time."

"It's a very squalid story, but it's kind of the dark side of
this whole idea of how to marry a millionaire," said Kirsch.
"I mean, it's a mythic idea among some women that you go
out and try to ensnare a good catch. But this was a woman
who was a bottom-feeder. And she was really doing everything she could and the only thing she could. To me, what
puts it into a fascinating context is that on one side she was
really just trolling for anyone who would send her $30 in the
mail, but on the other hand, she was aiming high."

Years later, in connection with the Blake case, private investigator Scott Ross actually put a number on the variety of
letters that Bonny sent out: eight different levels in all. "The
letters ranged from sending nude photographs and videos for
money at the lowest level to offering to visit the 'client' at
the higher levels," said Ross. "The higher the level of letter,
the larger the amount of money requested. The highest-level
letter was a request that the 'client' add Bonny to his will."

In 1993, much as she did to Philip Wright Worchester in 1980, Bonny convinced Oregon widower Timothy Larkins to replace his son, Randy, in his will with her name, and she didn't even have to marry him. "I give my residuary estate to Leebonny Bakley," wrote Larkins. Had the will gone through probate, Randy Larkins would have wound up with an inheritance only in the event that Bonny died first.

"But that wasn't the whole story of this woman because in fact she was working this scam almost as a way of making a living," said Kirsch. "It was like a bread-and-butter job."

Besly finally stopped playing the game in 1993, after his health went into decline and he'd been scammed enough. The letters trailed off, but he did continue to get a Christmas card from Bonny each year. They never did consummate the marriage.

In one of her final letters, Bonny taunted Besly with a rape scenario.

"I'm afraid that when we meet you're going to beat me up because of all the terrible things I've done to you," she wrote. "Someday someone may take revenge against me."

23

On the night of May 16, 1990, Christian Brando got drunk and shot his sister's boyfriend point-blank in the face.

According to Christian's later courtroom testimony, Cheyenne Brando complained to her brother earlier in the evening that Dag Drollet had been slapping her around. Drollet stood six-foot-three and weighed in at 270 pounds while frail Cheyenne was a foot shorter and weighed half as much, even though she was eight months pregnant with Drollet's baby.

Christian concluded that this was not a fair fight. He took it upon himself to even the odds and teach the Tahitian-born Drollet a lesson. He tanked up on spirits, got his gun and went into the living room to confront Drollet, who was lolling on the sofa watching TV. According to Christian, they quarreled, Drollet tried to wrestle away his .45 and Christian emptied a chamber into Drollet's head. When police found him, Drollet still had a cigarette lighter in one hand and the remote control in the other.

Marlon, who had been in the next room, ran in when he heard the shot. The rotund actor tried mouth-to-mouth resuscitation before calling 911, but the bullet from Christian's gun had gone all the way through Drollet's brain and exited out the back of his neck. Nothing could save him.

Even four hours later, Christian's blood-alcohol level was .19—nearly twice the legal limit for a DUI. Police arrested the thirty-two-year-old eldest son of the Oscar winner for *The Godfather*, and Brando called upon the best team of criminal defense lawyers money could buy to get his little boy out of the slammer.

When police recovered a virtual arsenal at his house—an M-14 assault rifle, a shotgun, a MAC-10 machine pistol, a .44 caliber carbine and a silencer—it did not help Christian's argument that Drollet's death was a terrible, freak accident. Given Christian's reputation for drinking and his hair-trigger temper, the firepower made the district attorney's office decide to charge him with premeditated first-degree murder.

During the summer of 1990, all of Los Angeles, including Robert Blake, watched the unfolding nightmare at the Brando compound with horror. A well-known television actor who had dinner with the former *Baretta* star at the time recalled Blake shaking his head in disgust at the televised court coverage. Instead of crying on the witness stand, Marlon should have been thinking more clearly the night that his son got in trouble, Blake said.

"Marlon should know better," Blake told his dinner guest. "You take the gun and you rub it in dog shit. You rub it in red pasta sauce. You make it *hard* for the cops to figure out who did it."

Blake had learned lots of little tricks of the trade during his *Baretta* days. The Method taught him to get inside a cop's skin, or a convicted killer's skin, as he did during *In Cold Blood*. Blake believed first and foremost in the craft of acting. Professionalism. Attention to detail. That's what spelled the difference between an artist and a televised twit.

During the late 1980s and early 1990s, Robert Blake gradually withdrew from the spotlight. He had offers, but he also had his professional pride. He didn't want to wind up a parody of himself as an aging TV sleuth. Nor would he consider a guest spot on another lame ensemble series or a bit part in a movie. Blake refused to step down to second-class citizenship just so he could get in front of a camera.

"I am an actor," he proclaimed. "It is the only thing I ever got any pride out of in my whole life. I didn't want to go to work for ten weeks on some movie and carry Warren Beatty's bags."

In May 1992, during his first TV appearance in years, Blake explained his absence from the public spotlight since

Hell Town. He told Maury Povich that it was all his parents' fault. Emotional and physical abuse inflicted on little Mickey Gubitosi had finally caught up with him, temporarily shutting down his acting career. That's who drove him to drugs. That's who made him drink. That's who caused him to explode and regret it all afterward.

Baretta was "one of the most destructive things I did in my life. . . . You don't do a series when you're a motion picture star," he said over and over and over.

He continued his confessional some weeks later on *Entertainment Tonight*. He'd quit TV so that "I didn't blow my brains out or eat somebody," he said.

> I came back because I felt like working. I quit because I couldn't stand it anymore. I acted for every reason under the sun, for fame and fortune and glory and money, to get a home or a family, to hide or get laid, or whatever. There is always a reason to be in front of the box. I just ran out of reasons and walked away.
>
> I got to that place where I realized I had spent my whole life hiding from the terrible things that had happened to me as a kid. Finally, I got into the right kind of therapy and got myself unglued enough so I could come back, so nobody can say, "He went out a loser. He is a fat old man with a cigar, sitting around telling stories about Hollywood." I am fairly proud of the way I lived my life. I consider myself a bull rider rather than selling peanuts in the stands. I came back to ride the bull. That's why I am doing this part in this movie, not a series or some other junk.

In the 1993 CBS miniseries *Judgment Day*, Blake portrayed New Jersey accountant John List, who murdered his entire family,[52] moved to Colorado, assumed a new identity,

---

52. List used a World War II 9 millimeter German handgun to kill his family.

remarried and eluded police for seventeen years. Critics called it his most chilling performance since *In Cold Blood.* As with *Blood Feud*, Blake had to defer his $250,000 salary until the film was finished. With Blake, salary escrow to prevent his tantrums had become standard operating procedure.

Tantrums never surfaced during the filming, however, chiefly because Blake was so deeply invested in correctly portraying the character that he no longer bothered with the guff he gave and got from the suits. "I could have been John List," he told interviewer Pat O'Brien. "There is no question in my mind that I could have been Perry Smith, that I could have wound up on death row or in a graveyard."

Even though he made no attempt to visit the convicted killer in Trenton State Penitentiary, where List was serving five consecutive life terms for methodically killing his wife, mother and three children, Blake said he knew what made List tick. "I'm very, very thoroughly convinced that John List had a sexual relationship with his mother and he had something even more devious and strange with his father," said Blake. "I just know it. Reading between the lines on what people said about him and examining the relationship with his wife and with women in general."

Blake had been in one sort of therapy or another since he was twenty-two years old. Was it any accident that his daughter, Delinah Raya Blake, was graduating from Pepperdine with her M.A.[53] in clinical psychology that year and entering a doctoral program at UCLA?

Some question did remain, however, as to just how deep Robert's own capacity for self-reflection went.

People say, "What is it like to play a murderer?" I've never met a murderer and I've been around death row a lot. I've met a lot of people who have done a lot of killing. I've seen a lot of murderers on TV but all I

---

53. Degree requirements include 3,000 hours of supervised counseling and a strong recommendation that all candidates complete a course of in-depth personal psychotherapy.

meet on death row is a lot of real people who wound up committing suicide even though they are still alive.

The fact that he killed his family was almost incidental to the crisis he was in. The fact that he pulled the trigger does not make him that much different than anyone else who is in deep trouble. We are conditioned by TV: "That was a murderer." But when I was on death row, I was struck by how *human* a murderer is, like you and me. Someone at the end of their rope. From time to time we all are. You could say Perry Smith was in trouble. John List was in trouble. But I'm in trouble too. I never met anybody who was not in terrible trouble, once you got to know them.

In January 1993, during his promotion of *Judgment Day: The John List Story*, Blake handed out twenty-six pages of autobiographical material to a semiannual convention of TV critics in Los Angeles. The autobiography began:

All right babies—just sit tight, and I'll tell you a story that will turn the hair on your ass to brillo. This ain't no Hollywood bullshit—this is the real blood and guts where all of us live. I don't care if you have a PhD or work at the AM/PM mini mart. I don't care if you drink champagne or drink beer or play croquet or bowl. This story is about what's inside of all of us, and it took me 59 years to get to it.

Everybody says why don't you write a book. Well, I ain't got time to write a book. This is a story I want people to read because it's a discovery that I made, that may help somebody out there someplace that's laying on the floor with their guts hanging out ready to stick a gun in their mouth.

Though he went into some detail about his father's cruelties and his mother's ineffectual passivity, his "revelations" had little effect. Most of them had been spouted at one time or another. A jaded press corps, which had been hearing about abused actors and their repressed memories of childhood trauma since Roseanne revealed all in a *People* magazine spread, was only mildly impressed. "In a press conference that became equal parts confessional, apology and public therapy, actor Robert Blake joined the ranks of celebrities with horror stories to tell about being abused as children," wrote *Richmond Times-Dispatch* TV critic Douglas Durden.

In the rambling vitriolic autobiography, Blake raged that his parents made him eat off the floor like a dog; that his father went into alcoholic hysterics, beating and abusing him while his mother coldly stood by and watched; that his older brother was gay, assaulted him and got his parents' approval and affection while Blake and his sister cowered in locked and darkened closets. Even as an adult, Blake allegedly slept each night with a flashlight.

It was grist for the tabloids, and Blake told the gathered critics that he had already given photos documenting the abuse to the *National Enquirer*. The headline from the February 2, 1993, edition of the competing *Globe* supermarket tabloid said it all:

> "Dad made me eat off the floor, mom sexually abused me and my sister and brother joined in." He says he spent $3 MILLION DOLLARS ON THERAPY BECAUSE OF IT!

Blake's relatives were divided on the veracity of his recollections.

"This thing of him eating out of the dog bowl—that's ridiculous," said his cousin Rose, who knew Elizabeth Gubitosi well during the final twenty-five years of her life. "She wasn't that mean. She was a mother. They fight with their children, but to make him eat out of a dog dish? The only one who ever heard of any of this was Robert. Nobody else in the rest of the family agrees."

"That's why everybody in Nutley was mad at him," echoed Steve Visakay, another cousin. "Robert made all of that shit up."

But his niece, Noreen Austin, who lived with her uncle and cousins in the years following Robert's divorce, disagreed.

"What Robert says about the awful way he and my mother

grew up is true," said Noreen, who stayed with the Blakes on Dilling Street for more than a year after Blake's sister died of cancer in 1985. "My mom never slept a full night in her life."

The unveiling of his repressed memories before the nation's TV critics opened a barrage of publicity for *Judgment Day* in the weeks that followed, interview cascading upon interview in which Blake managed to link his own sordid childhood with the imagined misdeeds inflicted upon the mass murderer John List.

"There have been long periods of times when I wasn't there," Blake told *Los Angeles Times* staff writer Susan King. "There were times when I could have done such terrible things that I could make John List look like Donald Duck. But I got the breaks and some people don't get the breaks. When you are really badly abused, most people wind up living very dead lives or they wind up living in the graveyard or they wind up on death row. John List was no different than all of these people."

And on *Entertainment Tonight*:

I think it is only an accident that I did not end up on death row or in the graveyard or the jailhouse, something like that, what with the baggage I carried through my life, what with the horrors that my parents or brother and sister did to me. Maybe in playing this part, there is a great deal of focus on child abuse. There should be a children's bill of rights. Hundreds of thousands of children like me are going through life, where life is abusing them the way they were abused as children. It would be nice if they could come to the conclusion as I did that they do not have to live out the third act of their life that way. That they were not genetically messed up, they were not born to be the wrecks of our society. Maybe if I do interviews like this, maybe there is somebody sitting out there with a gun in their mouth or something and I can say to them, you do *not* have to do that! You didn't do it! *They did it to you!* Go way back to the first five years of your life. Maybe the third act can be a gas, instead of a disaster.

I am having a hard time making decisions about the third act of my life. I am enjoying coming back to the real world. I have been very alone for a long time, I've been out in the desert talking to rocks and trees and mumbling to myself, and I have been in a lot of abuse therapy. All I know is I want to do things that make me feel good. I want to act, direct, do a play. Just smell the desert. This has been a very tough job.

Upon closer examination, there were problems with Blake's account of his childhood as there always had been over the years. Nowhere did he offer any verifiable details about the alleged childhood abuse. The closest he came was a story about a set of clothes that he wore for a movie that his mother would not let him keep, but which she then bought later on from a haberdashery so that his older brother could wear them. Blake said he had a still shot of himself as an eight-year-old on the set of one of his movies wearing these "fine clothes" and another in which his brother had on the same outfit. He also had a snapshot of himself wearing his sister's hand-me-down sweater. What was more, he was making this pictorial proof of his childhood horrors available to the *Enquirer*. The tabloid didn't see fit to print the photos.

The only surviving member of his family who could confirm or deny any of Blake's charges was his older brother, James, and he remained silent. He died two years later in Staten Island, taking his own childhood memories to the grave.

During his *Judgment Day* tirade, Blake drew the line at sharing specifics of his sexual abuse, though he told friends privately that he had been molested as a child, that the molester had been male and that was why he began packing a pistol wherever he went. "The gun was a big thing for him," said one actor who knew Blake well in the early 1990s. "He was molested as a young man, and this was his way of controlling a situation you cannot control. This is how he felt he could control his life and protect himself from what had happened to him: with a gun."

Whatever the truth of his accusations was, *Judgment Day* was a rating success during February sweeps, and Blake won his second Emmy. Robert made a rare public appearance that fall to pick up the award for best actor in a miniseries. In a spot interview with *Entertainment Tonight* on the red carpet, Blake said: "I have had more comebacks than you have hair on your head."

He basked in the limelight once again as he stepped up on stage to receive his award, and he told the audience that the blue tuxedo he was wearing he stole from the Universal wardrobe in 1975 when he was still doing *Baretta*.

It was his final major television appearance.

24

Bonny finally made it into the recording studio in 1990. She recorded *Rock-A-Billy Love*[54] with E. Robert Tellefsen—the stage name of her ex-husband Robert Stuhr.[55] Tellefsen and his Girls Band, which consisted of Bonny and a woman named Wendy G. Williams, made an album that was released on the obscure Norway USA record label. It contained covers of pop standards "Me and Bobby McGee," "Honky Tonk," and "Rock Around the Clock," but its standout selections were the two tribute tracks honoring the musical artistry of Linda Gail Lewis and Elvis. In the Elvis tribute Bonny sang the single most memorable couplet uttered on the entire album: "Rock and roll will never be the same/ Rock and Roll Leebonny is my name."[56]

And who could forget "The Flower of Love"?

> *Stick it up, stick it up, baby if you care*
> *Stick it up, stick it up, in the air*
> *Stick it up, stick it up, one more time*
> *Stick it up, stick it up, the flower of love is mine*

---

54. In the 1970s, Bonny had recorded another demo for a song called "Just a Fan," the refrain of which went: "I am chasing a celebrity. . . . There's no future in it I can see."

55. Stuhr was also responsible for getting Bonny hired as an extra in *Turk 182!* (1985).

56. Another bit of Bonny's poetry read: "When it comes to cars I like a Cadillac/It's the only way you're gonna get me in the sack."

While Bonny thought her songwriting might finally get a rise out of Jerry Lee Lewis, all she got was a smirk. Bonny was never one to be easily discouraged though.

James Rollin Thomas, one of Jerry Lee's road managers, broke her nose at a dive on the outskirts of Memphis one night. Paul Gawron had broken it years before, but there was no opportunity then to collect on the misdeed. Others might have seen her $1,606.95 in hospital bills as a problem, but Bonny saw it as opportunity. While she was still laid up, she was already planning reconstructive surgery that would give her a pert pug nose—a pop star's nose perhaps. She was still phoning DeMart Besly pretty regularly at the time and asked his opinion. He suggested a new nose "styled in the manner of Pinocchio."

Bonny sued and won a judgment of $20,000 against Thomas, but he couldn't pay, so she forced him to sign over his life insurance policy to her instead. Several years later, after Thomas died of natural causes, Bonnie received $87,000 as his beneficiary. She celebrated with a Caribbean vacation and wrote a postcard to her sister, Margerry, boasting: "Good investment, huh?"

Miraculously, Bonny had managed to make it through her twenties without being charged with anything worse than larceny or being convicted of anything more serious than forging a $40 check. The only time she had ever actually been jailed was in March 1989, when Memphis police busted her for drug possession. She claimed that she illegally purchased the prescription drug Demerol so that she could give it to Jerry Lee Lewis, but that made no difference to the sentencing judge, who fined her $552.50.

"She'd do anything to be around my brother," Linda Gail Lewis told author Deanne Stillman. "She was a darker, more sinister version of Kate Hudson's character [in *Almost Famous* (2000)]. There was no stopping Bonny. She was relentless."

"We all knew she was infatuated with celebrities," said Linda Gail's daughter, Mary McCall. "We all liked her. She bought us breakfast after gigs a number of times. We spent a lot of time at her house. Everyone trashes Bonny now, but I remember one person who was good to me."

Linda Gail had once sung backup to her famous older

brother, but by 1990 she was out of the inner Lewis circle. She had married an Elvis impersonator who developed health problems. To make ends meet, she went into business with Bonny for a brief time.

Advertising in a swinger publication called *EIDOS*, Linda's portrait was far more tasteful than her business partner's. Jerry Lee's sister wore a towel, exposing nothing more than a little forty-two-year-old thigh and some cleavage. But Bonny shrewdly calculated that her usual clientele would pay more for the possibility of sex with a celebrity, even if it was celebrity once removed.

When the *London Daily Mirror* learned about this latest of Bonny's many schemes on the eve of Jerry Lee's European concert tour, the tabloid ran an exposé spread over two pages under the headline:

Goodness Gracious! Jerry Lee's Hard-up Sister Is Selling Porn!

Bonny made no excuses for using Linda to get close to Jerry Lee. She wanted the Killer in the worst way and begged both Linda Gail and Judy Howell to help her. She even discussed ways of doing in Kerrie,[57] his sixth wife, to clear the path. When the Lewises finally did divorce in 1991, Bonny celebrated. Unfortunately, the fifty-five-year-old performer announced to the tabloids that he had no plans to marry a seventh time.

"I'm not interested in another girlfriend right now," he told the *Globe*, pointing out that he and Kerrie had Lee, a four-year-old boy, to raise together. "I don't want to do anything that could harm my future with my son."[58]

Two years later, Bonny raised the stakes further in her quest to capture the Killer when she told the *Globe* that Jerry Lee had fathered her third child. Bonny even named the little

---

57. Lewis, forty-eight, married Kerrie McCarver, twenty-one, on April 24, 1984.

58. Lewis's previous sons had as much bad luck as his wives. Steve Allen Lewis, three, drowned in 1962 and nineteen-year-old Jerry Lee Lewis Jr. was killed in a car accident in 1973.

girl Jerilee Lewis[59] in an effort to force the rocker to pay child support. Yet even those closest to Bonny conceded that it was extremely questionable that their sexual contact could have resulted in a child.

"You can't get pregnant from a blow job," said Margerry.

Nonetheless, the *Globe* article won Bonny an invitation to appear on a new tabloid TV talk show called *People Are Talking*. She was aglow with her impending celebrity until she got the word that the show had been canceled before she had a chance to go in front of the cameras.

According to Paul Gawron, the little girl was actually his—as were Bonny's two elder children, Holly and Glenn. Long after they were divorced, Gawron remained "Mr. Mom" as well as Bonny's administrative assistant. He had become chiefly responsible for sending and answering the thousands of letters that came into Bonny's drop boxes each month. Bonny spent less and less time on the business. She was much too busy chasing celebrities or getting married.

In addition to Paulakis, Gawron, Stuhr and Besly, she had also married an elderly truck driver from South Carolina named Robert Moon in the mid-1980s. She got a mail-order divorce in 1987 when she found that she could not cash in on Moon's life insurance policy. "I told her years ago, somewhere down the road, someone's gonna kill her 'cause she's playing everybody," Moon bitterly told one interviewer.

In 1991, she conned Missouri farmer Joseph Brooksher in much the same way she had Besly and Moon. The fifty-seven-year-old widower's mate of sixteen years had just passed away when Bonny solicited him through the mail. They "dated" for six months, then married. On their wedding night, she took his money and drove back to Memphis in his new Ford van. "I didn't even see her after that," Brooksher lamented to the syndicated tabloid TV show *Extra*. "She left in the night. I didn't see her no more."

Though she promised that she'd come back if he contin-

59. Born July 28, 1993, near Lewis' compound in Desoto County, Mississippi.

ued to send her money, Brooksher never did see her again. He didn't wise up in time the way DeMart Besly and Robert Moon had. The aging farmer claimed that he eventually spent four years in prison due to Bonny's bad checks.

Bonny did not always marry for money. Sometimes she did it for the hell of it. Somewhere along the line, Bonny met up with Glynn Wolfe before he died at age eighty-eight. They were reportedly married, at least for a few minutes, so that Bonny could join the twenty-eight other former Mrs. Wolfes in the *Guinness Book of Records*. When he passed away in a San Bernardino nursing home in June 1997, he held the record for having been married more times than any other American male. He was survived by nineteen children, but none of Bonny's were among them.

Bonny's biggest score came in 1993, when she wed William Webber, an eighty-three-year-old Port Charlotte, Florida, widower whom she made the happiest man in the world for a little less than two days. The nuptial bliss ended when she made a stop at his bank.

"All of a sudden the bank calls me up and says he's drawing everything out," said Bill Webber Jr., who lived out of state. But it wasn't his dad dipping into his savings. "*She* was withdrawing it," said Webber.

Bill Jr. left for Florida immediately, but by the time he arrived, Bonny and her sister, Margerry, had slipped out a second-floor window of Webber's condo and hightailed it back to Memphis.

A Florida judge eventually appointed a guardian for William Webber Sr. and froze his bank accounts, but not before Bonny made off with an estimated $350,000, according to the younger Webber. When Webber passed away in December 1999, his guardian said that the old man died of a broken heart.

Throughout these big scores, the day-to-day mailings, film processing and handwritten-letter production continued unabated. Paul Gawron was now middle management, with his own set of subordinates to supervise. Over the years Bonny had trained a whole new generation of younger women in the nuances of Polaroid porn, and she delegated as much as possible to Paul so that she had more free time. She was no longer minding the business as closely as she once had. Celebrity stalking had become her full-time vocation.

25

In 1994, Blake won the role of John Gotti in a CBS biography, but immediately began making nonnegotiable demands of the producers. He objected to a script that deified Diane Giacolone, the Brooklyn federal prosecutor who waged a five-year campaign to nail Gotti while it portrayed Mrs. Gotti as "a shrieking, self-centered bitch." The depiction, Blake deemed, was unfair to Mafia wives everywhere. With another Emmy under his belt, he was battling the suits again.

"I'm up against a bunch of executives who don't know shit from apple sauce, and I'm just about an inch from ripping open somebody's throat and sucking out their heart," he roared. "Those people at the network think because they work on the twenty-third floor, the wiseguys from the street can't get to 'em. The truth is, there'll be a friggin' crater where their houses used to be."

By this time Blake's recast autobiography bristled with a brand of tinseltown tough talk. "I wore a pin-striped suit and carried a gun," Blake said in his latest version of his allegedly troubled teen years. "I did time in jail. One night when we were robbing a liquor store, a cop almost blew me away."

Gotti's attorney Bruce Cutler refused to pull strings to get Blake in to see his client at the federal maximum security prison in Marion, Illinois, but without cracking a smile, Cutler suggested that *he* might portray Gotti in the movie if Blake decided to take a powder. "I'm not saying that out of arrogance," said Cutler. "I know what his beliefs are. I've told the people who know John Gotti: 'Over the next five years, there are going to be fifty Gotti projects. I may be the best Gotti you're going to get.'"

Kushner-Locke Company, which produced the CBS movie, tried to work with Blake and even changed the title from *Getting Gotti: The Diane Giacolone Story* to *John Gotti: A Gangster Boss*, but the concessions were not enough. Blake flatly told the press: "I sure don't need the friggin' Gotti people breaking my legs."

Anthony John Denison finally took the role abandoned by Blake and the producers switched the title back to *Getting Gotti*, giving top billing to Lorraine Bracco as prosecutor Giacolone. As for Cutler's prediction of fifty Gotti projects, only one other emerged: a 1996 HBO biography starring Armand Assante in the title role. To date, neither Assante nor Denison have had limbs broken.

Age and diminishing offers of acting roles did not lessen Robert Blake's hyperbole. If anything, he worked himself into a rage every time he spoke publicly. "You give me a fucking boat full of holes and twelve drunks and I'll row you to fucking China," he said. "But you put me on the *Queen Mary* and I'll fall over and break my leg. That's the way I am. I'm best when I'm coming off the canvas in the fifteenth round—then don't fuck with me, 'cause I'll kill Jesus."

Except for his infrequent TV talk show appearances, Blake's turn as the sinister subway official in the Wesley Snipes–Woody Harrelson–Jennifer Lopez caper film *Money Train* (1995)[60] was the last time that most Americans saw him. "When Robert got the role, I used to go to his house to help him practice," said longtime pal Mario Roccuzzio. "I was like an acting coach. He just couldn't quite put his finger on the key to the character. I asked him: What does the *Money Train* mean to you? He said it was like his possession,

---

60. *Money Train* briefly made headlines upon its November 1995 release, when vandals appeared to have mimicked a scene where a pyromaniac sets fire to a token booth. A booth operator was incinerated and then-mayor Rudy Giuliani joined Republican presidential candidate Bob Dole in calling for a boycott of the picture. When suspects told prosecutors the movie had nothing to do with their actions, the boycott was dropped, the movie made money and Hollywood felt vindicated.

that he had to take care of it. And I said, 'No, it's your penis, Robert, and nobody can mess around with it.' The light went on. He got it. That was the key to the character for him."

Blake took the credit for Roccuzzio's advice. "I want to make the train his cock," he told director Joseph Ruben. "When the train works right, his cock gets hard. When the train don't work, he can't fuck his wife."

Ruben was charmed. Blake was a real actor's actor in a world that had become overpopulated with pampered movie stars. He was "like a thoroughbred who hasn't run for a while," Ruben said. "We needed a bad guy who would have some weight to him. We wanted the audience to understand every time he's on the screen exactly why our guys [Snipes and Harrelson] hate him. Blake was able to deliver that and in a way that was totally unpredictable. He's just a very good, gifted actor."

But to the handful of journalists who still thought Blake worth writing about, he groused more like a choleric old workhorse than a thoroughbred. "It's very different today," Blake grumbled in *Detour* magazine. "Everybody's twelve years old. They've all got a fucking earring and a ponytail. The girl who serves the doughnuts and the producer both look alike and act alike, and from the back you can't tell them apart. And it's a very quiet place. A set used to be very noisy, with a lot of old fat guys with cigars who yelled at each other. Now everybody's got a little thing in their ear, and a little mouthpiece, and they all whisper to each other, eating cauliflower dip instead of bowls of chili and beer."[61]

Reviews were mixed for *Money Train* and its unbelievable plot about adoptive black and white brothers (Snipes and Harrelson) who plot to steal the transit authority's weekly

---

61. The catering at the *Money Train* premiere party was strictly New York: pizza, pastrami, eggplant Parmesan and egg creams spiked with brandy, though much of the movie was shot in L.A.'s Chinatown on a set six-tenths of a mile long that replicated a New York subway. L.A. luminaries Muhammad Ali, Larry Flynt and O.J. attorney Robert Shapiro were among the 1,200 guests who attended the very L.A. party in a 25,000-square-foot warehouse that was transformed into a New York subway station, complete with graffiti, turnstiles and claustrophobia.

trainload of subway fare revenue. The *Los Angeles Times'* Kenneth Turan called it "a by-the-numbers action-buddy picture," but the *Hollywood Reporter* complimented Blake and "his portrayal of a tough-talking transit chief who watches over his Money Train like it was his only daughter."

Blake was paid the same way for *Money Train* as *Blood Feud* and *Judgment Day*: if he cost the production time or capital because of tantrums, it came out of his paycheck. By now he was used to this arrangement and didn't care all that much about the money anyway. As he came up on his sixty-second birthday, Blake was far more concerned with getting back to center stage. He needed his close-up. When he got it, he was barely recognizable.

In 1993, Robert had undergone cosmetic surgery that Blake himself later described as giving him "a lizard face."

"If you make me look like a lizard, like everybody else, I'm going to kill you," Blake had warned his surgeon beforehand. "All I want is to look a little more rested, to take a little of the mileage off."

Instead, the extremely painful procedure left his face unnaturally tight and gave him the "permanent smile" he had dreaded. It also put him out of commission for months. The right ear didn't line up properly, and though his face was unnaturally taut, skin hung beneath his chin. He did not kill his surgeon, but there were those who thought he had a pretty good defense if he did.

"It hurt like a son of a bitch," he told *People*. "The doctors lie to you and say it's a piece of cake, but it ain't. They cut into your scalp, then down behind and below your ears. Then they pull the hell out of your skin."

That same year, he was cited for life achievement by the Young Artist Awards for his work on the *Little Rascals*. It was one of his proudest moments. His life seemed to have come full circle. Following years of psychotherapy, he concluded that his therapist had given him as little for his money as his plastic surgeon and that he was far better off writing the horrors of his childhood himself. He planned to write a book, but not yet. Memoirs were for people who'd finished up their careers. He wasn't quite over just yet.

He celebrated his birthday in 1995 with the slogan 62 AND FUCK YOU.

26

Margerry Bakley remembers well the night that Nicole Brown Simpson and Ron Goldman were murdered because she and Bonny were there. Well, not *there*, exactly. But they were close enough for bragging rights.

"We drove right by that Mezzaluna restaurant on the way to the airport," she said. "We caught the red-eye to Memphis at the same time that O.J. was catching the red-eye to Chicago."

The irrepressible Bakley sisters had come to town the previous week to help Dean Martin celebrate his seventy-seventh birthday. They were among the throng of party girls Martin invited to La Familia restaurant in Beverly Hills, where the Stallion from Steubenville held forth with some regularity in his waning years. While Bonny tried sidling up to Dean, Margerry flirted with Joe, the restaurant owner. He'd given her a small thrill by pushing a button that automated a sliding door leading to a hidden casino at the back of the restaurant. Shades of the Roaring Twenties! Margerry got her second thrill of the evening when someone switched the tape cassettes in the sound system, cutting off an old Dean standard in midcroon and replacing it with the Chairman of the Board singing it his way.

"And then there he was! Right beside me! And I have to tell you, those eyes are as blue as they all say. Old Blue Eyes," said Margerry.

She got so flustered she swallowed some of her wine down the wrong pipe and began coughing, to which Frank

Sinatra advised a waiter: "Turn down the air conditioning. Can't you see this lady's dying over here?"

It was a grand night. Rosemary Clooney was there, and Bruce Dern, and so many other luminaries. Bonny had worked this kind of celebrity magic before, but never on such a grand scale. Margerry could hardly believe her eyes. Her sister certainly knew how to worm her way into high-falutin circles. Just another night on the star circuit for Bonny Bakley—again, it didn't cost her a dime.

By the mid-1990s, Bonny Lee Bakley was roving ever farther out of control. She slept all day and played all night, and always let someone else pick up the check. She had a scam for every occasion. Need a free meal? Go with Bonny for seven courses and you wouldn't even have to pay for coffee. Need gasoline? Pick a card, any card—they all worked at the pump, no matter whose name was printed on them.

She received Social Security checks in all sorts of different names. It was just a matter of getting them cashed, and all that required was ID.

The mail-order business remained Bonny's bread and butter. And it wasn't the rip-off that everyone said that it was either. Bonny knew what she was selling: fantasy, pure and simple. According to her sister, her customers also knew what they were buying.

"Do you really think these sexy models that you see on TV telling you to call their 900 numbers are the ones answering the phones?" asks Margerry. " 'Course not! It's somebody like me on the other end, you know? There's some big fat girl or a faggot pretending they're a woman. But it's not these pretty models that you're seeing on the TV, okay?

"These guys, for $20, buy Bonny's photos thinking they're going to suck and fuck and then she's going to turn into a six-pack at the end of the night! Are you kidding me? It's a fantasy. It's all a fantasy."

Besides selling fantasy, Bonny found that lawsuits were another way to supplement her income. She would pop into her attorney's office fairly regularly with a possible personal damage action—everything from getting popped in the nose to falling down in a convenience store and injuring her tailbone. Bonny once asked her lawyer to sue a Memphis animal clinic for emotional distress because her dog had escaped from the clinic's kennel. When attorney Anthony Helm called the clinic to complain on behalf of his client, he was told the dog was no dog at all. "It was a wolf," the lawyer chuckled. "Bonny was entertaining, to say the least."

Meanwhile, United Singles Inc., as she now called her mail-order business, was thriving. In 1996, she reported an annual income of $24,000. That figure was highly questionable. Bonny had purchased a home and three rentals in the Memphis suburbs, all together valued at $352,000.

Was it any wonder that she had the license plates on her 1984 Mercedes 300TD personalized to read 1RSKTKR for "Number 1 Risk Taker?"

With the occasional windfall she picked up from her aged husbands, she was able to take lavish vacations. Bonny went to Hawaii, Mexico and the Caribbean with best pal Judy Howell. One day just before Christmas 1994, she said, "Let's go to Aruba!" They left the next day.

"I could never afford to go on one of her vacations, but she'd pay for everything and we'd be off," said Judy. "She'd get us in trouble, though."

Being a housewife from northern Mississippi, Judy had no notion of the topless-beach policy in Aruba, so when Bonny removed her bikini bra, Judy was shocked. "Then I started looking around and saw that everybody on the beach was doing it. So I thought, 'Why not?' Well, I lasted about two seconds. I turned about ten shades of red. I just couldn't do it. So I put my top back on and these guys behind us started laughing."

Bonny flirted on these trips, and pretty soon she and Judy would be invited out for a drink. Judy got worried. "Now, I'm a married woman and these guys wanted more than a drink."

She expressed her concerns to Bonny in private and Bonny just giggled. No problem: watch and learn, she said. After the guys paid for the drinks, they wanted to go gambling. When they arrived at the casino, the guys got out first and headed inside. That's when Bonny handed the cab driver a wad of cash and whispered: "Get us out of here."

"We left Aruba on New Year's Eve and came back through Fort Lauderdale, where we stayed at a hotel and ran into some Mafia types from Chicago," recalled Judy.

Again, the guys wanted Judy and Bonny to go nightclubbing. This time they did, and Judy freaked again. Bonny had a knack for getting herself and anyone with her into tight situations.

"It was like one of those speakeasies in the movies, where you knock on the door and they let you in," said Judy. "And there was anything and everything going on inside. Sexually, I mean. Everything! Sex, drugs and rock 'n' roll. They were doing it on the bar, in the corners, everywhere. This was exciting to me, but I knew we could be in for a lot of trouble."

Their Chicago escorts got a charge out of Judy's shocked expression when she beheld the orgy. "I can tell you've never been in a place like this before," one of them remarked.

"No, sir," said Judy, stiffening up. "No, sir, I sure haven't."

Once again, however, Bonny took the lead. She told their male friends she and Judy had some girl talk to tend to back in the powder room. Bonny escorted Judy out of sight and found a side door. Then the two of them skedaddled.

"I got back to Mississippi on January 8, and I've never had a vacation like that before or since," said Judy. "She paid for the whole trip with a mail-order guy's money. It's not like she tried to hoard her money. Bonny was generous. She didn't want anything. She just wanted me there as her confidante. If it weren't for Bonny, I'd never have gone anywhere."

In addition to long, luxurious vacations, Bonny liked to take long luxurious baths—the kind she had been denied as a child by Grammy Hall. At home, Bonny spent hours lying in the tub, talking on the phone. The rest of the time she scrutinized the *Star* and the *National Enquirer* for tidbits on the whereabouts of celebrities. She also studied astrology, numerology and cosmology. Bonny had a morbid fascination with death, maintaining that she could communicate with ghosts and had done so, in fact, after Dean died, when she called upon his spirit for advice on what to do next in her life. Though he didn't answer, she still believed in chatting with the dead, and yet, she avoided anything that reminded her of her own mortality. Bonny refused to eat in the same restaurant with any customer who appeared crippled or terminally ill. Rather than follow a hearse on the highway, she'd superstitiously detour onto an alternate route.

Bonny would also drive her Mercedes or that old Ford van she pinched from Joseph Brooksher for hours—sometimes days—along back roads. Bonny loved to party, the farther away from home the better. "She'd get up around 4:30 in the afternoon and start carousing," said Paul Gawron.

But on occasion, even a gifted grifter like Bonny slipped up. In September 1994, she was caught trying to pass two bad checks—one for $600,000 and the other for $2,000—on the account of a Memphis record company. The Shelby County grand jury indicted her for attempting to defraud the Volunteer Bank, maintaining that she knew full well that neither check was any good before she ever deposited them. Bonny had a different story. She opened her checking account, deposited the two checks, and they both came back stamped FICTITIOUS ITEM. She had no idea they were bad, she said.

"I was corresponding to a Mike Minns for several months from an ad in a matrimonial magazine," she told a Memphis general sessions judge. "He convinced me he was a rich businessman by sending me business cards saying he owned a radio station and also was president of a recording studio. I always longed to be a singer and he said he would manage my career and make me a star.

"I became vulnerable and gullible because I always dreamed of a celebrity status as a child and took singing and hypnosis classes in New York City as a teen. What made his story even more believable was on two different occasions he sent me $1,000 in cash along with his songs with orders for me to find a recording studio and make two different demos that he could play on his radio station and submit all over to others."

Bonny dutifully made the recordings, she related, and one day he called.

"He then said one song was a big hit in Europe and I

would be receiving a large amount for all the airtime soon. That's when he started sending me the said checks that I then halfway believed [to be valid] by now. I figured if it wasn't true the bank would know and throw it away. I didn't know there was a law like this. I don't even *want* a checking account anymore now."

She presented both her demo tapes and the letters that she'd received from Minns as proof that she'd been had, but the court wasn't buying. Bonny was convicted. She got a suspended sentence of three years at the Shelby County Correctional Center and was fined $1,000.

But Bonny just could not seem to stay out of trouble. Before her county case of bad checks had cooled, she and most of her immediate family, along with her half brother, Peter Carlyon, became the focus of a federal extortion case.

Bonny could not be slighted for turning her back on family. When Margerry needed a job, she put her to work on the phones, and when Peter needed employment she welcomed him into the inner sanctum of her mail-order operation.

Beginning in the summer of 1994, Bonny provided Carlyon with the names and numbers of many of her clients so that he, too, could bilk money from them. They agreed that for his work Peter would get $25 an hour plus a percentage of any contribution over $100. Bonny, being the thoughtful big sister, even gave Peter a special device to mechanically feminize his voice on the phone. From his very first client call, Peter was able to become that perfect sexy woman—the kind of femme fatale that subscribers to low-grade sex magazines desperately sought out.

Right off the bat, Peter, gloriously transformed into "Dorothy Shields," developed an amazing rapport with one of Bonny's established clients, a visiting college student from a wealthy Taiwan family.

For several years, the student had been one of Bonny's better clients. Living in Irvine, California, while he attended college, he relieved the pressures of a brutal study schedule far from home by perusing swinger magazines. Finding Bonny's ad, he wrote and, over time, Bonny bilked him for thousands. Unlike many of her marks, however, he was eventually gratified by a three-way home delivery. As Bonny recalled to the FBI, in the early summer of 1994, Bonny, her sister, Margerry, and thirteen-year-old daughter, Holly, all visited the client in Irvine, California. During the visit, all three "dated him," as she delicately put it.

Later that summer, however, it was "Dorothy Shields" making the power play for the client's prurient interests, convincing him to send $1,200 to a truck stop in West Memphis after her car supposedly broke down. It was also "Dorothy Shields" who was rapidly growing dissatisfied with the percentage of money she was getting for all her hard work and ingenuity on behalf of her big sister's business. After several months of making the calls for Bonny, Peter Carlyon concluded he could increase his income substantially by launching an independent venture.

So Peter set up his own shop, using Bonny's database. The client continued to be Peter's top client, which greatly disturbed Bonny, who had never consented to such an arrangement.

Bonny had no choice but to break the news to the client: "Dorothy Shields" was no lady. But he was in no mind to accept reality and continued sending "Dorothy Shields" money. Peter told Bonny that he'd made over $50,000 that year in his new operation, most of it from the client.

In April 1995, he traveled to Memphis to finally meet his mystery love. Peter was ready. He got his wife, Tammie, to pose as Dorothy, and Peter posed as an amiable relative who befriended the client and showed him the sights and sounds of Memphis. Peter introduced him to drugs and a friendly prostitute, and by the end of June, the trap was set. Peter and three friends cashed in on the client's lost weekend in Memphis by posing as Memphis police. They "fined" him $6,871 for illegal activities and he dutifully wired the money as soon as he got back to California.

Peter and pals regrouped a week later and gave the client another call. This time they were the FBI and he owed an additional $32,126.49 in federal fines. Once again, the client complied. Western Union asked why he was sending so much cash and the client replied truthfully—at least as truthfully as he understood it: he was paying FBI fines.

Pete's gang faced a snag when they tried to pick up the

money. Western Union demanded FBI ID to cash the moneygram. None was provided, and the money was returned to the client. Now they had to come up with a new strategy. Peter was stumped. It was time to call in the big guns. He called Bonny.

She was miffed that Peter would be so duplicitous as to scam her customer behind her back, but the prospect of sharing in the booty overcame her annoyance. For half the money, Bonny agreed to step in and show her little brother how the big dogs worked. If she wound up with anything less than her $15,000 however, she told her mother she would settle the matter with a gun.

Bonny crafted a letter, creating a bogus federal "Department of Immigrations," which purported to speak on behalf of the FBI. The letter detailed the client's offense: "aid and abedding prostitution." If he didn't pay fines of over $32,000 immediately, he faced deportation. United once more, brother Peter and sister Bonny traveled out of state to mail the letter safely so that it could not be traced.

The client finally began to grow suspicious. On July 12, 1995, he contacted the Memphis FBI office and told his story. After the father of one of Peter's pals in the Memphis police scam called the FBI with the same story, the bilking was over.

In the investigation that followed, FBI agents seized stacks of nude photos, pistols and a Samsonite briefcase from Bonny that contained liquid Demerol, prefilled morphine hypodermics and a vial of Dilaudid. Bonny maintained that she acquired the drugs from doctors for Jerry Lee Lewis and was merely safeguarding them for the day that Lewis finally came to his senses, left his wife for good and needed a little something to rekindle his passion for Bonny. Under this kind of nonstop law enforcement pressure, Bonny found it was getting harder and harder to play the dewy-eyed innocent. She had developed a bad back and carpal tunnel syndrome after years of writing thousands of phony love letters. She didn't smoke or drink and had given up drugs early, though she periodically went on a diet pill binge to keep off the inevitable thickening of middle age.

"I think they call them yellow jackets," said Paul Gawron. "When I was working sixteen-hour days getting out the mail order, I was taking her pills to stay awake and keep going."

It was not the best medication for one who complained to her doctor about irregular heartbeat, chest pains, migraines, insomnia, muscle spasms and degenerated disc disease. She took Atarax to get to sleep, Skelaxin and Cortisone for the disc condition and a variety of prescription and over-the-counter drugs for her other maladies.

Bonny knew she was obsessive-compulsive because her symptoms matched those of some of the basket cases she'd seen on daytime TV talk shows. She once listed them for her probation officer:

- Don't make sound decisions
- Too imaginative
- Hard to concentrate on one thing without other ideas popping into my head.

"Bonny talked too much sometimes," said Paul Gawron. "Sometimes she just told people things that they didn't need to know."

"She was always worried about saying or doing the wrong thing," said Margerry.

As Bonny approached middle age, she had evolved into a bleached blond, gut-churning "sex goddess."

When it came to intimacy, Bonny was alternately outrageously gross and coquettish as a kitten. But turning forty changed things. Lately, in her personal life, Bonny had been trying desperately to become a very different kind of woman. Respectable maybe, at least on the surface. In order to do that, she had to bag herself a celebrity once and for all, before it was too late.

27

Jerry Rubin called Robert Blake to tell him the ten-year anniversary of the Great Peace March was March 1, 1996, and a reunion was to be celebrated on the steps of Los Angeles City Hall where it all began. Former mayor Tom Bradley would be on hand to praise the dogged few who had stayed the course, and Robert Blake was to be feted with a chorus of "Amazing Grace" as one of the Great Peace March's saviors carrying the futile message of a nonnuclear future to deaf ears in Washington.

Blake had fought for a number of good causes in the eighties, but he was no longer interested. "I'm not as involved as I once was," Blake explained to Rubin. "But give my love to everyone."

He found himself increasingly watching from the sidelines as another generation—most of whom hadn't been born when Robert did his finest work—hit their marks in Hollywood.

He saw his son, Noah, trying to step into the old man's shoes and come up wanting. Noah's career was floundering in sitcoms like *Harry and the Hendersons* and guest turns on *Growing Pains, The Wonder Years,* or *Diagnosis Murder.* The boy would be better off getting more stage work under his belt. Of course, Noah wasn't really a boy. He was a man in his mid-thirties. When Robert was a man in his mid-thirties, he had a wife, two children, a mortgage and a bona fide career as a serious film and television actor. Noah was still playing in a rock band. So what happened?

To some, Blake was an icon. Dylan McDermott of ABC's *The Practice* listed Blake and Clint Eastwood as major influences on his career. Blake was now of an age where young actors sought him out, looking for guidance, and he gave it freely, but it wasn't always what they wanted to hear. To begin with, he told them, acting classes were a waste of time.

"You cannot become spiritual by talking about religion," he said in an interview in *Back Stage* magazine. "The more lame your imagination, the more technique you need. If you have the child's imagination, you need no technique."

Young actors paying out hundreds of dollars to some acting coach would be better prepared, he said, if they spent a night in a hospital emergency room or walked alone on a winter beach at three a.m. or stole a fifth of Jim Beam from their corner liquor store. "There's no greater concentration in the world than being a fucking thief."

As if to emphasize Blake's status as a has-been, CBS announced in 1996 plans to remake *In Cold Blood,* starring Julia Roberts' brother, Eric, in the Perry Smith role. "Compared to the '67 film our version is ruder—and I do mean R-U-D-E-R," proclaimed Roberts. Ruder it may have been, but according to the critics, better it was not.

On one level, Blake could have cared less. This remake mania that had swept over Hollywood in the previous decade was beyond free market commerce at its most heinous. It was just plain stupid.

Blake had been putting his own efforts into trying to bring more contemporary biographies to the screen, like that of United Farm Workers founder Cesar Chavez or tortured country music legend George Jones, whose lifelong battle with booze Blake hoped someday to develop into a greenlighted script. He called on contemporaries, like actress Sally Kirkland, who had some success creating their own production companies.

"I said, 'I don't know, Robert. I'm exhausted from tracking down my six gross points that they haven't paid me from the last one I produced,'" recalled Kirkland. "But I did encourage him. I think all actors have to eventually get their feet wet with producing themselves, because otherwise you go batty waiting for the phone to ring."

Sometimes it seemed like he'd do anything just to get a little media attention again. In 1996, Blake was a guest on the explicit radio sex advice program *Loveline.* During the half dozen appearances Blake made on Tom Snyder's *Late Late Show* on CBS in the late 1990s, he was "very highly strung," according to Snyder. Blake dug deep into his Hollywood memory, pulling out anecdotes about his shooting sprees with Steve McQueen or his drunken rampages with actor Nick Adams, both of whom had been dead more than twenty years. And as always, he blamed all of his bad-boy behavior on the alleged abuses that he had had to suffer at the hands of his parents when he was a child actor.

"He was always exciting. And dangerous," said Snyder. "Every night when he left the studio, the crew and I would speculate about what would happen to Robert. The feeling was that someday we would read or hear that he had shot and killed someone. And that if we did read or hear it, we would not be surprised."

Lost Highway (1997)—director David Lynch's eerie celluloid nightmare about a paranoid husband falsely jailed, then miraculously freed following his wife's murder—would be Blake's last feature film. In it he was billed simply as the Mystery Man—a strange gnome in mime's white face who hectors the husband (Bill Pullman) just before his wife (Patricia Arquette) is killed.

Before he agreed to take the part, Blake himself said he didn't understand Lynch's script. He wasn't alone. Even the perceptive Janet Maslin of the *New York Times* struggled to understand what Lynch was trying to say. In trying to describe the film's inexplicable story line, she said *Lost Highway* "constructs an intricate puzzle out of dream logic, lurid eroticism, violence, shifting identities and fierce intimations of doom."

Still, Blake said, "I told David I'll do the part if I can do my own makeup."

"He came up with the white-face himself," said Bill Pullman. "He wanted his ears pushed forward, so he put all this wax behind his ears every day to poke 'em out."

Blake's makeup became a high point of an otherwise bizarre and muddled movie. "A cellular phone and a video camera are all it takes to turn Mr. Blake's screen character into the scariest gnome since the red-cloaked dwarf in *Don't Look Now*," wrote Maslin.

Others didn't even know it was Robert. "I assumed it was some other Robert Blake," said *New Times* critic Andy Klein. "But, no, this is Baretta, looking totally different without his cockatoo."

Blake attended the premiere at the Cinerama Dome on February 18, 1997, surrounded by new-generation celebrities like Billy Bob Thornton, rocker Alanis Morissette and director Wim Wenders. Much as he did at the cast party for *Money Train*, at the bash that followed the premiere, Blake remarked on how radically things had changed since the smoke-filled rooms, creaking buffets and flowing booze of his day.

"Now it's a whole different world. You got thin people. From the back, they all look alike. They're all little quiet people, dressed dark, and they dip cucumbers in something. I feel like I belong in the La Brea tar pits."

On the romantic front, Blake still had a torch of sorts for his former wife. Sondra lived nearby. She moved into an apartment near Dilling Street, and Blake saw her from time to time, usually in plays or jazz clubs.

"He loved her for twenty years after they divorced," said longtime friend Mario Roccuzzio. "Robert loved Sondra. He adored her. She was the love of his life. It was like Sinatra and Ava Gardner, Romeo and Juliet. Only Sondra didn't feel the same way about Robert."

In 1997, she landed a guest shot on an *E.R.* which seemed to vindicate that she no longer needed her ex-husband's help getting TV jobs.

They remained friendly—friendlier than at any time in the last few volcanic years of their marriage. At one point, Blake even got the impression that she might want a second chance. "He once met her at the top of Mulholland, and they got back together, for about five minutes," said Roccuzzio.

Blake thought about it and discarded the idea of a rapprochement. He and Sondra were still poison to each other.

So when he saw her at the Jazz Bakery or Chadney's in the late 1990s, he'd duck out the back way like a teen trying to avoid an old girlfriend.

Blake remained enamored enough of the ladies that he still hung out at the Playboy Mansion, even though he no longer socialized much. He'd been a regular guest at Hugh Hefner's fabled Holmby Hills estate since the early 1970s, when Richard Brooks first introduced him to Hef. According to *Rolling Stone* magazine, Robert once peed in Hef's koi pond, but nobody stopped him. Hefner's standing orders were that security was not to interfere with him.

"I have seen him from time to time at the Sunday-night screenings, but he was an irregular attendee," said one mansion regular. "He was kind of a loner, not a big talker. He was like a lost sheep, not talking to anyone. I don't know who his friends were."

On a more ominous front, his passion for gun collecting had grown to the point that he boasted he had a different firearm for every room in the house. He obtained a concealed weapon permit from the Culver City police department, and he packed everywhere he went. He wore long, loose-fitting black jackets to hide the holster and the bulge, and spent hours shooting in the desesrt.

"Robert liked to take long drives out into the desert," recalled Mark Canavi, who worked for a time as Blake's personal assistant. "He would get into his van, and he would just barrel on the freeway and go up to places where he had shot Westerns as 'Li'l Beaver' when he was working at Republic as a kid."

Blake asked Canavi to accompany him once. Blake drove the two of them far off any well-traveled roads and then made an odd request.

"I mean, we're out in the boondocks," recalled Canavi, "and he stops the van. And he says, 'I've got to get out and pee.' I say, 'All right, fine, do what you have to do.' And he said, 'Do you have to pee?' I said no. And he said, 'I've got to teach you how to relax. I've got to teach you how to pee in the mud.' And I say, 'What the hell are you talking about? I don't have to go, Robert.' And he said, 'Well, it'd be all

right if I peed on one side of the van and you on the other.'
I said, 'Robert, I don't have to go!'"

Canavi thought the urination ritual odd, but odder still
was Blake's propensity for exercising in the nude. After Canavi been working at the Dilling Street house for several
weeks, Blake would show up sweating from his workout
buck naked and stand in front of Canavi, grinning. "I told
him to put on a towel or something," said Canavi. "I mean,
I told him it's inappropriate. And he just laughed."

Canavi quit after that. When Blake invited him to breakfast several weeks later, Canavi explained that he'd quit because he thought Blake might be coming on to him. Again,
Robert just laughed.

"He's so wacky at times that maybe he just wanted to see
how I would react," said Canavi. "I don't know. To this day,
I just don't know. Some people are like that. But I'll tell
you: he scared the hell out of me."

Stephen Cannell, Blake's old friend and production associate from his *Baretta* days, blamed Blake's reckless behavior on fading machismo.

"Old guys who see the end of the road coming get
goofy," said Cannell. "I mean, it happens." Nobody ever
guessed he'd soon get married again, least of all to a celebrity stalker.

ACT III

Stardust Memories

In the third act of my life, hopefully I will make up for the first two. I will have people around that love me.

—Robert Blake during a 1993
Entertainment Tonight interview

28

Over the Thanksgiving weekend of 2000, a veteran stuntman named Roy "Snuffy" Harrison hooked up with the son of another veteran stuntman at the Los Angeles County Raceway in Palmdale. They had both come for the "Day in the Dirt," a three-day extravaganza that attracted a broad swath of Hollywood, ranging from the movie stuntmen organizations that sponsored the annual holiday ritual to the kind of blow-dried studio executives that Robert Blake once took such pleasure in skewering as "suits."

The "Day in the Dirt" had become Southern California's unofficial grand prix of off-road motorbiking, and the rough and tumble of Hollywood—the Teamsters, the wranglers, the outlaws and their biker babes, the men and women who drove a thousand stunt cars at breakneck speeds—were out in force. If the people who took the fall for Hollywood had an unofficial annual reunion, this was it, and the father of the young man Snuffy Harrison had come to see was one of the best known among them.

Roy "Duffy" Hambleton had been leaping out of cars, off motorcycles and over cliffs for most of his sixty-three years. He'd once been married to Kitty O'Neil, a legendary stuntwoman who not only held the women's land-speed record but had been stone deaf since childhood. Her life story even inspired a TV movie that Duffy produced.[62]

---

62. Starring Stockard Channing as Kitty and James Farentino as Duffy, *Silent Victory: The Kitty O'Neil Story* aired over CBS in 1979.

Once Harrison corralled young Hambleton, he told him that he'd recently been speaking with Robert Blake, who had been a onetime stuntman himself back in the 1950s. Robert had come up with a terrific idea for a movie based on the "Day in the Dirt," said Harrison, and Blake had thought instantly of Duffy.

Robert Blake loved dirt biking. He'd once told *Daily Variety* reporter Will Tusher that, next to sex, taking a motorcycle out in the middle of the desert was about the best way he knew to lose weight. "That's the equivalent of them fat ladies that put them belts on and shake," he'd said. "I don't think there's a better exercise in the world than dirt-bike riding. Every muscle in your body is going all the time, and at great intensity."

Hambleton didn't do much biking himself anymore. That was for younger, fitter men. When he'd worked as Blake's stunt double on *Baretta* and *Joe Dancer,* he could have ridden circles around anybody in Hollywood, but now he lived a relatively quiet life in semiretirement on a three-acre spread out in the high desert southeast of Palmdale. He'd recently battled leukemia and prostate cancer, and hadn't worked in a while.

He had an ornery reputation too—worse than Robert Blake's, if that was possible. Kitty O'Neil had long since divorced Hambleton, accusing her ex of trying to kill her. He'd once taken a life insurance policy out on her before one of her land-speed runs, she said, and the lug nuts were mysteriously loosened on her wheels. Even more curious was the fact that the parachute that was supposed to help her brake had been laced with battery acid.

O'Neil maintained in an interview with the *National Enquirer* that her ex-husband had boasted of killing others—an assertion that he apparently had made to others over the years: "Duffy's a wicked man. He often bragged about killing other men, including one for Robert Blake and one man because of [revenge for] his father. He tried to kill me! That's why I left him."

Duffy denied attempting to murder his wife, of course, but never denied having a temper. He'd busted many chops in his time, packed pistols, brawled and generally trafficked with all kinds of low life. When two San Bernardino County sheriff's deputies had come snooping around his ranch in recent months, investigating a report of a thief seeking refuge there, Duffy pointed a rifle at them and told them both to get the hell off his land. He would soon be going to trial on that one.

But he got along well enough with Blake. Robert thought Duffy might be interested in getting back into show business, if it were strictly on an advisory basis. Snuffy Harrison asked if young Hambleton could get a message to his old man to call Blake.

After they parted, Harrison scanned the crowd for Bobby Bass, another stunt veteran. He'd been told that Bass was supposed to be there, even though the stuntman had developed Parkinson's disease to such a degree that he could no longer work.

Bass was even better known in the business than Duffy Hambleton. The sixty-four-year-old stuntman was a legend. He'd crashed cars, leaped out windows and taken punches for everyone from John Wayne to Sylvester Stallone in a career that spanned thirty-five years and more than forty movies. Was it Susan Sarandon and Geena Davis who drove their car over a cliff at the end of *Thelma & Louise* (1991)? No, sir, that was Bobby Bass.

Bass creamed muscle cars in *Smokey and the Bandit* (1977), taught Mel Gibson how to butt heads in *Lethal Weapon* (1987), fell out of aircraft in *True Lies* (1994) and tempted death in *To Live and Die in L.A.* (1985), for which he was honored by his peers for performing the best vehicular stunt of the year. And like Hambleton, Bobby had once done stunt double work for Robert Blake on *Baretta*.

His last film was the Arnold Schwarzenegger thriller *End of Days* (1999), but Parkinson's had slowed him to where he could only coordinate stunts. He still put in appearances at events like "Day in the Dirt," though, and Snuffy scanned the crowd, expecting to find him.

He did not. Nor did Harrison run across a third stuntman that Blake told him that he was looking to hire: Gary McLarty.

Harrison had been pestering McLarty to call for two

months. One morning in September, McLarty had pulled out of his driveway at his Sylmar home and did a double take. Snuffy Harrison was waiting for him. He flagged McLarty down to tell him that Robert Blake wanted to talk with him. He even handed McLarty Blake's unlisted telephone number and said he ought to give him a call.

He never did call Blake, but in a way that was understandable. Though the jobs might not be rolling in as fast as they did when he first started back in the mid-1960s, McLarty was still looking for work as either a stunt coordinator or a stuntman. He was preoccupied with making a living, not a has-been's pipe dreams about a dirt-bike movie.

McLarty had cracked up countless cars in well over one hundred movies and TV shows during nearly forty years in the business, including *Convoy* (1978), *Beverly Hills Cop* (1984), *Last Action Hero* (1993) and the biggest demolition derby of them all, *The Blues Brothers* (1980).

He was there the day director John Landis staged a chase sequence in which a police car went out of control on Lake Street in downtown Chicago. It rolled over, hit a cameraman's station wagon and knocked it one hundred feet. People nearly died in that one. In the next Landis movie that McLarty worked on, people *did* die.

Gary was best known as one of the pilots who crashed a helicopter leading to fatalities on the set of *Twilight Zone— The Movie* (1982), the most infamous stunt in Hollywood history. Before dawn on July 23, 1982, actor Vic Morrow and two child actors were sliced to pieces when a helicopter crashed next to them in the Santa Clara River bed during a Vietnam War escape scene. McLarty testified for the prosecution after Landis and four others were charged with involuntary manslaughter. He was to be the prosecution's star witness.

But Deputy D.A. Lea D'Agostino credited McLarty with losing the case after he testified that Morrow wanted to do the more dangerous stunts himself. It was Morrow who resisted efforts to use a stunt double. Following a closely watched ten-month trial, the jury acquitted Landis and the others.[63] Landis rewarded the five women and seven men for their verdict with an exclusive advance screening of his next film, *Coming to America* (1989).

Rather than being blackballed from the industry, McLarty continued to get jobs. A working stuntman could pull down a couple hundred grand a year. In addition, McLarty could handle second unit work and had both his SAG and AFTRA cards to boot. At one time or another, he had done just about every job there was to do in Hollywood, from acting to directing. With his twenty-eight-year-old son, Cole, starting to get noticed for his own stunts in films like *Speed 2: Cruise Control* (1997) and *Stigmata* (1999), McLarty appeared to have founded a dynasty.

Like Hambleton and Bass, Gary McLarty first came to know Robert Blake from his stunt work on *Baretta*. With his thick black hair and short but muscular torso, McLarty even resembled Blake. He'd also worked with him on *Coast to Coast* and still ran into Blake from time to time along Ventura Boulevard or at one of any number of industry events.

They were friendly enough, but McLarty was short with him. He had a lot on his mind. He'd recently been through a nasty divorce, aggravating an already precarious fiscal situation. Despite forty years of credits, producers just weren't that interested in hiring a sixty-year-old stuntman. His most recent film job had been *The Mod Squad* (1999), and it showed in his bank account. McLarty's income had dropped from a whopping $217,000 in 1995 to just over $5,000 in 2001. He needed a real job, not Blake's dirt-bike project in the bush.

Blake's initial call to sixty-five-year-old Snuffy Harrison had come out of the blue sometime in the late spring. Harrison hadn't seen Blake since his *Baretta* days either. The two of them had been getting together at least once each week ever since.

---

63. Harland Braun was one of the defense lawyers in the *Twilight Zone* case.

The former *Baretta* star called Harrison so often that Snuffy became a kind of professional liaison. He certainly didn't mind. Like Hambleton and Bass, Harrison had health problems: a heart condition that made it impossible for him to earn the kind of living he once did. In addition to the TV work on *Baretta*, Snuffy had once flown with *Charlie's Angels*, crossed swords with a guest star on *Fantasy Island*, and coordinated the stunt work on the prime-time soap *Pacific Palisades.*[64] His movies included *The Untouchables* (1987), *The Abyss* (1989) and *Total Recall* (1990), but there hadn't been any more feature films for quite a while.

Snuffy liked Blake. He was different from most stars. Blake had his ego, to be sure, but he understood who got the pictures made. Blake had never been above hanging with the crew. He appreciated the hard, painful effort that it took so that a stunt looked like the real thing on camera. And he genuinely cared about the little guy who did his job, signed his time card and headed out the studio gates to the nearest cocktail lounge to unwind.

Lately, they'd been on the phone to each other more than a dozen times during the week before and after the first of October. That was the week that Blake snatched his kid back from that broad he knocked up a couple years back. . . .

But that was a whole other story.

---

64. With thirteen episodes in the can, the Aaron Spelling project was supposed to be Joan Collins' comeback following *Dynasty*, but never made it to air.

29

Back in Arkansas, Bonny was growing restless. She wanted to return to California now that she was officially Mrs. Robert Blake, but her probation didn't end until January 29. After the child-snatching fiasco in September, there was no way she was ever going to get her probation officer to let her leave the state early. She was stuck inside of Little Rock with the Memphis blues again.

Bonny had finally married a celebrity, though, and that was worth celebrating. Blake quit changing his phone number every other week and grudgingly took her calls now. He assured her that little Rosie was fine. He did point out that Bonny really needed to change the child's name to Rose Lenore Sophia Blake, in honor of Blake's cousin Rosie Newick back in New Jersey.

"She bought all sorts of stuff and sent it out to Blake to have a playroom made, so that when she got there, the baby would have her own nursery," recalled Margerry. "She sent high chairs, cribs, clothes. We're talking shipping costs and everything. She even sent out a camcorder. She didn't have the baby with her, so she told Blake, 'Take pictures so I can see them. It's our daughter's first Christmas.'"

All told, Bonny spent $3,000.

"And this slob goes and gives everything to the Salvation Army, including the camcorder," said Margerry. "Bonny was furious. She'd never spent anything like that on any of her other three children, and he just goes and gives it all away! She felt like she couldn't say anything, though, because money didn't seem to mean the same thing to him."

Blake had bonded with the baby in Bonny's absence. He even let the little tyke sleep in the same bed with him, which was more than Bonny could say for herself. To make herself more appealing to him, she began looking into plastic surgery. In the early 1990s, she had spent $5,000 to have laser eye surgery and remove the crow's-feet from around her eyes. A face-lift would remove the unsightly lines from around her mouth and neck.

She'd also read about a new procedure in which a small incision could be made at the navel and a tube inserted beneath the skin, to pump up her breasts. They would stand at attention the way they had when she was a teenager competing in the Miss Nude Northern New Jersey pageant. She put the surgery on her "to do" list, along with the annual Botox antiwrinkle treatments that she'd started having done the previous winter in Florida.

"She would do whatever Blake wanted to please that creep," Judy Howell said.

Bonny also switched her hair color from blond to brown because she thought it would make Blake happy. She shopped at thrift stores for vintage clothing because she believed he wanted an old-fashioned girl. Instead, he took to calling her "Raggedy Ann." She was hurt but undaunted.

Bonny was now a star's wife, and she meant to make the most of it. She sent Christmas cards to everyone she could think of who mattered, and wrote in them, like the one she sent to Larry Flynt: "Hi! I just married Robert Blake. We need to get together." She did not bother to send a card to DeMart Besly to hit him up for holiday cash as she usually did, though. Besly had died on Christmas Day 2000.

For several years DeMart's health had been failing. He had no direct heirs and he wasn't going to put Bonny in his will, no matter how many times she asked. He left most of his property to a young couple from Darby who had moved in to take care of him near the end. But Besly did leave something to an aging niece.

Dawn Dupré lived a Bohemian existence with her eighteen-year-old cat in Santa Monica. At first she was miffed that all Uncle DeMart had left her were several yellowing old manuscripts. He fancied himself an author in addition to his many other accomplishments, and Dawn wound up with most of his unpublished efforts. One had a note attached to the cover that read, "This may be worth something someday." It was the book titled "Ubiquitous Bonny, Mistress of Sham."

Dawn cracked it open and read the unbelievable tale of her uncle's final fling with a younger woman—and what a woman! There were photos too, some so awful they made Dawn blush. An amateur graphologist, Besly had analyzed Miss Bonny Lee Bakley's handwriting and concluded that he'd married the worst Jezebel on the planet. Besly predicted Bonny would die someday in a most unpleasant way, and probably at the hand of one of the many men she'd ripped off. According to Besly, the playwright George Bernard Shaw made the point perfectly half a century before Bonny was born:

> Old men are dangerous because they have no future. Old men are no longer afraid. They can treat all convention with contempt and can say and do terrible things.

Back in Little Rock, Bonny was preoccupied with getting her mail-order business shipshape so that Paul could take over come February. "She slept all day and was up all night," said Gawron, who continued to live with Bonny and raise her three older children. "I think she just, you know, didn't like her life. When I saw her, she'd get up around four thirty p.m., we'd go out to dinner, come home, do the mail order and I'd go to bed so I could get Jerilee off to school in the morning."

When she wasn't sleeping, Bonny moped around the house. Paul couldn't figure it out. She'd gotten what she wanted, hadn't she?

"All these years you've been chasing after a rich guy," he said. "Now you got a rich guy. So what's up?"

"Well," she began, "I don't want him to think I married him just for his money."

Paul laughed. "Well, you did. You know you did."

A week before Christmas, something strange happened at

Bonny's place. Holly wanted to go fishing, so she sent Glenn out to fetch her tackle box from the back of Bonny's car. Down among the leaders, floats and split shot was bait of a very different variety. Glenn pulled out several bundles of a white powdery substance and took it in to his mother. What was their antidrug mom doing with enough cocaine to stay loaded for a week?

Bonny had no explanation. She hadn't put it there. It was far more likely that Glenn or Holly was responsible, since they'd both been busted for drugs up in Memphis. Both of them vehemently denied it. That set Bonny to wondering: Was it possible that Robert had planted it? If she was caught with cocaine while she was still on probation, the offense would automatically tack at least another year onto her sentence. And Blake had demonstrated by his actions that he was not anxious to have her come out to California to join him and the baby.

One morning, she blurted out over the breakfast table: "Think this guy's going to kill me?"

Paul did a double take, but then he lectured her about her evil ways. "You know, everything you're doing is exact opposite of what the Lord would tell you to do," said Paul, newly eloquent in his faith following his recent conversion. "The Lord says He'll give you anything you ask for, but you got to do it according to the rules. You're breaking every rule in the book. Satan has always tried to copy God. You may get what you want here, but you may die the next day after you get it."

Paul wasn't exactly boosting her morale. Gawron thought she was profoundly depressed. What he didn't realize was that Bonny Lee Bakley was in love. "See, Blake wasn't controllable like the mail-order guys," observed Judy Howell. "They are desperate; he wasn't. She always felt like she had to be in control until she fell in love, and then she was *not* in control."

"Everything pissed him off," said Margerry. "He'd scream, 'Nobody talks to Robert Blake that way unless they're six feet under or out of state!' So Bonny would try to make a joke out of it and say, 'Well, I *am* out of state.'

And it pissed him off even more. He took everything too damn serious."

Bonny taped every word Blake said. For as far back as she could remember she had been taping her phone calls. She had every celebrity she'd ever spoken to on tape: Redd Foxx, Chubby Checker, Robert DeNiro, Peter Falk . . .

And now she had Robert Blake.

She played one of her more voluble exchanges with her new husband for her probation officer. He thought Blake must be on something.

"The probation guy goes: 'Are you sure this guy's not drinking or doing drugs? He's too erratic,'" recalled Margerry. "One minute he's nice. The next minute he's screaming and hollering. There was something wrong with him because you never knew whether he was being nice or being nasty. He was up and down, all the time, always threatening to kill himself:

"'I'm going to *kill* myself! I'm going to blow my brains out. But don't worry. *You're* coming with me! I've already got a bullet with your name on it.'

"This was said over and over again. And it wasn't something to be taken lightly. I warned Bonny. It was a threat. It was a constant threat."

Bonny didn't agree. He was just being Robert—all bark, no bite. She wasn't about to screw up her marriage just as it was about to begin.

As for money, she didn't need to beg him for cash. United Singles Inc. was now grossing $50,000 a year, and there was no reason why it couldn't make more. She'd built up the business and now had $17,300 in a savings account in Little Rock and another $14,200 in checking and savings at the First Tennessee Bank in Memphis. She also owned two homes in Memphis as well as the one she had purchased in Thousand Oaks, California, in 1997. Her total real estate holdings had increased in value to $450,000. Blake could say what he liked, but Bonny was a woman of independent means.

She gave Paul last-minute instructions to get off a round of letters and check her nearby mail drops. Then she began packing. Her probation ended right on schedule on January 29.

That same day, Robert Blake went to the Culver City Police Department to renew his concealed-weapon permit. Then he awaited his wife's arrival.

<u>30</u>

Robert had to wait until March before Bonny showed up.

Instead of flying directly to L.A., she left in February for Dover, New Jersey, to visit her sister and conduct some business. She had mail drops near Dover, and they hadn't been checked in a while. Envelopes with cash were undoubtedly waiting. If she was going to see Robert, she figured she ought to bring as much spending dough as she could because he sure as hell wasn't going to pay for anything.

When Bonny did finally fly to L.A., Blake didn't even meet her at the airport. He was busy and would have little to do with her. She spent most of her first week at the Beverly Garland Hotel. She had no idea what Robert was doing.

He finally told her she could move into the split-level guest house behind his main residence. Given his bachelor ways, that was probably a blessing because the place was a mess except for one room. Rosie's nursery stood apart as sweetly decorated in blues and yellows, with teddy bears everywhere.

The guest house was cozy enough for Bonny's purposes anyway: it had its own kitchen and den in addition to the bedroom in the loft and sliding glass doors that opened to the grassy backyard behind the main house. She would have preferred living in the main house with Robert, but he said no. He still didn't want to sleep with her.

"This is too new for me," Blake told her. "I'm used to living alone."

That was fine. Bonny could be patient. But she did want to see the baby, and she didn't want to feel like a prisoner in her own home.

"He didn't let her use any of his cars," said Margerry. "He'd make that Earle drive her around. She didn't like Earle, and she didn't want him taking her places and being nosey. She didn't want to talk to the guy. She didn't really care for him."

Bonny began to see yet another troubling side to Blake's complex personality. His personal assistant, Earle Caldwell, followed him around like a puppy dog, and Blake seemed more solicitous of Caldwell than he did of Bonny. Blake struck her as being peculiarly close to Earle—so much so that: "She thought maybe Robert Blake and him were gay, having an affair or something," said Margerry.

Earle Caldwell was certainly loyal. Blake found him a year earlier at Sam's Stereos, where the forty-five-year-old installed sound systems for a living. When Sam's went out of business, Robert offered him a job. Earle looked strong enough to crush someone's skull yet he didn't have the stomach to step on a snail. He said he was married, but his wife lived 300 miles away in San Mateo. Earle also had a girlfriend who lived near his Burbank apartment. An odd arrangement by Memphis standards, Bonny thought, but then, this was L.A.

Unknown to Bonny, Robert had sent Earle to Arkansas in December on a mysterious mission around the time that Glenn and Holly found cocaine in the tackle box in the back of Bonny's car. Blake also didn't tell his wife about the shopping spree that he sent Earle on a few weeks after he returned from Arkansas. According to a list Earle scrawled on a yellow scrap of paper and stuffed in the cup holder on the dashboard of his Jeep, Blake wanted him to purchase two shovels, a small sledgehammer, a crowbar, some old rugs, duct tape, Drano, pool acid and lye. Earle also made the notation "get blank gun ready" after an entry that simply read ".25 auto."

In addition to running errands and acting as Bonny's bodyguard (or, as Bonny told her sister, her "shadow"), Earle cleaned Blake's extensive collection of weapons. Blake boasted that he had a different gun for every room in the house, and Bonny could see the truth of it with her own eyes.[65]

In a rare departure from his usual contempt, Blake had once warmed enough to Bonny in the weeks before their November marriage to get her to pose for photos holding various pistols from his collection.

"He wanted her to caress the barrel, like it was his dick," said Judy.

When Bonny told Margerry about the photo session, Margerry told Bonny she was crazy. "I said, 'Bonny, don't let him do that to you! You're on probation! He's either going to turn them into your probation officer and tell him you're playing with guns or he's going to kill you and say you did it yourself because your fingerprints will be on the gun'."

Bonny just giggled and told her sister not to be ridiculous. Now she wasn't so sure. She began thinking maybe she'd made a mistake. Perhaps she should have stayed with Brando. At the same time she was settling in at Blake's place, she phoned Christian and sent off a love letter enclosing photos of the baby. Brando remained her backup in the event things didn't work out with Blake. Because Brando was young, tall and handsome—everything Robert was not—Blake hated him. Whenever Bonny brought up his name, Blake sarcastically referred to him as "Golden Boy."

She began demanding to see little Rosie Lenore Sophia. When Robert finally relented, it was only for an hour and under the watchful eye of a supervisor Blake hired to make sure Bonny didn't abscond with the baby.

Try as she might, Bonny was beginning to see her initial hope of establishing a real family with Blake dashed. After less than two weeks in California, she told Blake she had to

---

65. During a subsequent search of Blake's Mata Hari Ranch, police only recovered a Smith & Wesson model 4013 stainless steel .40 caliber semiautomatic handgun and its magazine, containing six hollow-point copper-jacketed rounds.

go back to see her sister in New Jersey and attend to business in Memphis.

Though he did not approve, Blake was well aware of his wife's business. Instead of tapering off, Bonny's scams picked up steam after the marriage. She had hundreds of victims, broken into four categories:

- Old & rich
- Young & rich
- Doctors
- Attorneys

In a nineteen-page computer printout of Bonny's business notes from Friday, March 30, 2001, typical entries read:

- He is old, dignified, a Master Mason, University Order of the Amaranth . . . thinks he is rich. He is a trustee of a firm & I would become the trust trustee if I married him. Was going to send me $1,000 at one time. . . .
- He has race horses, retired, 46, has two settlements coming. One couple worth thousands & other couple, million. Number not listed.

It was inevitable that Bonny would discover the Internet as another source of income. On the "Women Seeking Men kinky personals" Web site,[66] Bonny's ad appeared next to a topless photo taken of her when she was still in her early twenties. The ad read:

I'm looking for a new love. You must be too because you are reading this ad! I'm lonely due to a recent broken engagement. I'm told I'm very pretty but don't worry. It hasn't gone to my head. I'm not real particular about men's ages or looks. I feel this is not important as long as you're nice. I'm 22 and can travel to meet you if you can't. Write soon and cheer me up!

---

66. The Web site posts pictures and provides forums for men and women to advertise sexual services, a perfect venue for some of Bonny's schemes.

I have time to answer all and visit some until I meet the right one, then I'm done. Miss Bonnie Bakley . . .

Before she left L.A., she set up a mail drop at a postal shop on Ventura Boulevard, a few blocks from Blake's house, and did her first mailing as Mrs. Robert Blake. That same week, forty-six-year-old Stu McNally of Van Nuys found an unsolicited letter in his mailbox that began, "Hi single guy."

Bonny claimed she was being evicted from her apartment and needed about $200 for rent, but would settle for $20 to play the lottery if that was all Stu could afford. "Don't worry, I'm not fat," she wrote. "I promise I never will be. I'm into sex with the right man who I want to have a relationship with. I do hope it's going to be you."

It was signed "Miss Lee Blakely."

Bonny arrived at Margerry's apartment on March 25. She said that Blake hadn't given her a dime.

"He said he gave her $10,000 a month since the baby's birth, $20,000 to pay a big debt and $30,000 to come up to New Jersey to visit me," said Margerry. "Maybe that's why she had to go out to Wal-Mart and buy a $30 air mattress so she could sleep on the floor of my son's bedroom. She never had $30,000. I have a copy of her TRW report. There were never any debts paid. Bonny paid her own way. Always."

She stayed with her sister through the end of March and the first week of April. Seeing an opportunity to turn her sister around, Margerry took her to church. They had both been raised Baptist, but Margerry had recently converted to Catholicism. The church changed her life. She thought it might change Bonny's too. During Bonny's first Mass, Margerry told her she could cross her arms, go up front and get a blessing from the priest, even though she wasn't a member of the church.

"Everybody could use a blessing," Bonny said, and joined the procession.

The following week Bonny accompanied her sister to Mass again. This time there was an anointing of the sick—"a spiritual healing mostly," according to Margerry.

"I said, 'Why don't you go up? Maybe it'll help your

carpal tunnel syndrome.' I thought she was too much into astrology and all that crazy stuff, but she was all for it!"

Shortly after that, Blake called, saying he wanted her to come back to California. Bonny was hesitant. If she came back, she told him, she was bringing her sister with her and she was going to drive herself in her own car so that she wouldn't have to put up with Earle chauffeuring her everywhere.

Robert was fine with that, especially the plan to bring Margerry along. He proposed that they meet in Phoenix and go for a holiday on the Colorado River—a sort of belated honeymoon.

Bonny could hardly believe her ears. There had to be a catch.

No, not at all. Robert had made all the arrangements. They'd spend a little time in the casinos up around Laughlin and get some sun, relax, go boating up at Lake Havasu. He knew that Bonny loved to swim. What better place to swim than the Colorado River?

Bonny grinned as she put down the receiver and winked at her sister. Got him!

"I could see right through what was happening all along," said Margerry. "I didn't agree with what my sister was doing to him. There was a point when I felt sorry for what she was doing to him. But murder is wrong. There is a better way to deal with things. You reap what you sow."

31

Duffy Hambleton thought Blake's idea was a good one. Out in the Lucerne Valley where Hambleton lived, there was certainly plenty of interest in dirt biking. A "Day in the Dirt" movie sounded like a winner to a semiretiree who hadn't worked in a while. When he got Snuffy's message about arranging a meeting with Blake, Hambleton decided to go.

They met one afternoon in mid-March at Du-par's restaurant on Ventura Boulevard in Studio City. "The third booth from the front was where he always sat," recalled a waitress who identified Blake as one of her regulars. "He ordered the same thing every time: grilled cheese sandwich, fries and a Sprite."

Duffy arrived with a younger friend named Nate Henry, but when Blake saw Nate, he became antsy. He told Hambleton that he had to speak with him privately. Nate shrugged, offering to wait. Blake and Duffy went across the street to another restaurant.

There, Blake asked Duffy if he would mind coming to Blake's house with him. He had something that he wanted to show him.

At Blake's Mata Hari Ranch, Blake got right to the point. He hadn't called Duffy about making a movie. Blake began hauling out photos of nude women and lurid letters from which he read excerpts aloud. They were obscene pleas for money. These photos, these letters—Blake told him—they were mailed out to men all over the country by *Blake's wife*! He knew she was bad when he married her, but he didn't know how bad. She was worse than a whore, and Blake had made the mistake of having a child with her. Now he was worried that his little girl would grow up to become a porn star like her mother.

"She'll have a fucked-up life," Blake complained bitterly.

Blake hated this woman. He wanted her dead. He unzipped a gun casing and displayed a .25 caliber semiautomatic pistol. He told Hambleton that it had no identifying markings and was thus untraceable. If Duffy would do the deed, there would be a handsome payday: $100,000.

Hambleton did not say no.

Blake took him for a drive around the neighborhood. He pointed out a nearby Italian restaurant—Blake's favorite, as it turned out. Vitello's, it was called. Blake cruised slowly down the alley behind Vitello's as well as up and down the nearby streets. He pointed out quiet, secluded spots where Blake might park his sleek black Dodge Stealth one evening. Then Duffy would quickly sneak up on the passenger side and—pow! End of wife.

Hambleton still did not say no, but he had a suggestion. He told Blake that if he stopped at the nearest 7-Eleven store and picked up an AT&T prepaid phone card, Blake would be able to phone Hambleton in the future and there would be no billing record for the calls.

Blake drove Duffy back to Du-par's. A patient Nate Henry paid his waitress and drove a silent Duffy Hambleton back to the desert.

But Blake and Duffy would meet again.

Snuffy Harrison called the headquarters of Stunts Unlimited, the unofficial hiring hall for Hollywood's best-known stuntmen. He wanted to call Bobby Bass at his home in Harbor City to ask the former *Baretta* stuntman to give Robert Blake a call, but the secretary wouldn't give out Bass' number. Instead, she told Harrison she'd call Bass herself and ask him if he wanted Blake's telephone number.

"No," said Snuffy before hanging up.

Snuffy finally got Bass' number and called him himself. Bass hung up on him too.

But Snuffy was not an easily discouraged middle man. He

also tried Gary McLarty again in mid-March. This time Snuffy was more urgent, and McLarty gave Robert Blake a call.

On March 19, the two met at Du-par's. Blake was sitting in the same booth where he had seen Duffy Hambleton. Robert asked Gary to come with him for a ride in his Stealth. They went to Blake's ranch and out came the letters and the lurid photos, proof of mail fraud. On top of that, this woman was now living on his property, though she would be gone until sometime in April.

Blake took McLarty to the separate guest house at the rear of his property and showed him where Bonny lived. She slept upstairs, in a loft. Downstairs were sliding glass doors that could be easily popped out. It would be little trouble for someone to break in.

"And bump her off while she was asleep," said Blake. Just walk right in and "pop her while she was asleep in her bed," he reiterated. "She's killing me, so I want you to kill her."

McLarty wondered if he'd heard right. Was he being asked to kill Blake's wife? And if so, did it have anything to do with McLarty's own troubled past?

In 1991, McLarty had shot and killed fifty-year-old ex-con Donald Deppe, who had been living with McLarty as a houseguest. Deppe had a history of threatening people, and that was enough for the courts to rule that the shooting was self-defense. Still, that made McLarty a bona fide killer, justified or not, and Blake knew it.

They went for a walk around the neighborhood. The serene shady parklike streets around the Mata Hari Ranch were an odd contrast to the violence McLarty heard coming out of Robert Blake's mouth. He laid out a scenario in which he'd escort his wife down to the water's edge along the Colorado River, near Bullhead City, Nevada. It would be nighttime—no one around. McLarty could hide in Blake's van. Then, from out of nowhere, she could be shot. Blake offered proof of how serious he was by pulling a small automatic pistol out of a zippered gun case. McLarty was noncommittal. Blake drove him back to Du-par's.

So, Blake wanted to know, how much would this cost him?

McLarty didn't answer.

"How's $10,000 sound?" Blake asked.

Again, McLarty didn't answer.

Three days later, Blake was on the phone wanting to know McLarty's answer.

The answer was no.

"Why not?" Blake demanded.

Because it was murder. McLarty didn't want anything to do with it. He hung up, thinking that was the end of it.

Duffy met with Robert Blake two more times, but this time Blake had to come to Hambleton. They rendezvoused at a coffee shop in the tiny desert town of Pearblossom.

Blake still liked the idea of doing it somewhere near Vitello's, but now he had another plan that might even be better. He suggested the same roadside scenario as before, with Blake at the wheel and Bonny sitting next to him. But instead of having to deal with the police, they could drive her out to a prearranged spot in the desert, where Blake would have a couple graves dug and a guy standing by to shovel the dirt.

A *couple* of graves?

At that point, gears began whirring in Duffy's head. How convenient it would be to kill the killer and bury him next to the victim. Then there would be no question about payoffs. Blake could keep his $100,000 and still be rid of his problem.

Even if Blake wasn't that devious, Hambleton still had his leukemia to think about. It was only a matter of time before he went to his own grave anyway.

"I probably wouldn't be alive long enough to spend the money," he told Blake.

Not to worry, said Blake. He'd take care of Hambleton's family.

Duffy made his decision. No deal. He thought he knew who that second grave was for, and he wasn't quite ready to take his last dive.

32

When she heard many months later about Blake's meetings with the stuntmen, Margerry had her own guess as to who that second grave was for, and it wasn't Duffy Hambleton.

"It was for me," she said.

On April 5, 2001, the Bakley sisters set out for L.A. in Bonny's Mercedes, stopping first at the vital statistics office in Little Rock. According to Arkansas law, Bonny had one year from the date of her daughter's birth to change her name without additional court costs. As a sign of good faith, she changed Christian Shannon Brando to Rose Lenore Sophia Blake as of April 6, 2001.

They continued driving from Little Rock to Dallas, where Bonny planned to conduct some business. On the way, they heard frequently from Blake via cell phone.

"What's taking so long?" he demanded.

Bonny threw him back one of Perry Smith's best-known lines from *In Cold Blood*, when the two killers are trying to make money by retrieving empty Coke bottles off the shoulders of the desert highway. "Well, they don't throw out bottles like they used to," said Bonny, hoping Blake would get both the film reference and her sarcasm about how financially strapped she was.

It went right by him. Instead he told her how anxious he was to see them both. Margerry didn't like the alternately fawning and controlling tone of Blake's voice. He creeped her out, and she told Bonny as much. When they got to Texas, Margerry opted to turn back.

"I feared for both of our lives on the way west," said

Margerry. "That is why I left from Dallas. He had bad intent. I told her I am not going out there and risking my life and leaving my son without a mother. When he asked me to join them miles away from civilization, I refused to go. I was convinced that if he got Bonny and I alone in the desert, he'd kill us both."

Bonny continued on to Phoenix to meet Blake, but kept changing her plans. She had a possible score in Phoenix and didn't want Blake watching how she worked.

"Bonny had a criminal mind, no question," said Judy. "If she had put it to a different use, there's no limit to what she might have been able to do."

One of Bonny's junior partners operated out of the Phoenix suburb of Tempe, and she had a prize client: a shy 300-pound computer nerd named Wally. She and her partner used to joke about "Wally's World," which seemed to consist of a computer screen, an Internet hookup, a refrigerator and regular delivery of dirty pictures.

Wally did not like human contact. Once a week, at the same time, he would leave an envelope containing cash on his front porch, and Bonny's partner would drop off a new assortment of beaver shots. The arrangement had been going on for months. Bonny reasoned that, as long as she was going to be in town anyway, she would take the scam to the next level.

Without consulting her partner, Bonny paid Wally a visit. She knew he wouldn't come to the door, so she left a suitcase containing some of her most outrageous lingerie on the front porch along with a note saying she'd be back later.

When she returned, the suitcase looked as though it hadn't been touched, but her note was gone, so she left another. Several notes later, Bonny got the message. Wally would never emerge from his world. Bonny admitted defeat and headed for the border.

During her Phoenix sojourn, Blake called her cell phone constantly. When was she going to get there? When could he expect to see her? How much longer?

She told him she'd meet him in Kingman, on the Arizona side of the border, then called back again and finally settled on Blythe, just across the California line. On April 19, she met Robert and his loyal sidekick, Earle, and they spent the night at a Blythe motel.

It was not a propitious beginning. Bonny sprinkled the tub with bath salts, floated off in a dream and flooded the bathroom. Blake yelled at her, and she apologized. She was so elated about seeing him again that she'd forgotten to turn off the water.

"She would go to the bathroom and stay in there forever and he didn't like it, but that was her thing," said Judy. "What she was doing was primping, maybe studying herself to see how she appeared to men."

The threesome continued north along the Colorado River to nearby Parker, Arizona, the following day, checking in at the Blue Water Inn and Casino. Bonny and Blake had adjoining suites while Caldwell had a separate room. They rented boats, went fishing and gambled. Bonny gave Earle $70 to play the slots and he won enough to pay her back, but she wouldn't take it. The big old goof started to grow on her.

Blake told Earle to drive Bonny's Mercedes back to Dilling Street and deposit it there along with most of her luggage. She wouldn't need much to wear, he said, laughing.

Earle said he'd remain in L.A. if Blake didn't mind, but Robert insisted that he return. Bonny felt safer when he was around, he said.

Once Earle returned, they moved on to Lake Havasu— Blake driving his old Ford Econoline van while Caldwell followed in his Jeep. After Havasu, they continued farther north to Laughlin and Bullhead City.

On the banks of the Colorado at Bullhead City Blake finally became amorous. He'd told Bonny a week earlier about a fantasy he had of a woman drinking tequila from a bottle just before French-kissing him and then administering oral sex. Bonny made a face. She was not fond of tequila or anything else stronger than white zinfandel, but she said she'd give it a go if he substituted rum for tequila.

"When they got to the desert, Robert bought her a cheap bottle of 151 rum," said Margerry.

They waited until dusk and headed for the Colorado River. When Bonny asked what had become of Earle, Blake told her not to worry. He'd sent him up river to go fishing.

Bonny looked around and, seeing as they were alone, undressed and lay down in the sand. Blake dropped his trousers and was about to mount her when Caldwell showed out of nowhere, complaining that he was sick. He bent over and threw up in the bushes.

Bonny watched in confusion as her husband, naked from the waist down, leaped up and ran to Caldwell's side. He stood with his arm around Caldwell.

"It's okay, it's okay," Blake said in a low, comforting voice. "Don't worry about it. I'll have someone else do it."

That's when Bonny noticed that Caldwell had a gun in his hand.

"She thought maybe Robert Blake and him were gay, having an affair or something," said Paul Gawron. "In her eyes, everything got related to sex. So she thought they were close, whispering in each other's ears, touching and stuff like that."

Bonny later told Margerry, Judy and Bobby Stefanow that she had concluded Caldwell was supposed to show up and kill her that evening. He didn't have the stomach for it, which is why he threw up when he stumbled upon them, apologizing to Blake for his last-minute jitters.

Judy told her she was nuts. If Blake was pulling these kinds of stunts, Bonny should just pack up and get out. Bonny sighed.

"At least I'd die happy," she said.

They spent a week in the desert before heading to Sequoia National Park. On April 27, the Blakes and ever-present Earle Caldwell checked into a $240-a-night two-bedroom cottage at the Gateway Restaurant and Lodge just outside the park. Blake knew the area well. He owned property nearby on the Kaweah River and often went there when he wanted to get away.

"They were having fun," Caldwell reported later. "They were in the river, splashing around, swimming, having a good time."

He recalled the two of them holding hands, kissing and picnicking on the riverbank. The guide they hired to take them into the park got the opposite impression.

"Robert totally ignored her," guide Gary Tomlin told the

National Enquirer. "Never held her hand and insisted they sleep in separate beds at their motel. There would be total silence between them as they walked. He never touched her or did anything romantic."

Blake took the queen-sized bed while Bonny slept on a cot. They were just as chilly toward each other in the great outdoors as in the tepid indoors.

Late one afternoon, the trio climbed to the top of Moro Rock, a landmark lump of granite sticking out of the Giant Forest area of Sequoia. A steep quarter-mile staircase of a trail ascends 300 feet to the summit, where spectacular views can be had all the way to the Pacific Ocean to the west and Mt. Whitney to the east. Once they had climbed to the top, the three looked around and saw that they were alone. Robert told Earle, "I'm cold," and sent him all the way back down to the van to fetch Blake a jacket.

Once she and Blake were alone, the passion began. Bonny later told Bob Stefanow that they were finally getting intimate when Earle returned, and she was sure he had a gun in his hand. It was almost dark, but Bonny could see Caldwell begin to shake and sob. He bent over and threw up. In a reprise of Bullhead City, a half-naked Blake quickly stepped over to his driver.

"It's okay," Blake told him in a soothing voice, hooking his arm around Caldwell's shoulders. "I'll take care of it. I'll get someone else."

The odd couple plus one also scaled 400 steps to the top of Sequoia's Hospital Rock,[67] guided by a Tulare County fire chief, but once they returned to the bottom, macho Earle told everyone he was going to race all the way back to the top by himself. When he returned, he became so sick that Blake ran into the bar at the Gateway Lodge, shouting that his bodyguard had collapsed. The bartender called 911. Paramedics diagnosed altitude sickness and drove Earle down to the Kaweah Delta hospital thirty miles to the west.

---

67. So called because in 1873 early settler James Everton stayed here to recover from a gunshot wound he got after stumbling into a shotgun snare that had been set to trap bear.

Blake, saying he was too tired to follow the ambulance, sent Bonny in his stead. Earle was treated and released, and Bonny brought him back up the mountain. Bonny started to warm to him a little more. He really wasn't such a terrible person.

According to Margerry, Bonny spent as much time talking with Caldwell about Blake's idiosyncrasies as she did talking with Blake himself—a man she was now describing as volatile, masochistic and misogynistic. Bonny's delusions finally seemed to be fading. She told her pals that her celebrity husband was turning out to be nothing more than an egocentric crybaby with a hair-trigger temper.

Even though the Blake party was booked at the Gateway Lodge through April 30, they checked out a day early and headed home to Studio City and the final week of Bonny Lee Bakley's life.

33

On May 1, for the first time since the day before their wedding, Bonny made love to her husband upon their return from Sequoia. It wasn't mind-blowing or intensely passionate, not for her at least. Blake was not exactly a reciprocal lover. Bonny told her phone pals that sex with Robert had deteriorated over the past three years from "good to bad to worse," and yet she put up with it, as he still represented unprecedented stability to her.

"I asked her why in the world she was staying with him and she told me she just wanted to be happy in her life for a change," said Margerry.

She wasn't happy having Earle Caldwell around, though. The same day that she and Blake finally had postmarital sex, Earle set out on a weeklong trip to San Mateo. He didn't leave voluntarily. Blake told him to take some time off because Bonny didn't want him there. She considered herself tolerant about such things, but after how chummy she'd seen Blake get with his bodyguard in the mountains and out on the Colorado River, Bonny decided that enough was enough.

"Do you think he's gay?" she hissed to her ex-husband Paul.

"I've never known the guy," said Paul. "I've never spoke to him. I don't know anything about him. All I know is what you say, and I don't believe half of what you say anyway."

Blake assured Caldwell that he wasn't being fired and that there would be a job waiting for him when he got back. He just thought that it would be a good break for Earle to take a little time off and visit his wife, whom Caldwell hadn't seen in months.

For his part, Earle thought he and Bonny were just starting to hit it off during their sojourn in the Sierras. In addition to his primary duties as her bodyguard, he saw himself as peacemaker between Bonny and Blake. He later quoted his volatile boss as instructing him: "I'm sixty-seven years old. I got this beautiful baby. As long as the baby's happy, I'll do anything. We'll get this to work."

But there were enormous problems to overcome, beginning with their schedules. Bonny and Blake rarely saw each other. She stayed up all night and slept until noon while he hit the sack early and rose at dawn. They constantly quarreled over money. Despite the prenuptial agreement in which Bonny effectively signed away all her rights to his fortune, Blake regularly accused her of trying to steal from him, just as she had all the other men in her life. As a result, Bonny never asked for money. She began operating her porn business from his Mata Hari Ranch—not out of choice, according to Margerry, but necessity.

"I don't want him to think I married him just for his money," Bonny told her sister repeatedly.

Bonny still rarely got to see Rosie, whom Delinah now raised as if Rosie were her own daughter and not her half sister. Blake kept postponing Bonny's requests to see the baby, appearing to do everything in his power to sever any remaining ties between mother and daughter. Bonny's hectoring had now escalated to a din on the matter of Rosie, and guaranteed a pitched battle between herself and Blake even on the best of days.

Bonny was also convinced that Blake had her phone bugged because he knew details of her most private phone conversations. That's how Judy Howell figured Robert knew they were planning to reclaim Rosie.

"She and I planned a kidnapping," said Judy. "We were going to get that baby back. I think that is what got her killed. I feel guilty. I think he was taping us, or overheard it and it forced him to do something."

During a 4½-hour phone conversation on the evening of Monday, April 30, Judy advised Bonny in a step-by-step scheme to retrieve Rosie and return her to Memphis. Blake had already promised to take Bonny to see the baby the night of Thursday, May 3, but Bonny feared it would be a repeat of her last visit, when one or more "supervisors" stood by to make sure the visit was short and that Bonny had no tricks up her sleeve.

"I could handcuff myself to the bottom of the sink at Delinah's house and they would call the cops and then I could take the baby and leave," Bonny suggested.

"Don't do something stupid," counseled Judy. "You go see the baby Thursday night and insist on taking her home with you. If they resist, go outside and call the police. They'll let you take your own baby."

Judy came up with three possibilities for the rescue of baby Rose: If Blake let her have the child, Judy would fly to L.A. and take Rose home to Memphis. If he did not, Bonny would somehow steal Rose and spirit her off to the airport herself. If neither option worked out, Bonny would call the police, show them the birth certificate and take legal custody.

"She never could do anything alone. She always had to have someone with her," said Judy. "She was supposed to call me after she did or did not get to see the baby."

But the call never came because the Thursday visit was postponed until Monday. Angered by the delay, Bonny put up such a fuss that Blake promised her that they wouldn't be leaving Rose with Delinah. They'd bring the baby home to Dilling Street with them. Cryptically, Blake added that if anything ever happened to either one of them, the baby should go to Delinah.

Bonny gushed, but then began to worry. Later that same day when she told her sister what had happened, Bonny said: "It was too easy. He's going to do it. He's going to kill me."

Yet in the next moment, she would wax on over the possibility of a fairy-tale ending. Buttressing those hopes, Blake asked her to join him in house hunting. They began cruising the San Fernando Valley each day, ostensibly looking for a new place to move once Blake sold his Dilling Street home.

"That week, after they had returned to L.A., Blake began

driving around the Valley with Bonny every day, mumbling something about 'looking for just the right spot,'" said Judy.

Bonny told Margerry the same curious story. "Blake drove up and down different streets, and if he found a spot he liked, he pulled over, got out and told her to stay in the car while he looked around—like he was casing the area," Margerry said. "Bonny asked him what he was doing, but he said, 'Just lookin' around—no big deal.' Bonny didn't know what to make of it."

But even those oddly pleasant drives were punctuated by arguments and mood swings. According to Blake, he and Bonny had been arguing all week long about Holly and her boyfriend coming to stay with them. Holly's boyfriend had been busted four times for DUI and Holly had her own history with drugs and alcohol. Blake's worst fear was that her entire family would begin moving in, one by one, until they overran the entire compound. Soon, he'd be tripping over Margerry, Holly, Paul, her younger brothers Joey and Peter—it would never end. Blake didn't want Holly or her boyfriend near his property, but Bonny vehemently stuck up for her daughter. The pressure between the two continued to mount.

On Thursday, May 3, Bonny called her mother and related a chilling conversation she'd had with Blake the night before: "I've got a bullet with your name on it!" he snarled.

"I'm not just some dumb country girl, you know," Bonny retorted. "I must be kind of smart. I got *you* to finally marry me. I got myself a movie star and nobody thought I could do it."

"Girl, you better remember who you are fucking with," said Blake. "I'll kill your ass!"

To add to the growing tension, Bonny made a disturbing discovery in Blake's exercise room, located just down the stairwell from Bonny's room. A red-and-blue sleeping bag had been carefully laid out on the floor, but it had obviously not been slept in, according to Margerry and Judy Howell. Bonny inferred that the sleeping bag was a not-so-subtle allusion to Blake's final TV appearance, in *Judgment Day: The John List Story.*

"John List was from New Jersey, just like Blake," said

Margerry. "He executed his mother, his wife and his three children, and then placed them all in sleeping bags."

Nearly five years after the release of *Lost Highway*, Blake's real-life drama would also soon revolve around the nightmare of his wife's murder—a fact that Bonny's friends and relatives maintained was no coincidence.

"Everything that happened in Blake's movies happened to Bonny," said Judy Howell. "Everything about him came from his movies, including the way he talks: his 'dese' and 'dats.' 'You can take dat to dah bank, and dat's dah truth.' His life *is* his movies."

Margerry talked to Bonny half the day Friday, May 4.

"That last day she was on the phone with me from eight a.m. to two thirty p.m.," said Margerry. "My sister would talk to me for seven, eight hours at a time every day and, I mean, I'd fall *asleep* on the phone with her. I would pretend my battery was dead and hang up."

She kept repeating that Blake was going to kill her because of her demands about the baby. "He told her, 'I've already got a script written out for you,'" said Margerry. Bonny was disturbed, but unnervingly calm about her predicament. She had become so fatalistic that she even told Margerry which reporter to contact at the *Star* supermarket tabloid, and which of her photos to distribute to the media upon her death.

Bonny tried to call Judy later in the day, but just got her answering machine. Bonny's normal giggle was absent from the message she left: "Wish you were home. I am a little bit worried. I will call you back later."

Robert took her out to dinner that night. They ate at Vitello's, sitting at table 42. When the pianist saw Blake come in, he smiled and played Robert's favorite song, "I Remember You."

34

Ron Ito knew the minute he got the call that the Bonny Bakley case was going to be more than a sixty-dayer.

It was just before midnight of May 4, 2001, and in the LAPD's Robbery Homicide Division, the clock starts ticking the moment a detective is handed a new case. If it's not solved in sixty days, everything gets written up. Every call, clue, search, interview, tip, lead, gumshoe adventure—it all goes down on paper. The idea is that the unsolved crime can then be turned over to someone new if the original cop on the case moves on to other work. Some people call this continuity. To Ito it was a migraine.

"You're called out in the middle of the night," he said. "It's cold and wet. You're in an alley and some guy is lying there, no ID, no witnesses. And *you* have to find out who the killer is in sixty days."

If Ito ever needs a reminder of how maddening a sixty-dayer can become, all he has to do is look out Parker Center's back door to Judge John Aiso Street, formerly San Pedro Street. When the respected L.A. Appellate Court jurist was murdered in Hollywood nineteen years earlier, Ito drew the case as a rookie.

"Judge Aiso was about eighty when he died," he recalled. "I put a lot of time and effort into that one. I even had $125,000 in reward money. And to my horror, I could *not* solve it. It has never been solved."

Ito assumed the judge was pushed down by a bum who was either too loaded or schizophrenic to realize what he'd done, or who wound up dead himself before he could confess to killing Aiso. Regardless, Ito now had to endure a running joke in Robbery Homicide: "Hey Ron! Which of your cases is the next street gonna be named after?"

Ito smirked. L.A. still didn't have a Robert Blake Avenue. He knew the Bonny Bakley murder wasn't going to be a sixty-dayer. This one looked more like a sixty-weeker.

"Sometimes you have a real whodunit," said his partner, Brian Tyndall. "Sometimes you get a smoking gun. Ron and I never seem to catch those."

Brian Tyndall was as bald as Kojak and a sharp-dressed man, favoring blue pin-striped shirts, red rep ties and suspenders. He wouldn't join Ito as his partner on the Bakley case for another two months, however, because he was heading up a probe into a long-running police corruption scandal at LAPD's Ramparts Division.

For the time being, and especially in the first few hours following the murder, Ron Ito was on his own. Poring over the initial police report, Ito picked out the facts quickly. Bonny's assailant shot her twice at close range: once in the head and once in the shoulder. She'd been sitting in the passenger seat of Robert Blake's Dodge Stealth when the killer stepped up to her open window and fired. Robbery didn't appear to be the motive, as nothing was taken. And despite the relatively busy location—a residential street a block from a popular restaurant early on a Friday evening—there were no witnesses.

Robbery Homicide Division captain Jim Tatreau soon assigned detectives Steve Eguchi and Robert Bub to assist Ito in the early days of the investigation. The three detectives were called out from the North Hollywood Division to interview Blake. The actor remembered some things very specifically while other facts were indistinct. That wasn't especially unusual with a surviving spouse who had just been through the trauma of seeing his mate moments after her murder. But other oddities leaped out to the detectives.

For one thing, Blake said he left a gun behind in the restaurant. He had a concealed-weapon permit to carry it, and explained that he did so because Bonny wanted protection. But how many people walk off and forget a loaded .38 caliber pistol?

For another thing, he was the only one who seemed to recall there being any gun. Neither Steve nor Joe Restivo, the two brothers who operated Vitello's and had known Blake for years, saw any gun. The waitress who took the Blakes' orders didn't see it. Neither did the busboy or the bartender or any of the other patrons.

Moreover, Blake told investigators that when he and Bonny first left the restaurant, he didn't see anyone. Then, a little later, he revised that. The investigators' report read:

> Blake said he saw an older male after exiting the restaurant. This person was walking in front of them in the same direction and turned right into a house. Blake never saw him come out. Blake said this individual caught his attention because the manner in which he was dressed reminded him of his father.

It was at this point that Blake suddenly remembered leaving the gun behind at Vitellos's. His chief concern was not the danger that a loaded weapon might pose in a crowded restaurant, but that he might lose his concealed-weapon permit. Actor James Caan had apparently lost his permit, Blake told police, and he didn't want his revoked too.

"Holy shit, I left my gun in the restaurant," he recalled telling Bonny. "I'm going to lose my license. I'll be back in thirty seconds or something like that."

"'Okay, honey,'" Blake recalled her telling him. Then he added, "Bonny liked that gun."

When he returned a few minutes later, Bonny was still sitting in the front seat of his Dodge, but he said she appeared to be asleep. When the cops asked if she had been attacked while Blake was retrieving his gun, he answered, "Are you asking me or . . ." Then he caught himself.

"That's how it must of happened," he said, adding that she had appeared "perfect" when he first left her.

Next, he said, he knocked on a couple of neighbors' doors.

"There wasn't a motherfucker [who] would answer the door," he grumbled.

At the corner of Kraft and Woodbridge, across the alley

from the restaurant, Blake finally found his Good Samaritan—film director Sean Stanek, a local resident.

"You've got to help her," Blake implored Stanek. "You've got to help my wife. She's bloody, she's beaten. Oh my God. She's bloody, she's bloody, my wife is bloody. They beat her up, she's been beaten."

Stanek asked where she was and Blake pointed diagonally across the street at a Dodge Stealth parked in front of a Dumpster. He stared at Blake, noted his dilated eyes and wondered if he weren't just a drunk, angry husband who'd been slapping his wife around and taken it a step too far. Blake's hands didn't appear scratched or bleeding, so Stanek went to a phone in his back room and called 911 while Blake waited in the living room.

"Tell them to come!" Blake shouted.

While Stanek was still on the phone, Blake headed out the front door and back to Vitello's. He later told police he was going to see if there was a doctor in the house, but then, Blake had told Stanek that he was going to make a phone call.

"I thought it was strange that he wasn't going back to his wife," said Stanek.

Back at Vitello's, Blake stood inside the entry alcove and yelled for a doctor. He got an off-duty nurse instead. Teri Lorenzo-Castaneda stopped eating when she heard Blake call out. Blake was asking a waiter for a glass of water as Castaneda rushed up and asked him what was wrong.

"It's not me. It's my wife," said Blake.

"What's wrong with her?" asked Castaneda.

"I don't know," Blake answered.

He hurried out the front door. Castaneda was at his heels, still asking him all the way down the block what was wrong with his wife.

"I thought it was strange that he only said there was something wrong with his wife, rather than telling me his wife was injured and bleeding," Castaneda later told police.

When they were within several yards of the car, Blake finally came as close to telling the nurse what was wrong as he was ever going to.

"She isn't moving," he said. He told Castaneda the story

about going back to retrieve his gun, but kept getting the name of the restaurant wrong: Vitello's, where he had eaten three times a week for more than ten years, had become "Aroma's."

But Castaneda had heard enough. She ran ahead to the car and found Stanek already hovering over the passenger seat, trying to wrap a towel around Bonny to keep her warm while he remained on the line with a 911 dispatcher via his portable phone. Stanek tried talking to Bonny, but all he heard was labored breathing. Oddly, he also noticed that her right shoe was missing.

"What is wrong with her?" Blake shouted as he ran within a few feet of the car, but never close enough to see what Stanek and Castaneda were doing. "What happened to her? What happened?"

Castaneda took over from Stanek, trying to administer first aid, but she already knew it was a lost cause. Bonny bled from her mouth, eyes and nose, as well as from a neat round hole in her right temple. As the nurse checked for a pulse, Bonny gasped her last breath. Still frantically trying to bring Bonny back from the dead, Castaneda asked Blake one more time: "What happened?"

"We ate at Aroma's," Blake repeated. "Did we get robbed?"

At that point, an ambulance rolled up. Blake sat on the curb, hyperventilating. Stanek sat down beside him.

"What happened?" Stanek repeated the question.

Blake told the story again: he'd gone back to the restaurant to retrieve something. When he returned "not even a minute" later, there she was.

"They must have beat her up," he told Stanek. Then he wanted to know: had she been robbed too?

Stanek got to his feet and walked to the hood of the car, where paramedics had left Bonny's purse.

"Did she have a wallet?" Stanek asked Blake.

"No, no, she doesn't have a wallet," said Blake. Then, a beat later: "Yeah, yeah, she—she does." Stanek heard Blake mutter under his breath that he knew that this was going to happen.

Blake asked for a glass of water and Stanek ran back and

forth from his house three times to refill the glass for Blake, who gulped it down and then began throwing it back up.

When the police arrived, they put Blake in the back of a black-and-white and drove him back to the station for further questioning. On the way to the station, he went off on tangents during the interview, relating a story from the time when he was only nineteen years old and saw someone beaten with a hammer when he welshed on a gambling debt. Blake appeared to be equating that incident with his wife's death.

And the non sequiturs continued back at the station too. "Bonny started to use that car [her Mercedes] and now she is dead," said Blake.

He spoke of a John from New Jersey who tried to kill Bonny in 1999 after working with her for years in the porn business. John attempted to crash a car while both he and Bonny were in it, "like a suicide pact."[68]

Blake spoke of a suspicious two-door blue van that was parked outside his house one night and how he had armed himself with a Blackhawk revolver and a flashlight before going to investigate. When the driver saw him, the van suddenly backed up and took off around a corner. Blake didn't get a license number.

Blake then spoke of another person who walked by the house one night and how both he and his bodyguard, Earle Caldwell, noticed the suspicious nature of the pedestrian.

But the most fantastic stories he spun were about his wife and her peculiar method of making a living. All of the detectives remarked on how thoroughly he trashed his dead wife's life and reputation mere hours after her brutal murder.

Sitting in the backseat of the squad car, Blake said, "It's

---

68. John Ray was a legally blind business partner whom Bonny eventually married while she was living in Memphis. The "suicide pact" was actually an incident when Ray was sitting in the passenger seat as Bonny was driving late one night and he suddenly grabbed the steering wheel, trying to run her off the road. According to Margerry and Paul Gawron, it was an act of revenge because of Bonny's promiscuity, not a suicide pact.

all my fault," then repeated a comment he'd made to Stanek while sitting on the curb beside the Dodge Stealth: "I knew something like this was going to happen."

When one of the detectives asked him what he meant by that, Blake began, "Well, she . . . " Then he stopped. "I'll tell you when we get to the station," said Blake.

But as near as Ron Ito could tell from reading the report, he did not tell them when they got back to the station. In fact, he pretty much had said all that he was going to say, because a short time later, Robert Blake's lawyer showed up.

35

Margerry Bakley learned of her sister's death when tabloid reporters showed up at her apartment door in Dover, New Jersey, shortly after midnight on May 5, 2001.

"CNN was on. My mother was on the other line. The doorbell's ringing and it's the *Star* magazine. And my mother goes, 'The son of a bitch shot her. He killed her. She's dead.' And as she was saying that, CNN was [broadcasting] the loading of her body into the ambulance."

In Memphis, Paul Gawron had a similar reaction: "I got a phone call from somebody in L.A., a newspaper, some reporter, and he said, 'Bonny's been shot.' The words out of my mouth was, 'Oh, my stars!' My first thought was, 'He did it. He actually did it. She was afraid and he did it.'"

Some were not so quick to pass judgment though, and they weren't just Robert Blake's lawyers. Bonny had a most unique background. She had made any number of enemies in her fast and furious forty-four years. Upon reflection, three months later, Gawron began to consider the same range of suspects as Blake's attorneys and wondered if they might have a point.

"I wouldn't exempt her own family, tell you the truth," Gawron said.

Someone broke into attorney Anthony Helm's office and stole a phone log and a dozen of Bonny's porn shots from one of his filing cabinets the day after her murder. Helm, who had handled Bonny's legal problems for more than a decade, reported the theft to the Memphis police when the tabloids began calling.

"Indirectly I got an offer from a tabloid through an attorney," he said. "It involved $100,000 for the photos."

Helm turned the offer down, but began wondering if the thief who broke into his office had received that same offer.

"I never thought something like this would happen," Helm said. "I may have been a little bit naive."

"I'd be the first one to apologize if it wasn't true too, but I know he did it," Margerry Bakley said shortly before she signed her own contract with the tabs. "Blake murdered my sister. It's as simple as that."

The *Star* paid Margerry $20,000 for her exclusive story and Judy Howell earned enough to pay cash for a new Chrysler P.T. Cruiser. For months afterward, Bonny's mother, Marjorie Lois Carlyon, would not speak to the press because she too had signed a lucrative, exclusive contract with the *National Enquirer*.

"I feel Blake was planning Bonny's murder from the day after they got married," Carlyon revealed in the pages of the *Enquirer*. "I am 100 percent sure that Robert Blake was responsible for murdering my daughter."

Gawron too joined the gravy train. He released to the tabloids one of Bonny's secretly recorded phone conversations with Blake. In the months that followed the murder, Bonny's daughter Holly, her brother, Joey, and her half brother, Peter, would also sell testimonials to the highest bidder. As a single mom with no job and no income, Margerry made no apologies.

"It's what Bonny would have wanted me to do," she said.

Besides, like the coverage of O.J., the Bonny Bakley story was tailor-made for the tabloids. If anyone was going to be vigilant and get to the bottom of the murder mystery, Margerry reasoned, it would be the tabs. It wasn't going to be the *New York Times* or the *Wall Street Journal*.

The Good Samaritan in whose arms Bonny Lee Bakley died could have cleaned up too, but he chose not to.

"It's been a painful time for me," said Sean Stanek. "I know I could make a lot of money on this if I wanted to and totally cash in on my fifteen minutes of fame. I mean Kato [Kaelin] just got a knock on his door from O.J. and he had million-dollar offers. Well, I was covered in Bonny Blake's blood. It was a horrible experience to go through."

For his part, Noah Blake appeared for free on *Larry King Live*, defending his father by saying Bakley "was afraid and wanted him to carry" the gun.

"My dad is innocent, period," Noah said emphatically, even though he seldom saw his father and had never met his late stepmom. "He doesn't need to prove that. He is not obligated nor is he obliged to address a thousand-trillion rumors. He was scared for himself. He was scared for me. He was scared for my sister. He just had no idea what had happened and he was really scared. He still is, you know, pretty shaken up about this."

Delinah was less forthcoming. Except for a controlled postarrest interview she gave to the producers of TV's *Biography* series for a largely fawning profile of her father and his long career in Hollywood, Blake's unmarried elder daughter remained mum.

Sondra was the least candid of any of the Blakes. While she consented to a round of interviews on the morning news programs, she was accompanied by feminist attorney Gloria Allred, who cut off all but the most innocuous softball question. Once she gave her generalized vote of support for her ex-husband, Sondra shrank back into the same traumatized cocoon of silence that she had occupied for twenty years.

But Blake's lawyers more than made up for the family's silence.

"The only thing Robert should be sentenced to do is free public service TV spots for Planned Parenthood," said attorney Barry Felsen, the entertainment law partner at Goldman & Kagon, the law firm where Robert Blake did most of his legal business for almost thirty years.

"He should go on camera and say, '*Always* use a condom,'" continued Felsen—an ironic sentiment that was echoed by Blake's son, Noah, who took some delight in turning the tables on a father who had admonished him for years to always use contraception.

But Felsen didn't just lecture his client on birth control. Before Ron Ito could get Blake alone in an interrogation room, Felsen had put in a call to Harland Braun.

While he limited his practice to criminal law, Braun's client list could easily pass for that of an entertainment law firm. Over the years, his celebrity clients included Roseanne Barr, the late Chris Farley, Steven Seagal, rapper Eazy-E, actors Ed O'Neill, Gary Busey and Harry Morgan and former NBA star Dennis Rodman. He also represented L.A. congresswoman Bobbie Fiedler in a political bribery case, several of the cops in both the Rodney King beating case and the LAPD's Ramparts scandal, as well as Elizabeth Taylor's doctor, who had once been accused of overprescribing medication.

But Braun's specialty since leaving the Los Angeles County D.A.'s office in 1973 was murder—the more high profile, the better. Even his enemies sang Harland's praises.

"He speaks in sound bytes," said Deputy District Attorney Lea D'Agostino, whom Harland once addressed as "scum" during the highly publicized *Twilight Zone* manslaughter trial of the mid-1980s. "People think we should be mortal enemies, but we're not. If I were in trouble, I'd certainly want someone who is as dedicated on my team."

Even before the LAPD's Scientific Investigation Division trucks were rolling toward Dilling Street on May 5, Braun hired Woodland Hills private investigator Scott Ross to run a parallel investigation to that of the police. It wasn't that Braun didn't trust the LAPD to do its job. He simply wanted to give them plenty of fresh leads to investigate—and if there was ever a woman with fresh leads to investigate, it was Bonny Lee Bakley.

The detectives' chief dilemma at the moment was that they had too many suspects, and Braun knew it. Braun went on the offensive, carting box after box of Bonny's belongings to Parker Center, claiming that her porn business alone proved that Ito and his fellow detectives would be rushing to judgment if they singled out Robert Blake as their sole suspect. As he came across mailing lists containing the names of hundreds of men Bonny had fleeced over the years, he boxed them up and sent them along with the porn. While he was at it, Braun called a press conference and distributed media releases. For those who asked—and for those who wouldn't—he happily flipped through photo albums stuffed with snapshots of Bonny at her horniest and most hirsute. He provided audiotapes of her conversations about bilking men and meeting stars and, last but not least, he laid out just a sampling of the hundreds of men who had good reason to want to see Mrs. Blake erased from the planet.

As if that wasn't enough, Braun also went after her family, claiming they were the worst kind of grifters. One of the first questions his newest client asked him was whether he thought Bonny or one of her friends or relatives might have contracted to kill Blake.

"Of course," Braun answered. "There's no moral content to any of these people. Once she's in Hollywood, what does she need Robert Blake for? She gets rid of him, she'd be Mrs. Robert Blake. She's established herself."

Once he had the Robbery Homicide Division scrambling to paw through and catalogue the entirety of Bonny's porn trove, Braun suggested that Bonny did herself in, hiring a hit man to off Blake only to wind up double-crossed. Was it so far-fetched that a woman such as the ubiquitous Bonny Lee Bakley might pay, say, half of a $50,000 murder contract up front and become the victim herself when the hit man figured out that $25,000 in hand (especially from a rip-off artist like Bonny) was worth a billion in the bush?

Harland spun a theory that made Blake the unwitting stepping-stone to far bigger Hollywood fish. Bonny's scams might have yielded even more money, power and notoriety, Braun said, if she could have used Blake's name to gain entrée to higher Hollywood circles. She certainly hadn't abandoned her criminal ways, the lawyer reasoned.

The plain fact, he claimed, was that once Ito's team looked beyond Blake or his bodyguard, Earle Caldwell, as possible suspects, "you got too much evidence. It's all over the country. You wouldn't know where to start."

Braun called Bonny "hypervigilant" and blamed her paranoia on stalkers, not her husband. She hid her car at the back of Blake's house and used Caldwell as her own bodyguard, he said. In the months before her death, Blake and Caldwell both told Braun that a young man with a crew cut had been parking his black four-door pickup down Dilling Street and had been watching the house. In addition,

Caldwell told Braun that Robert "was getting weird phone calls."

Somebody was after Bonny, Braun said, and it wasn't Braun's client.

Strategically, the flip side of slamming Bonny was that it was humanizing Robert.

"Once he found out it was his child, you've got to understand, this is a Sicilian[69] guy whose blood is important," said Braun. "So if this child was his blood, I mean, this is an old-fashioned guy. This is not a guy who's going to not pay child support. This is a guy that will sacrifice his own happiness for his blood."

Furthermore, the police had been unable to connect Robert to the crime with fingerprints, fibers, blood, gun residue, hair or the murder weapon. "If he had done it, the physical evidence would be there," said Braun.

Those who knew the sandy-haired lawyer with the trademark tortoiseshell half lenses understood that kicking Robbery Homicide's institutional ass was not personal. Braun learned early to spin the media. In 1981, two doctors who discontinued intravenous feeding of a critically brain-damaged man were charged with murder. It could have been just another plea bargain, but Braun went public with it and prompted a firestorm of publicity on the right to die with dignity. Braun won. Since then his media massaging had made him very nearly as big a star as many of the celebrities he represented.

---

69. "My father is not Sicilian," said Noah Blake. "He's Neopolitan."

36

There were many puzzles to solve in the days following Bonny Lee's death and Braun was quite right about one of them: physical evidence was weak. If Blake did it, he either had help or he had planned a brilliant cover-up.

The murder weapon—a German-made 9 millimeter Walther P-38 pistol of World War II vintage—was found in a Dumpster near the murder scene, but other than traces of gun powder residue that Blake could have picked up from his own .38, there was nothing to connect him to the Walther. Blake said he'd done some target practice earlier in the day and the residue could have been left from that.

Ito kept coming back to the .38 pistol that Blake packed at the restaurant. Now where did he leave it exactly? Under a sweatshirt on the seat beside him, according to Blake. Yet nobody else—not one person inside or outside of the restaurant—could remember seeing the bundle.

In examining Blake's Dodge, one of the detectives made note of a space just beneath the hood where a .38 pistol or a Walther might fit snugly. The Scientific Investigation Division also found motor oil on the front bumper of the Dodge—oil that could conceivably have been used in cleaning or lubricating a gun. Beyond that, they had nothing—or at least nothing that they were willing to share with Blake's lawyers or the press.

The day after Bonny's death was May 5 or, as most Southern Californians knew it, Cinco de Mayo—Mexican Independence Day. Margerry learned from a tabloid reporter who lived in Blake's neighborhood that the planning of the celebration actually began early that year. Flyers were distributed in driveways and mailboxes all over Studio City warning residents that fireworks would be set off on the eve of Cinco de Mayo and that pets or people averse to loud bangs ought to stay indoors. The noisy display was to begin at nine thirty p.m., which also happened to be minutes before Bonny's murder.

Margerry passed that information along to Ron Ito, but even more important, she told him about another loud noise that she had heard over the telephone earlier that day. During Bonny's last, long transcontinental phone marathon, Margerry heard an explosion on Bonny's end.

"What was that?" she asked.

"I don't know," said Bonny.

For the next few minutes, Bonny scurried around to see what the noise might have been, but came back to the phone without an answer. Maybe it was a sonic boom, she concluded, and carried on with the conversation.

"From what I hear, before somebody murders somebody, they test fire a gun," Margerry recalled months later. "They always fire off a shot to hear how loud it sounds. And you know, Blake admitted to firing a gun that day."

Ito and his crew moved into the Mata Hari Ranch with a search warrant on May 5. The cops found a treasure trove of old cassette tapes in Blake's house, some belonging to Bonny and some to Blake. Much of it was music, some not. Their differing tastes in music alone demonstrated just how far apart they were.

Bonny's collection of seventy-three tapes consisted mostly of oldies: Roy Orbison, Elvis, the Platters and, of course, Frankie Valli and Jerry Lee Lewis. But there were also some surprises, including taped conversations with the brother of *Hustler* publisher Larry Flynt, and dozens of Bonny's dialogues with Christian Brando and Robert Blake.

Blake had two hundred seven tapes, including old-time radio serials like the *Lone Ranger*, the *Green Hornet* and *Gangbusters*, as well as jazz sides from Mel Torme, Charlie Parker, Harry James and Sinatra. Robert's taste was eclectic enough to include Jerry Vale and Janis Joplin, but he also taped his own singing lessons. There were also disturbing oral accounts of both his troubled past and his present day nightmares.

"In these tapes, he frequently talks about violence and occasionally talks about murder," wrote Detective Ito. "In one tape, he describes how he dreamed he was surrounded by 'semicrappy people' who were making demands on him and killed a man at a restaurant."

Blake also collected articles from the *Wall Street Journal* and the *Los Angeles Times* on the latest developments in paternity law. Across a white legal pad he'd scrawled, "I'm not going down."

One of Ito's partners found $10,000 in $100 bills in a dresser drawer in the walk-in closet of the master bedroom. Another detective found an additional $2,000 in $100 bills in another dresser in Blake's bedroom. Around the same time, Harland Braun was making a remarkable preemptive statement to ABC News concerning his client and the cash. He said that Blake withdrew $45,000 in the months leading up to Bonny's murder, but that he handed it over to Bonny so that she could wrap up her probation problems in Arkansas and visit Margerry in New Jersey.

When Blake drove up to his house in his pickup during the detectives' search, he found a pair of uniformed officers at his front gate. He was dressed in typical Blake fashion: red sweatpants, dark T-shirt and black baseball cap. When he tried to enter his house, a half dozen detectives quickly gathered around him and joined hands, encircling him and preventing him from moving.

"Stay where you are, Mr. Blake," he was told.

The detectives began to pick up the questioning where they'd left off the previous night, but Blake remained silent. The odd conclave moved inside the fence at the side of the Mata Hari Ranch, and the standoff continued for another hour, until Blake tried to return to his pickup. The cops said no deal. They had a search warrant for that too.

Blake's lawyer finally showed up in a Mercedes and whisked him away to the hospital, where according to Braun, he was admitted for treatment of high blood pressure.

Blake checked himself out of the hospital the following day, May 6. The first thing he did as an outpatient was to meet with Braun's team of private investigators. The second thing he did was pay a return visit to Vitello's to parley with co-owner Steve Restivo. While Restivo refused to detail what was said, the *National Enquirer* reported that the restaurateur was overheard after the meeting muttering, "I'm not going to lie for that man."

On Monday, May 7, Ron Ito and Steve Eguchi interviewed Earle Caldwell. Caldwell told the detectives about the trips to the Colorado and Sequoia, about Bonny's paranoia and Blake's penchant for firearms. Asked if he had ever seen Blake whip out his .38 and set it next to him at a restaurant—say, Vitello's for instance—Caldwell said he had never seen Blake remove his gun in public.

Caldwell's alibi checked out with several friends. He had, indeed, been in San Mateo the night Bonny met her doom. The most curious thing about the interview was not what Caldwell said, but how he said it. It seemed as though every other sentence began with: "I'm supposed to tell you this." It was also worth noting that he showed up for the interview with his lawyer, Arna Zlotnik, and that he refused a polygraph because he didn't believe they were accurate and he knew that they were not admissible in court.

The following week, Ito interviewed Joey Bakley and Gary McLarty, the stuntman Blake had solicited several weeks earlier to rid him of his wife. According to McLarty's son, Cole, his father almost threw up when he heard about Bonny's murder.

As one week passed into another, and the mound of evidence against Bonny that Braun replenished regularly was slowly investigated and set aside, it became crystal clear to Ron Ito that he had exactly what he feared the most: a sixty-weeker, and then some.

He then called on Brian Tyndall to give him a hand. Together, they spent the next year moving from lead to lead, state to state and revelation to revelation. They handled the case as they'd handled their careers, moving steadily and carefully forward, idling long enough—some would say way too long—to protect themselves from becoming another LAPD casualty like former O.J. investigator Mark Fuhrman.

37

Bonny wanted to be cremated and shipped back to New Jersey, but Forest Lawn wound up being her final resting place. It seemed appropriate somehow. Forest Lawn is home to Bette Davis, Jack Webb, Lucille Ball, Freddie Prinze, Charles Laughton and a host of other stars. Her soul might long for the nudist colony of her youth, but the groupie in her had to feel right at home, sandwiched for eternity between tough guys like George Raft and Telly Savalas, and pop idols Ricky Nelson and Andy Gibb.

"Bonny wanted more than anything in the world to be hooked up with a movie star," said Anthony Helm, the Memphis attorney who represented Bonny for more than a decade. "I hate to say that she was an airhead, but she reminded you of someone who was shallow. Yet the more you talked to her, the more you got the idea that your first impression was wrong."

She was both brassy and painfully shy, stopping at nothing to get next to a star, but struck dumb once she achieved her goal. Now she had been struck dumb forever.

A pool media camera provided footage to the networks of the somber funeral proceedings of May 25, capturing Robert Blake's first public appearance since his wife's murder. Delinah held the baby while a dour Blake spoke. Blake looked dapper but withered in the warm spring morning, and his thatch of jet-black hair contrasted with the stretched white leather of his badly lifted facial features. The naturally grim expression he constantly seemed to wear looked like the scowl of a scarecrow. He had very little to say beyond a vow to never let little Rose ever forget her mother.

"I stand before God to make this pledge," he said just before the casket was lowered. "As long as I have breath, I will do everything to make my daughter Rosie's life the best I can.

"It's because of Bonny that Rosie was born. It was her will, her conviction, not mine, her dedication that brought Rosie into this world, and for that, I thank God and I thank Bonny."

He made no public vow to track down her killers the way O.J. Simpson had once done, but neither did he anoint her grave the same way that he once did his father's. Even so, Margerry Bakley nearly gagged on the opposite side of the country as she listened to him speak.

"There's no love at that funeral," she told Fox News moments after Blake's speech.

For more than a week, Bonny's mortal remains had become the prime pawn in a growing feud between the Bakleys and the Blakes. It began when the Los Angeles County Coroner released the body to an L.A. funeral home. The original plan called for a large but tasteful New Jersey funeral following an autopsy, with Bonny making her final journey to her rural roots. Arrangements were made, but no one anticipated a media mob scene so intense that the funeral director couldn't even get close enough to his own parlor to get Bonny's body out of the hearse. After Blake's private investigator Scott Ross witnessed the crush, he advised his client to forget about going back to New Jersey.

"I've never seen anything like this," Harland Braun told the Associated Press. "Emotions in this case are running so high."

Blake called off a family-only service for his slain wife, and for a time, no one knew what was going to happen to Bonny.

"We had a private religious service planned," Braun said. "A priest was coming and Robert was going to be there with his three children. But now we're afraid if he showed up there would be a riot."

As consolation for burying her in L.A. instead of in New

Jersey, Blake offered to pay for Bonny's relatives to fly in for the funeral, but bickering broke out over the cost. Whatever rapprochement that might have been achieved collapsed overnight. None of the Bakleys showed. In the final irony of her life, Bonny was buried by strangers amid celebrity corpses, receiving more media attention in death than she had ever hoped to receive while alive.

In the weeks following the slaying, Blake and his bodyguard never discussed Bonny. "We look at the sky, we watch the birds. We don't talk about it," Earle Caldwell told CNN. As far as any suspicions he might have about Blake's responsibility for his wife's death, Caldwell said it "never even crossed my mind."

"I interviewed Caldwell," said the AP's Linda Deutsch. "He was very loyal to Robert. He said that to his dying day he would swear that Robert didn't to it."

Meanwhile, Harland Braun's anti-Bonny juggernaut rolled on. It came as no surprise that Braun played into the hands of the *New York Post*, which weighed in with the single most egregious headline during the month after the murder. On June 1, one day before Rosie's first birthday and six days after Bonny was buried at Forest Lawn, the *Post* carried a report that Harland Braun's investigative team had spread out across the U.S., scouring for even more skeletons in the Bakley family's closets. The headline read:

Blake Bids to Shovel More Dirt on Wife's Grave

Braun leaked tapes, letters and Bonny's damning FBI file to the press over the months that followed, making sure that no one would ever forget how sordid her life had been. By midsummer, his campaign to dehumanize Bonny had its desired effect. Virtually any conversation regarding the Bakley murder anywhere in the country began with the words, "Nobody deserves to be murdered, but . . ."

And slowly, Robert Blake faded from the headlines.

By mid-July, another scandal had caught the middlebrow imagination of Americans: the mysterious disappearance of Congressman Gary Condit's young intern Chandra Levy. For the balance of the summer of 2001, the Blake scandal faded indirectly in proportion to the nation's growing interest in Condit and Levy.

None of the gaggle of reporters and cameramen who jostled the funeral director for a look at Bonny's casket or crowded in to catch Robert Blake's parting words at the funeral even noticed when Blake belatedly applied for and won guardianship of his daughter. On July 13, 2001, he got from Bonny in death what she was never willing to relinquish in life: full custody of Rosie.

At the same time, Margerry asked the courts to name her administrator of Bonny's estate, but Blake challenged her, both in L.A. and in Memphis. After all, he was the one, he claimed, who had kept up the payments on Bonny's rental in Thousand Oaks, which was more than Margerry or anyone else in the Bakley family was doing.

"Based on Margerry Bakley's extensive criminal records involving theft and fraud and illegal business activities, I fear and believe that if the court appointed her special administrator, she would not administer the decedent's estate in the best interests of my daughter, Rose, or the other heirs," Blake wrote in a three-page court declaration.

"You can never win against money unless you have it, and I don't," said Margerry, adding tearfully, "He does."

Amid the last of the media fanfare, Blake moved out of his sprawling Mata Hari Ranch, as he had always called his Studio City home, and moved into Delinah's Hidden Hills hideaway, where omnipresent media trucks could not park. By summer's end, the Bakley case was history.

"I think it's a cold trail," said Harland Braun.

"I don't think he did it," said comedian Mark Canavi, who had been present on that warm August night in 1998 when Bobby met Bonny. "It's one of these things that's going to remain unsolved."

In August 2001, Blake put his beloved Mata Hari Ranch[70]

---

70. Originally listed for $1,098,000, the price on the 4,909-square-foot home dropped to $950,000 by December and $850,000 as of February. It finally sold in the spring of 2002 to a star of NBC's *E.R.*

up for sale. Very much a do-it-yourself home, it had a perpetually unfinished ambience and a brooding quality that neither landscaping nor new coats of paint could ever erase.

For Blake, almost nothing of his former life remained. Before he moved away from the Dilling Street neighborhood he'd called home for seventeen years, Blake had become a pariah. Many former neighbors shunned him. He became even more of a recluse, relegated to a gated community at the northwestern end of the San Fernando Valley, far from the public eye.

In the meantime, the sixty-eight-year-old actor's friends, family, acquaintances and enemies alike wanted to believe that Bonny's real killer might simply have gotten away with murder. The idea that so pathetic a creature as Robert Blake might be responsible was just too repugnant to contemplate.

"He's all alone and lonely," said Blake's former next-door neighbor. "He's crying all the time and says his neighbors have turned against him."

By September 11, when the disastrous terrorist attacks occurred, the last traces of Blake's former life vanished. In a letter dated September 27, 2001, Blake returned his concealed-weapon permit to the Culver City Police Department.

Dear Chief (Ted) Cooke:

What with the stock market, lawyers' fees, and other matters, I am unable to maintain the residence in Culver City.[71] I am therefore voluntarily surrendering my gun permit.

I want to thank you for being a decent, stand-up human being. When I was a boy, there were more like you, but they don't seem to make them anymore. My best to you and yours.

Sincerely,
Robert Blake

---

71. Blake owned rental property in Culver City, which allowed him to obtain his permit on the pretense that he actually lived within the city limits.

In the fall, Braun resurfaced briefly to give the syndicated entertainment/news program *Extra!* his latest theory: an armed robbery suspect who had been arrested in June on an unrelated case might have been Bonny's killer.

Meanwhile, Ito and Tyndall whittled a little bit more off of the case paperwork each day. They kept in touch with Margerry, Judy and the rest of Bonny's telephone cabal. Sixty days had, indeed, turned into sixty weeks. The only public voice besides Margerry's that still occasionally sounded off about the forgotten case was Cary Goldstein, the Beverly Hills divorce lawyer who had helped Bonny force Blake to marry her.

"I have spoken with a source inside the investigation who has informed me that the case is definitely not cold. He said it is hot," Goldstein would tell reporters from time to time.

And though they all printed his words, no one really believed them.

Until the afternoon of April 18, 2002, that is, when Brian Tyndall and Ron Ito came calling at Robert Blake's Hidden Hills hideaway, an arrest warrant in hand.

Afterword

Los Angeles County district attorney Steve Cooley charged Robert Blake with murder, conspiracy and solicitation. Blake's bodyguard, Earle Caldwell, was also charged with conspiracy to commit murder in connection with the May 4, 2001, shooting of Bonny Lee Bakley. In the weeks that followed, opinions among Blake's friends and family about his past, his innocence and his future ricocheted from the San Fernando Valley to Santa Monica with assessments as varied as the actor's notorious mood swings.

"I know he is incapable of an immoral action and in our friendship I saw him prove that over and over again," said actress Beverly D'Angelo, who costarred with Blake in *Judgment Day.*

"There has been an orange jump suit waiting for him for a while," said actor Ed Begley Jr., a Blake acquaintance since his *Baretta* days.

Mackenzie Phillips, a child actress in her own right on the 1980s sitcom *One Day at a Time,* recalled a randy Robert Blake during the filming of an episode of *Baretta* when she was only fourteen.

"I was handcuffed to Robert," she said. "We were prisoners in the back of a truck and Gary Busey and Strother Martin were our kidnappers."

Phillips' aunt, who was also her guardian, hovered like a mother hen, warning her niece: "I have *got* to keep that Robert Blake away from you!" She sensed that Blake would have liked to be much more than handcuffed to the young actress.

"She was convinced he was trying to get me into bed, and I'm pretty sure he was too, and I was just a kid. I remember that every time he saw my aunt he'd say, 'I better back off'. . . . He was a very strange man. My aunt and I just got so creeped out by him."

After the *Baretta* episode in which he appeared with Phillips, Busey subsequently became friends with Blake when they both entered a twelve-step program together.

"We went through recovery together," he said, "so we understand the brotherhood of survival."

They almost shared the brotherhood of Bonny too, according to Harland Braun, who is Busey's lawyer as well as Blake's. In shuffling through some of Bonny's papers in the days following her murder, Harland came across a jaw dropper and phoned Gary Busey at his Palm Springs retreat.

"Are you sitting down?" he asked.

"Sure," said Busey.

Harland read from the back page of one of Bonny's last catalogued scam sheets. Under the category of YOUNG AND RICH was an entry that said: "Find Gary Busey's phone number. Call his mother, Virginia, in Tulsa, Oklahoma. He's next."

At first Busey laughed. Then he remembered the blowsy, blushing blonde he'd seen Robert Blake squiring at a Malibu restaurant months earlier and took a deep breath.

"She was giving me the eye," he recalled. "Not in a come-on way, but in the way that says, 'Wow! This is neat. I'm meeting Gary Busey.' Now I know why."

While some in Hollywood maintain that Blake must have been drunk or drugged to get involved with Bonny Bakley, Busey chose to believe that Blake was, and is, still sober. As one familiar with the inside of more than one jail cell, Busey advised Blake: "Pray every day and thank God for what He has given you to go through. I know Bobby will go through it and stand up to it, and whatever he receives he will receive with acceptance and respect."

Others offer a more cautious stance on Blake. "I had coffee with him a couple of times and I thought he was dangerous," recalled a Century City psychologist. A few mochafrappacinos with Blake was all she needed to make her informal diagnosis: a seething misogynist who needed help. "I knew two women who dated him," she said. "I warned them against him."

"I give him credit for being too smart to get involved in something like this," said Blake's old *Baretta* producer Jo Swerling. "Just getting involved with a woman like that in the first place I find very hard to believe, and then this murder. We had a name for that type of operation in the navy. When something was screwed up beyond all imagination through poor planning and poor execution, we called it a goatfuck. I can't see Robert being involved in a goatfuck."

"He misses his boots," said comedian Mort Sahl. "But he's very disciplined. He's always been a strong guy, even on the worst locations. He is a straight-ahead soldier."

"The last time I spoke with Robert was back in May," said Tommy "Butch" Bond, Blake's old Rascal buddy. Butch told *Court TV* that he went on the defensive for Blake after Bonny's death, telling radio and TV stations how impossible it was for the little Mickey Gubitosi he knew to have ever committed so heinous a crime.

"I know how Bobby Blake really is, and as far as I'm concerned, there's no murder in his heart," said Bond. "It's true that he was emotionally disturbed—always has been—but he doesn't have murder in his heart. If he were going to do any damage to anything or anyone, it would be to himself."

About a week after Butch had hit the talk show circuit, the phone rang. It was Bobby Blake.

"Honest to God, Tom, I didn't do it," the actor told Bond.

"I believe you, Bobby," Bond replied.

"They're after me," Blake continued.

"You know, Bobby, I'm here for you. If you need any help, give me a call."

A week later, Blake called back asking Butch if he knew a good attorney, but he apparently later found one because Bond did not hear from him again.

"I am just absolutely amazed what has happened with the media," said actress Sally Kirkland, a Blake confidante who, in addition to having once been nominated for an Oscar,[72] also describes herself these days as a yoga master, former debutante and an ordained minister with the Movement of Spiritual Inner Awareness.

"I feel that there should be much, much more fairness involved," she said. "I have never *seen* this Robert Blake, this person that I read about in the papers. I have never experienced him, and I come from a place from having known him a long time. So I just want to go on record that this is not the Robert Blake I know. My prayer would be that the media would stop making money and exploiting this and getting rich on it because it is just not fair. It is not America the democracy I know. The Robert Blake I know is a kind, gentle, fabulous actor who helps and cares about young people."

If influence on young people is the measure of a man's character, then publicist Dale Olson pegs Blake near the top. "I consider Robert to be one of my closest friends and I am in total denial of his ability to do this," said Olson. "Everybody is saying that he will commit suicide, but he won't do that to his children. He did a fabulous job in raising Deli and Noah. They relate more to him than to Sondra.

"He doesn't let anybody know what he is really like. He's created the persona of a tough guy, an iconoclast, like Robert Mitchum did and just like Russell Crowe is creating today. But everybody has the wrong idea. He is a gentle, kind, thoughtful, sensitive and extremely humane man."

"They compare Robert to O.J. Simpson," said Blake's cousin Steve Visakay. "The difference between Robert and O.J. is that Robert is going to be convicted of murder. That's it.

"Blake is a guy with no personality. On TV, nobody liked him and he always had a bad mouth. He had that movie-star mentality. He was Mr. Big Shot. He bad-mouthed his family. He's not a popular figure, not in Nutley, and not in Hollywood. He did it to himself."

And if that weren't damning enough, Visakay points out

---

72. Best Actress nomination in 1987 for *Anna*.

one other fact that runs counter to Dale Olson's contention that Blake is not suicidal. "What does run in this family is suicide," says Steve Visakay, who maintains that Blake's real father—Visakay's uncle Sal Gubitosi—and the abusive father who raised him, James Gubitosi, both shot themselves while a third Gubitosi brother, Louis, leaped from a seven-story building to his death at age thirty-four.

"So you better watch out for Robert," Visakay concluded. "Don't let him loose."

Mario Roccuzzio, an actor Blake met nearly forty years ago when he was doing *The Connection* onstage in L.A., loves Blake and counts him among his closest friends, but also sees him as a much darker figure. "Bobby can be the most evil man on earth," says Roccuzzio. "He is evil—evil like the devil. He can destroy you—and I'm not talking about Bonny now. He can destroy you with his words."

Blake had hung a poster of Frank Sinatra in his exercise room, where he did his morning calisthenics. Roccuzzio demonstrated how similar the temperaments of the two men have always been by meshing the fingers of both his hands, as if he were about to pray. "Frank could be ruthless, and so can Robert," he continued.

He could also be tender. "He was always outside working in his backyard, and whenever I would ride by, he would always go out of his way to chat for a minute and pat my horses," said a neighbor who lived a few doors down from the Blakes on Long Valley Road in Hidden Hills. "He was very knowledgeable about horses and always asked questions about their breed and temperament. From what I could see he was a very caring father toward both daughters."

It was Robert who took little Rosie out for walks.

"He has a *very* powerful presence," said the neighbor. "His eyes are very intense, and he is built like a Mack truck. I never knew that he was almost seventy. He seems much younger. But again, what struck me the most is how genuinely nice he was. His backyard seems so empty now. I'm actually really sad he's gone."

Though many seemed upset over Blake's ordeals, others treated the opportunity more lightheartedly. Trumpet player Jack Sheldon, a longtime pal who refused to discuss his friend in an interview, couldn't resist zinging Blake from the stage during a recent Thursday night session at the Jax jazz club in Glendale. Between sets, he told his audience: "So, you guys, what do you think about Bobby Blake? Do you think he did it? If you think he *didn't do it*—well, then, this restaurant is in Pittsburgh! Bobby Blake, he gives new meaning to the phrase, 'Hey, can you wait in the car?'"

During his first day in lockdown, Robert Blake ate oatmeal for breakfast, cold cuts for lunch and hamburger casserole for dinner. The cell he was placed in is removed from the general population—a routine procedure for celebrity prisoners, yet still particularly depressing for a man who maintained throughout his life that he lived a childhood full of fear, entombed frequently in a dark closet as punishment.

Separated from family and friends and even other inmates, Blake had no radio, no television—no daily contact with the outside world. According to his lawyer, he was permitted to read, but his dyslexia made it tough going. His obsession with a fitness regime was out of the question. He got just one to three hours of "roof time" a week, when he was allowed to get some fresh air and exercise at the top of one of the twin towers of the Los Angeles County Men's Jail.

In the beginning, visitors lined up to get in a little Plexiglas phone time. Sally Kirkland was first to visit. "He quite literally was crying for joy when he saw me," she said, "and I was crying for joy because of the light in his eyes. I think the only reason why I got in so easily [and others did not] is maybe because the deputies started naming off my credits."

Being inside wasn't all bad for the actor. Blake gave up smoking, lost ten pounds and did his best to resume some part of his exercise regimen. He became philosophical with his visitors. "Don't worry," he consoled a weepy friend. "I've had a full life."

Although he couldn't lift weights to the strains of Sinatra or tap-dance naked while staring at himself in a roomful of mirrors, the little exercise he was allowed to do helped him sleep.

Blake called Mario Roccuzzio at six p.m. each night.

"If I ever get out of here, I'm going to come and live with you," he jokingly threatened.

"Well, you're going to have to sleep on the couch, and I ain't giving up my room," Roccuzzio shot back.

Blake told Roccuzzio that he was selling his house in Hidden Hills, tagging the furniture for giveaway and offering Roccuzzio first dibs.

"There's an armoire—furniture from four houses," said Roccuzzio. "I'm making out like a bandit."

Blake doesn't think he'll ever get out of jail, said Roccuzzio, because he thinks the judge in his case believes "I am unsafe with the baby and [the judge] has it in for me."

Though they talk about the case, mostly he and Blake reminisce.

"We go back to our younger days," says Roccuzzio, recalling his first meeting with Blake in 1959. As the star of a play in which his character was a junkie, Blake was sitting in a tree outside the theater getting into character. "We go back to those times. We talk about going to clubs in the fifties and sixties."

Somewhere along the line, Robert Blake became a lost soul. Neither twelve-step programs for alcohol, cocaine and cigarettes, nor decades of psychotherapy, meditation or invoking familial spirits filled the huge void in his psyche. Ironically, it was Bonny who brought him hope in the form of Rose. But at the same moment, Bonny also brought him down.

On Monday, April 22, 2002, Blake was arraigned. His indictment labeled him the triggerman on the night of the murder, intentionally "lying in wait" to kill Bonny. The "special circumstance" nature of the indictment allowed prosecutors to seek the death penalty, but D.A. Cooley announced he would not do so. "Special circumstance" indictments are a major roadblock to bail, however.

For one so averse to "suits," Blake was about to face a closetful of them. Lead prosecutor Patrick Dixon had been a Deputy D.A. since 1976 and was named "Prosecuting Attorney of the Year" by the Los Angeles County Bar Association in 1998. First chair went to Greg Dohi, a cool Harvard graduate who balanced Dixon's occasional outbursts and is considered a formidable opponent by the defense.

"He's too young to win the case on his own. He looks too unseasoned, so they brought in Dixon—for his gray hair as well as his skills," said a member of Blake's defense team.

On April 26, Earle Caldwell's loyalty seemed to have paid off. Blake posted $1 million in cash to release Caldwell on bail. He also hired and paid for Caldwell's defense counsel, attorney Arna Zlotnik.

According to Braun, granting Caldwell's bail and hiring Zlotnik for the bodyguard were both business decisions based on a California law that requires employers to stand behind an employee on any criminal charge arising from their employment. But to many observers, Blake seemed to be buying Caldwell's continued loyalty. The police's hopes of turning Caldwell into a prosecution witness had been dashed by cash competition. According to one LAPD source, Blake had also opened his checkbook to help Caldwell with rent and other financial obligations.

In each of a half dozen affidavits filed in support of his search warrants, Ron Ito always ended on an ominous note: "The fact that Mr. Blake is wealthy and has hired private investigators in the past in order to intimidate people gives [me] reason to believe that he has the resources, the ability and the inclination to contact witnesses and intimidate them."

Ito's suspicions about Blake's motives did not end there. They extended beyond Robert to Delinah, who the detective believed must have conspired with her father to steal Rose from Bonny.

"I believe that his daughter Delinah must have been aware of Mr. Blake's efforts to take baby Rose and eliminate the baby's mother," wrote Ito in a sworn affidavit with which he sought a warrant for Delinah's phone records.

On the same day that Robert Blake ponied up $1 million for Caldwell, Delinah spoke out for the first time in a *20/20* interview with ABC's Barbara Walters.

"What do you tell Rosie about what happened to her father?" asked Walters.

"We tell her that daddy is away, daddy's taking care of

business. . . . He talked to her on the phone the other day and he was singing to her. I think I said, 'Are you done?' and she said, 'No! More.' And she held the phone to her ear and just kept listening."

"What do you tell Rosie about her mother?"

"She doesn't ask because she never knew her mommy."

Delinah professed complete faith in her father, a man she knew could never have committed the crime.

On April 29, 2002, six days before the anniversary of Bonny's death, a one-year statute of limitations had expired and Bonny's estate was free to sue Blake and Caldwell for her wrongful death. In addition to Holly, Glenn and Jerilee, baby Rose is named as a plaintiff in the suit against her father.

At a bail hearing May 1, Blake spoke up publicly for the first time in his own defense. "For the past year, I have been silent while this town and my country and the police said whatever they want about me," Blake told Superior Judge Lloyd Nash. "Now it's my turn to fight back. This is my right to fight back for my life. For the past year, practically everybody had tried to take that away from me—the news media who I once respected, the police who I once respected, my country which I once respected."

Blake said he needed to be granted bail so that he could prepare his defense. Severe dyslexia hampered his reading briefs and legal documents in his jail cell.

"I can't fight in that cement room with thousands of pages that I can't read. [I] need to be working on this case from the outside. I'd like to be out and see Rosie and the sunshine of the world."

The D.A.'s office opposed bail. In Ito's arrest report, he cited a travel agent Blake had consulted about traveling to Mexico. He had $10 million in assets and drawers full of cash at his Dilling Street home. What would prevent him from fleeing the country as other aging indictees had done before? What would keep an accused killer from using his cash and connections to silence witnesses or wreak havoc against enemies, real or perceived? Blake had allegedly told at least two stuntmen as well as retired LAPD detective William Welch about his intention to "whack" Bonny. Why wouldn't he whack someone else, given half a chance?

Braun remained skeptical of claims that Blake tried to hire stuntmen to kill Bakley. If it were true, he asked, "why didn't they call the police?"

On May 9, 2002, Robert Blake's thirty-five-year-old daughter won temporary guardianship of her baby half sister Rose.

"When the judge said, 'I give Delinah custody till July 25,' she put her arms up like it was a fuckin' football game," said Margerry. "You know, where you pull your hand back like in a fist, like you just scored a touchdown? That's what she did. Right in front of the court." A July 25 hearing was scheduled on Delinah's petition to be declared permanent guardian of the child, who celebrated her second birthday on June 2, 2002.

Three days later, Joey Bakley was arrested and charged with grand theft and identity theft, stemming from years of living in San Diego under several aliases—thirteen felony counts in all, dating back to alleged crimes from as much as a decade earlier. He pleaded innocent and was ordered held without bail.

On June 12, 2002, CNN unloaded another bombshell in a case that seemed to carry more ordnance than a B-52. Since the day Bonny was murdered, a former *Los Angeles Times* reporter named Miles Corwin had been tagging along with lead investigators Ron Ito and Brian Tyndall, taking notes while the pair interviewed witnesses and collected evidence. When first meeting witnesses, Ito even introduced Corwin, who had been covering the police for several years for the *Times,* as one of his partners.

Braun went ballistic. "It is consistent with what we have been saying all along," he began. "It is a Hollywood case and people come forward to make a bigger role for themselves."

He continued, "Somebody screwed up big time. This is the real world, and that was a screwup. Someone didn't think ahead. This is different than the book business that he wrote on South Central L.A.[73] This is Hollywood and this can be dangerous. How about Corwin transporting Blake's clothes, and being at the house when it was searched and part of the scout team? The police are going nuts. We haven't even laid a subpoena on Corwin for his notes. And they say [former chief Bernard] Parks approved it. Let's see the approval and the guidelines."

At a June 18, 2002, bail hearing that lasted less than twenty minutes, Blake's styled coiffure needed a dye job. His hair had the two-tone look of a skunk: silver at bottom, jet-black on top. His expression was tense, frozen and tight-lipped, as if he'd been botoxed and never quite recovered. He looked far more tired than during his first bail hearing, but the result was the same: no bail.

Delinah and Noah showed up to support their father. In tight tie-dyed jeans and powder blue shades, Noah looked as if he were at an audition instead of a bail hearing. His sister on the other hand was somber, jaundiced and hostile. Asked how her dad was holding up, she snapped, "How would *you* like to spend Father's Day in Jail?"

"They grow up in the shadow of their parents and many of them develop an inferiority complex," said Dr. David Levy,[74] one of Delinah's professors at Pepperdine University. "They feel that they can't compete with their parents, or they feel like they're not being seen for who they are. They feel like they're seen only in relation to their parents. So they frequently develop difficulties in their sense of either self-esteem or self-identity. They want to be seen as separate and unique, but the problem is other people want to see them in relation to their parents."

Blake loyalists also showed up, including Roccuzzio,

---

73. *The Killing Season: A Summer Inside an LAPD Homicide Division* (Fawcett) by Miles Corwin.

74. Before he became a psychologist specializing in the problems of child actors, Levy was himself an actor and was nominated for an Emmy for a guest role on *Cheers* as one of Dr. Frasier Crane's group-therapy patients during a session on low self-esteem.

John Solari, his *In Cold Blood* costar Scott Wilson and *Cocoon*'s Wilford Brimley. Blake must have been happy that Caldwell remained a loyalist as well. Dressed in a dapper gray suit and bright blue Hollywood power shirt, Caldwell told Judge Nash he would retain Arna Zlotnik rather than accept a court-appointed attorney, even though Blake was paying Zlotnik's legal fees. The judge stressed that down the line the arrangement could work to Caldwell's disadvantage. Earle didn't care.

A week later, on June 28, Blake, with his hair and complexion as gray as the outlook for his near future, was again denied bail. Although Nash agreed to hear another application later in the year, Blake bristled like the Hollywood bad boy he once had been.

While Blake's hopes ebbed in the courtroom, Margerry Bakley's flowed in the courtyard outside where she—not the star of *Baretta*—now stood before the cameras. She turned her bile toward Blake into a pitch for a new Internet venture that hosts victim-oriented Web sites, including bonnybakley.com and chandralevy.com. With a sense of righteousness befitting a political candidate, she read a prepared statement that tied her sister's tragedy to Chandra Levy, Danielle Van Dam and even the World Trade Center disaster. When unfriendly reporters suggested that she might be making a high-tech profit off of her late sister, Margerry insisted that 20 percent of the proceeds would go to My Friend's Place, a home for homeless and runaway kids, just like Bonny once was.

Great, but how did she feel about Blake?

"If somehow this man gets out, it changes everything," she said. "I don't want my niece with this man. He not only threatened to kill my sister for an entire year before he killed her, he's threatened to commit suicide and I believe he is unstable enough to do that. I am afraid he would take the life of my niece and his own life."

In a dramatic shift of position, Margerry then asserted that she wanted custody of Rose. "I would love to just take her away and go live in the country with her and just get her out of this lifestyle," she said. "This [Bonny's murder] is going to follow this baby around with the rest of her life.

She has enough to deal with—and she doesn't even know what she has to deal with yet. I don't think keeping the maternal side of the family away from her is the right thing to do."

Shocked by Margerry's sudden maternal instinct regarding her sister's daughter, Harland Braun retorted: "If she takes that baby, she'll turn her into a prostitute."

The next day found Braun pontificating from the plush confines of his Century City office, now a command center for the national media. "It's just the typical day in the life of a lawyer," joked Braun as he meandered past the labyrinth of cameras, lights and tripods to his office, where he had just been interviewed by Peter Van Sandt from CBS' *48 Hours*.

In an office across the hall, a reporter from the *Los Angeles Times* pored over Bonny's pornography portfolios. Meanwhile, Braun's investigator Scott Ross popped a videocassette into a VCR. Always a stickler for detail, Ron Ito had taped the police search of Blake's house the day after the murder. Braun's interest, however, had less to do with the evidence than the people. Miles Corwin could be seen dogging the steps of LAPD investigators—an egregious and, Braun believes, fatal breach of police procedure. He hopes the tape wrecks the prosecution's case.

"The hard thing will be to get into the story of Bonny Bakley. That's going to be tough," said Braun from behind his handsome mahogany desk. Again, he may rely on the VCR to tell the story. "I was even thinking of using the *48 Hours* piece about Bonny—put that on for an hour, and get it over with."

Just as Blake has been haunted by comparisons to O.J. Simpson, Braun has been ceaselessly compared to O.J.'s counsel Robert Shapiro. Recently at a restaurant, Braun ran into radio commentator Michael Jackson. As he was leaving, Jackson called out to Braun across the crowded room: "O.J. did it!"

Braun said he plans an "Un-O.J." defense. He won't surround himself with a phalanx of high-powered consulting attorneys, nor will he hire now-familiar O.J. criminologist Henry Lee—although he'd like to.

"I want to stay as far away from O.J. as possible" he said. "I don't want payback for O.J."

Unlike O.J.'s dream team, Braun claims to be unimpressed by Hollywood. "I don't go to Hollywood parties," he says. "When I represented Chris Farley, they had to tell me who he was. I represented Steven Seagal and I didn't know who he was. I am not Robert Shapiro. That's his shtick!

"But in this case, they're Hollywood. We're Hollywood. We're *all* Hollywood. Now are you going to convict someone of murder because someone in Hollywood [referring to retired stuntmen Gary McLarty and Duffy Hambleton] comes and tells you the story? Remember, in Hollywood these are people who go to restaurants not for the food, not for the service, but because they might be seen there. Now, would you ever convict someone based on the testimony of people who are that stupid?"

One key issue Braun wants addressed in court is a rumor that Delinah Blake is infertile and that her father impregnated Bonny because she wanted a baby. "It's ridiculous, and Deli will testify to that in the trial," said Braun.

Since the murder, Delinah has been conspicuously silent, speaking only with local KCBS-TV news reporter Paul Dandridge and ABC's Barbara Walters in brief, innocuous interviews that skirted every key issue. Since Margerry announced her hope of challenging Delinah for custody, the thirty-six-year-old psychologist's mental and physical health is suddenly in the forefront.

Yet Braun becomes noticeably vague when asked about Delinah's alleged stint in rehab or the serious medical condition to which she alluded in her marriage-annulment declaration. "I can't remember what it is," Braun says, "but it's not serious."

Braun's hope for a happy ending centers on Delinah. If she takes full responsibility for Rose, moves to another home and remains independent from her father, the remnants of Robert's shattered life may have a chance. When—not if—Robert gets out of jail, says Braun, he should assume a new role as if he were the baby's grandfather, and not live beneath the same roof as his daughter.

There is clearly a schism within the Blake camp about how to deal with the media.

"The civil lawyers are risk averse," said Braun, referring specifically to Barry Felsen. "The problem is, this is a murder case and there are big risks. From the moment Bonny was dead, I was on TV talking about it. Can you imagine if I had waited for all the Hollywood types?"

The careful story placement, hype and access control so endemic to the entertainment industry is toxic in a capital case, Braun believes.

"There is a time when you have to strike: boom! The civil lawyers have never sat next to a guy who has been convicted of murder and hauled away. To them, everything is always settled behind closed doors. No one knows who wins or loses. Everyone scratches each other's back. This is serious stuff. We don't have time for focus groups. Give me a break! We have to run this like a political campaign."

And then there is the question of the Barbara Walters interview with Delinah Blake. "They made a mistake," said Braun. "It got on for only about ten minutes. If you're going to do TV, you do Larry King. He is not going try to impress you with how smart he is."

Robert Blake's preliminary hearing begins in the fall of 2002, and as the evidence unfolds, the guessing game begins on when Harland Braun will cut a deal for his sixty-eight-year-old client. But it is because Blake is sixty-eight that Braun says he feels certain the case will go to trial.

"There is no compromise with a guy who is his age," he says. "There is nothing to deal with. Whatever sentence he gets, it is going to be for the rest of his life. Solicitation [of murder] alone is nine years, so there is nothing to do but go to trial."

In the meantime Robert Blake cools his bootless heels, crafts his ultimate monologue about his childhood victimization and continues on that never-ending quest to heal his inner child. From his now-familiar place behind the Plexiglas in the Los Angeles County Jail's visiting area, he recently summed up his sense of resignation to old pal Mario Roccuzzio: "They can't do anything to me that hasn't been done before."

* * *

Three months after the murder of Bonny Bakley, the authors met for dinner at Vitello's restaurant to discuss our approach to our *TV Guide* investigation of the May 4, 2001, execution-style shooting of Bonny Lee Bakley.

Run by the Restivo brothers, Vitello's is an inconspicuous neighborhood trattoria, frequented by employees of nearby CBS Studio Center as well as the offices and stores along Ventura Boulevard—the main retail artery that traverses the entire length of the San Fernando Valley. Like several L.A. restaurants that cash in on their proximity to Hollywood, Vitello's features two entrées named for local celebrities: the Fusilli Robert Blake and the Poulet Garry Marshall. In the name of research, I ordered the Fusilli Robert Blake, but Mary had her eye on the chicken.

"Can you tell me about the Poulet Garry Marshall?" she asked the waitress.

"Why don't *you* ask him?" replied the waitress. "He's sitting right behind you."

Sure enough, the creator of TV's *Happy Days,* director of such comedy hits as *Pretty Woman* (1990) and *The Princess Diaries* (2001), and older brother of director/comedienne Penny Marshall sat in the next booth, enjoying an early supper with his daughter. He wasn't at all surprised that we had come to Vitello's to begin our examination of the Robert Blake murder mystery. He pulled a letter from his sports coat that he'd recently received from *People* magazine, wanting to know if Marshall knew Blake personally.

"I wouldn't know Robert Blake from that chair," Marshall said jovially, "but because both of us got a dish named after, everybody figures we must be pals."

It's been said a million times, but Hollywood really *is* a small town. Bonny Bakley knew this and exploited it mercilessly, until her facility at getting ever closer to the star of her choice finally killed her.

Garry Marshall knows and greets the Restivo brothers by their first names—Joe and Steve. He even cast Steve Restivo, a sometime actor, in a small part in *The Princess Diaries*: Count Vitello. A few blocks from Vitello's, Marshall and his family operate a neighborhood theater, where they stage new plays, and a few blocks in the other direction, Robert Blake raised two children and a niece before reluctantly descending into what seemed to be an uneventful retirement.

Of course, it is still L.A. and neighbors—even close neighbors—tend to keep to themselves. On Robert Blake's block, none of his neighbors had a clue what went on inside his house or inside his head.

Like detectives Ito and Tyndall, we traveled throughout the country in pursuit of the truth. In Memphis we found Jerry Lee Lewis' road manager, not in a studio, but in a restaurant. He was our waiter. Paul Gawron just happened to answer the door when Mary knocked at what she thought was a neighbor's house. In Missouri, our investigation brought us to a local truck stop, where the sheriff and most of the town came to our aid.

Robert Blake called us once. He left a message on an answering machine in November, three days after what would have been his and Bonny's first wedding anniversary. He said he had been long interested in writing the story of his life and that he wanted to talk, but would first have to consult with his lawyer. Not his defense lawyer, Harland Braun, but his entertainment lawyer, Berry Felsen. He made no mention of his late wife.

During his promotional tour in 1993 for *Judgment Day*, Blake once remarked that people who commit atrocities like multiple murderer John List are probably damned. "I wonder if they live at all, though, after they do something that suicidal," Blake said. "I wonder if they ever live again, or if they just remain vertical."

The only Blake who finally and hesitantly open up to us was Noah, who spoke at length about his rocky relationship with his father and alluded to deeper troubles within the family as he was growing up, but ultimately lapsed into a Gubitosi *omerta*.

If you are still breathing, you still have a chance, argued Margerry Bakley, whose own troubled past continued to plague her in the summer of 2002. At least in jail, she noted, Robert Blake can count on getting three meals a day.

"We don't have the race card and the poverty card doesn't work," she said, referring to both the murder and child-custody cases. "I have no money and Blake does. This is really all about the haves versus the have-nots, and the have-nots always seem to finish with nothing, just the way they began. You can't just change the mind-set of America. America loves a winner, and my sister wasn't a winner. Getting justice is just not that simple.

"But whether people believe it or not, I continue to pray each day—not only for my family and Rosie and Delinah, but I also pray for Robert Blake."

Bibliography

"Actor Apologizes for 'My Big Mouth,'" *Los Angeles Times*, April 20, 1981.

ALPERT, DON. "Robert Blake Ran Away . . . Into Screen Stardom," *Los Angeles Times*, December 27, 1959.

ARMSTRONG, LOIS. "Money's Cold Comfort Now to Robert Blake, Sleeping With 'A Stranger Called Success,'" *People,* September 19, 1977.

BARTHEL, JOAN. "What Is 'Willie Boy'? It All Depends," *New York Times*, October 6, 1968.

"Battle of Brando, Ex-Wife Takes New Twist," *Los Angeles Times*, March 10, 1972.

"Blake, Robert." *Current Biography*, 1975.

BLAKE, ROBERT. "For Kids, 'Baretta' Endorses Booze Over Pot, Any Day," *Los Angeles Times*, March 30, 1977.

BLANKSTEIN, ANDREW, AND ANNA GORMAN. "Leads Pursued in Slaying of Actor's Wife," *Los Angeles Times,* May 23, 2001.

BLOSSER, JOHN, AND PATRICIA TOWLE. "Blake Bribed Bonny's Ex-Hubby to Trash Her at Trial," *National Enquirer*, May 5, 2002.

"Brando's Son Faces Murder One," *People,* June 4, 1990.

BROWNFIELD, PAUL, AND CARLA HALL. "Tragedy Hit as Blake Faded Comfortably from Fame," *Los Angeles Times*, May 21, 2001.

"Cast As a Killer," *People*, May 6, 2002.

CHAMPLIN, CHARLES. "Blake's Hanging in There," *Los Angeles Times*, January 8, 1983.

————. "'In Cold Blood' Movie Roles Go to Two Unknown Pros," *Los Angeles Times*, January 4, 1967.

————. "Robert Blake: Actor Ready to Move Mountains," *Los Angeles Times*, August 5, 1973.

————. "Robert Blake Shifts Gears for 'Hamster,'" *Los Angeles Times*, October 8, 1978.

————. "Robert Blake Turns His Life Around," *Los Angeles Times*, June 6, 1992.

————. "Wildcat in a Celluloid Jungle," *Los Angeles Times*, April 24, 1977.

CHAVEZ, PAUL. "Actor's Representatives Say Mysterious Figure Had Been Seen at House," the Associated Press, May 8, 2001.

CHUA-EOAN, HOWARD. "In Cold Blood, Part 2: Hollywood Has Another Murder Mystery As Police Hunt the Killer of a Former TV Star's Vilified Wife," *Time*, May 21, 2001.

COGAN, David. "Too Distraught for a Polygraph," *New York Daily News*, May 8, 2001.

COOK, BRUCE. "Stalking the Hamster of Happiness," *American Film*, January 1979.

"Cops: How Blake Did It," *National Enquirer*, May 29, 2001.

CREWS, HARRY. "Television's Junkyard Dog," *Esquire*, October 1976.

CROGAN, JIM. "No Blood Found on Blake," *Los Angeles Daily News*, April 28, 2002.

DEUTSCH, LINDA. "L.A. Police Chief Says Bakley Murder Probe Could Take a Long Time," the Associated Press, June 6, 2001.

DUNN, CLIF H. "The Day Blake Stuck Gun in Ex-wife's Mouth!" *Star*, June 5, 2001.

DUNN, CLIF H., AND JACK CARTER. "Baretta Paid Me to Be His Hit Man," *Star*, May 29, 2001.

"Endangered Species," *People*, March 1, 1993.

"Explosive Enquirer Tapes and Letters Reveal the Depth of Blake's Fury," *National Enquirer*, May 7, 2002.

"Enquirer Tapes Provide Major Evidence on Blake," *National Enquirer*, May 7, 2002.

"Family's Shocking Charge Against 'Baretta' Star: Robert

Blake Murdered Wife," *National Enquirer*, May 22, 2001.

FAUSSET, RICHARD, AND MICHAEL KRIKORIAN AND KURT STREETER. "Wife of Actor Robert Blake Shot to Death," *Los Angeles Times*, May 6, 2001.

GENTILE, DON, AND JOHN BLOSSER. "Robert Blake Murder: The Blackmail Letters That Got Wife Killed," *National Enquirer*, June 29, 2001.

GOLDBERG, ORITH. "Blake Named a Suspect: Attorney Turns Property Over to Detectives," *Los Angeles Daily News*, May 11, 2001.

GOULD, MARTIN. "Blake Kidnapped Infant Daughter," *Star*, June 5, 2001.

GOULD, MARTIN, AND MAGGIE HARBOUR. "Candid Tape Bares Robert Blake's Dark Secret," *Star*, May 29, 2001.

GREENBERG, PETER. "Thrown Out of Five Schools and One Window . . ." *TV Guide*, May 10, 1975.

HALEY, LARRY. "Robert Blake's Rage: Wife's Secret Tapes," *National Enquirer*, May 29, 2001.

HALL, CARLA, AND MASSIE RITSCH. "Actor Grew Even More Reclusive After Wife's Killing," *Los Angeles Times*, April 19, 2002.

HARBOUR, MAGGIE. "Blake Killed Wife to Give Daughter Baby," *Star*, May 28, 2002.

———. "Dead Wife's Family Gives Up Fight for Tot," *Star*, May 7, 2002.

———. "Robert Blake's Kinky & Violent Sex Life," *Star*, June 19, 2001.

"Heaven and Hell," *Detour*, November 1995.

HICKS, JACK. 'I Was As Crazy As I Acted. Bad Crazy," *TV Guide*, April 23, 1983.

HOWARD, JANE. "Actors and Townspeople Felt 'Squirrely,'" *Life*, May 12, 1967.

"In Cold Blood: Robert Blake's Hard-luck Hollywood Life Takes a Bizarre Turn When His Wife, Who Had a Shady Past, Is Murdered," *People*, May 21, 2001.

JONES, JACK. "Brando Flies from Paris; Mystery over Son Grows," *Los Angeles Times*, March 11, 1972.

KEVENEY, BILL, AND KELLY CARTER. "Questions

Swirl Around Slaying of Blake's Wife," *USA Today*, May 10, 2001.

KILDAY, GREGG. "Robert Blake Scores a Point or Two," *Los Angeles Times*, August 2, 1975.

KING, SUSAN. "The Rage Within," *Los Angeles Times*, Feb. 21–27, 1993.

KNAPP, DAN. "Tell the Establishment That Robbie Boy Is Here," *Los Angeles Times*, May 3, 1970.

Last Will and Testament of Bonny Lee Bakley. Probate Court of Shelby County, Tennessee, case no. C-4468.

"Leebonny Bakley Buried During Brief Ceremony at Forest Lawn," *City News Service*, May 25, 2001.

Bonny Lee Lewis v. Joseph Lee Brooksher. Chancery or Circuit Courts of Shelby County, Tennessee, case no. 155244-R.D.7.

LI, DAVID K. "Blake Was Accused by Cops: Att'y," *New York Post*, May 30, 2001.

LI, DAVID K., AND ERIKA MARTINEZ AND ANDY GELLER. "Robert Blake's Moving Farewell to Bonny Lee: Was It All An Act?" *New York Post*, May 26, 2001.

LINDERMAN, LAWRENCE. "Robert Blake: The Playboy Interview," *Playboy*, June 1977.

"Little Beaver Hangs Up Bow to Join Army," *Los Angeles Times*, May 30, 1953.

MOULTRIE, DALONDO. "Parks Accuses Media of Smearing Bakley," *Los Angeles Times*, May 17, 2001.

MURPHY, MARY. "Roles for Award Winners," *Los Angeles Times*, March 3, 1972.

"My Murdered Sister Lived in Fear of Baretta," *Star*, May 22, 2001.

NELSON, ERIK N., AND HELEN GAO. "'Baretta's' Wife Slain; Actor Blake Returns to Car to Find Her Shot," *Los Angeles Daily News*, May 6, 2001.

NEWTON, EDMUND. "O.J. All Over Again," *New Times Los Angeles*, June 7, 2001.

"A Nightmare Lived Again," *Life*, May 12, 1967.

O'NEILL, ANN, AND ANDREW BLANKSTEIN. "Police to Obtain Tape of Bakley and Blake's Talk," *Los Angeles Times*, May 23, 2001.

"Open Case: Ten Months Later, the Murder of Robert

Blake's Wife Remains Unsolved," *People*, March 11, 2002.

"Paradise Lost," *People*, May 1, 1995.

PARK, JEANNIE, AND ROBIN MICHELI. "As He Copes with His Son's Murder Rap, Marlon Brando Is Dealt a Second Blow: Daughter Cheyenne's Suicide Try," *People*, November 19, 1990.

People of the State of California v. Robert Blake, aka Michael Gubitosi, and Earle S. Caldwell. Superior Court of the State of California for the County of Los Angeles. Felony count, case no. LA040377. Filed April 22, 2002.

Petition and Order for Appointment of Guardian Ad Litem Under the Probate Code. Robert Blake, petitioner. Los Angeles Superior Court, filed July 13, 2001.

POLLOCK, DALE. "Robert Blake on 'Coast': Candor or Hype?" *Los Angeles Times*, March 8, 1980.

Premarital Agreement by and Between Leebonny Bakley and Robert Blake. Signed October 4, 2000.

REDELINGS, LOWELL E. "The Hollywood Scene," *Hollywood Citizen-News*, March 10, 1960.

"Robert Blake Says He'll Make Daughter's Life 'The Best I Can,'" *USA Today*, May 29, 2001.

"Robert Blake Still Mainly Battles Himself, But His 'Blood Feud' Causes a Scrap," *People*, May 8, 1983.

"Robert Blake Was An Unpopular Hell-Raiser in High School," *National Enquirer*, June 29, 2001.

ROSENBERG, HOWARD. "Blake Doesn't Have a Prayer in 'Hell Town,'" *Los Angeles Times*, September 11, 1985.

RYAN, JOAL. "No Bail for Blake," *E! Online News*, May 1, 2002.

SCOTT, VERNON. "Robert Blake Mirrors Child Actor Tragedies," *Hollywood Citizen-News*, November 11, 1959.

SHARBUTT, JAY. "NBC Pulls 'Hell Town' from Lineup," *Los Angeles Times*, December 17, 1985.

SHAW, DAVID. "The Battles of 'Baretta,'" *TV Guide*, June 10, 1977.

SHIPP, PATRICIA. "Robert Blake, 67, in Bizarre Tug O' War over Love Child," *National Enquirer*, October 24, 2000.

———— AND PATRICIA TOWLE AND MICHELLE CA-
RUSO. "Bodyguard Botched First Attempt to Kill
Bonny," *National Enquirer*, May 7, 2002.

———— AND ALAN SMITH. "Robert Blake Had Secret
Meeting with Marlon Brando on Eve of Killing," *National Enquirer*, June 5, 2001.

SIGESMUND, B. J. "It Sounds like An Episode of 'Baretta,'" *Newsweek*, May 8, 2001.

SINGLETON, DON. "Blake Thanks His Slain Wife at Her
Grave," *New York Daily News*, May 26, 2001.

SMITH, ALAN. "The Day Robert Blake Threatened to Kill
Me," *National Enquirer*, May 14, 2002.

SMITH, CECIL. "Curve Thrown at Emmy Show," *Los
Angeles Times*, May 20, 1975.

STILLMAN, DEANNE. "A Murder in Hollywood: The
Robert Blake Affair," *Rolling Stone*, May 23, 2002.

STREETER, KURT. "Police Make a Second Search of
Blake Home," *Los Angeles Times*, May 10, 2001.

TAUBMAN, HOWARD. "The Theater: 'Harry, Noon and
Night,'" *New York Times*, May 6, 1995.

*Temporary Custody Agreement by and between Leebonny
Bakley and Robert Blake*. Signed October 4, 2000.

*Tennessee Department of Correction Investigation Report of
Bonny Bakley*. April 1996.

THOMAS, KEVIN. "Polonsky Talks About 'Willie Boy,'"
Los Angeles Times, June 22, 1968.

————. "Shoot-Out Marks Grand Central's Hollywood
Debut," *Los Angeles Times*, March 26, 1973.

THOMPSON, DAVID. "Robert Blake's 21-Gun Salute,"
Globe, June 6, 2002.

"3 Cited by Italo-Americans," *Los Angeles Times*, July 2,
1975.

TOWLE, PATRICIA. "Blake's Bizarre Marriage to Bonny
Lee," *National Enquirer*, May 7, 2002.

*Blanchard E. Tual, Administrator of the Estate of Bonny Lee
Bakley on behalf of the heirs of said decedent v. Robert
Blake, aka Michael Gubitosi; Earle Caldwell, Doe 1,
Doe 2, Doe 3, Doe 4, Doe 5, Doe 6 and Does 7 through
50*. Complaint for damages for wrongful death. Los

Angeles Superior Court, case no. EC 034380. Filed April 29, 2001.

TURNER, RICHARD. "In This Corner, Robert Blake—Lying . . . Scraping . . . Scuffling Once More Against the Odds," *TV Guide*, March 2, 1985.

TUSHER, WILL. "Breakthrough Interview with Robert Blake: A New Kind of Hollywood Hero," *Photoplay*, October 1975.

———. "Robert Blake: Baretta's at Home in the Valley," *San Fernando Valley Magazine*, September 1977.

———. "Robert Blake Says: 'Making Love Is the Best Way to Lose Weight," *Photoplay*, September 1977.

"Two Unknowns Seek Movie Fame as Killers 'In Cold Blood,'" *Life*, May 12, 1967.

"Unknown Actor to Play In Cold Blood Killer," the Associated Press, November 18, 1966.

U.S. v. Bonny Bakley. District Court for the Eastern District of Arkansas, case no. 96-M-3022.

U.S. v. Bonny Lee Bakley. District Court for the Eastern District of Arkansas, case no. Lr-Cr-96-53. Filed March 12, 1996.

U.S. Department of Justice–FBI Report. Bonny Lee Bakley, et al. 9A-ME-48753.

PENGUIN PUTNAM INC.
Online

Your Internet gateway to a virtual environment with
hundreds of entertaining and enlightening books
from Penguin Putnam Inc.

*While you're there, get the latest buzz on
the best authors and books around—*

Tom Clancy, Patricia Cornwell, W.E.B. Griffin,
Nora Roberts, William Gibson, Robin Cook,
Brian Jacques, Catherine Coulter, Stephen King,
Jacquelyn Mitchard, and many more!

**Penguin Putnam Online is located at
http://www.penguinputnam.com**

PENGUIN PUTNAM NEWS
Every month you'll get an inside look at our upcom-
ing books and new features on our site. This is an
ongoing effort to provide you with the most
up-to-date information about
our books and authors.

**Subscribe to Penguin Putnam News at
http://www.penguinputnam.com/ClubPPI**